BEST NEWSPAPER WRITING 1987

D1277550

Copies of *Best Newspaper Writing 1987* are available for
$9.95 each from The Poynter Institute. Earlier editions are also
available in limited quantities. Some discounts apply. Please
write for details.

For Billie Keirstead
All praise for the precision and style
of this series belongs to her.

About this series

AUGUST 1987

The Poynter Institute for Media Studies proudly publishes the ninth volume of its series *Best Newspaper Writing,* valued since 1979 by students, teachers, and professionals as an indispensable text on clear, effective, and graceful newswriting.

In 1977, the American Society of Newspaper Editors (ASNE) made the improvement of newspaper writing one of its primary long-range goals. In the following year, the society inaugurated a contest to select the best writing in several categories from newspapers in the United States and Canada, and to reward the writers with prizes of $1,000. The Institute volunteered to spread the gospel of good writing by publishing the winning entries along with notes, commentaries, and interviews. That first volume, *Best Newspaper Writing 1979,* sold out long ago and has become a collector's item.

As in past years, *Best Newspaper Writing* is a joint venture of the ASNE and the Institute. Each spring, a panel of ASNE editors meets in St. Petersburg for two days to screen nearly 500 entries and choose the winners. The first six editions of *Best Newspaper Writing* were edited by Roy Peter Clark, an associate director of the Institute.

Dr. Clark was one of the first newspaper writing coaches and has been a national leader in the growing movement to make American newspapers more readable, more interesting, and more accurate. Trained as a Chaucer scholar at the State University of New York at Stony Brook, he came to the *St. Petersburg Times* in 1977 from Auburn University. He joined the Institute, then known as Modern Media Institute, to direct its Writing Center.

Clark conducted writing seminars for newspaper professionals and for advanced liberal arts graduates seeking careers in journalism. He also worked with high school students, college journalism teachers, school newspaper advisors, and their student editors. Clark has developed a pilot program for fourth- and fifth-graders, which has had remarkable success in teaching elementary schoolchildren not only to write well, but also to love writing. Clark describes his philosophy and methods in his book, *Free to Write: A Journalist Teaches Young Writers* (Heinemann, 1986).

In 1985, Clark was joined on the writing faculty by Dr. Don Fry, his mentor and former colleague from Stony Brook. Fry graduated from Duke University and the University of California at Berkeley. He is a distinguished scholar of early English literature and an outstanding teacher of writing and ethics. He serves as a writing coach and consultant to many newspapers, lectures frequently at universities and national meetings, and testifies in libel trials as an expert witness on the precise meanings of words. He has published a number of articles on the qualities of good writing, coaching, and libel.

Clark and Fry co-edited the 1985 volume of *Best Newspaper Writing,* and Fry has edited the two subsequent volumes. The 1986 edition added a new feature, a bibliography of the best articles and books on news writing. This year Jo Cates, the Institute's chief librarian, begins an annual bibliography of newswriting, editing, and coaching.

The 1987 categories included deadline and non-deadline writing, commentary, and a new topic, obituary writing. A committee of 16 editors, chaired by Anthony Day, editorial page editor of the *Los Angeles Times,* judged this year's entries:

John Carroll, *Lexington* (Ky.) *Herald-Leader.*

Don E. Carter, Sea Island, Ga., formerly of Knight-Ridder Newspapers.

Robert P. Clark, Harte-Hanks Newspapers, San Antonio, Texas.

Colleen Dishon, *Chicago Tribune.*

Meg Greenfield, *The Washington Post.*

David Laventhol, *Newsday,* New York.

Ross Mackenzie, *The Richmond* (Va.) *News Leader.*

Patrick McCauley, *The Huntsville* (Ala.) *Times.*

Eugene Patterson, *St. Petersburg Times.*

Eugene L. Roberts, *The Philadelphia Inquirer.*

Howard Simons, Nieman Foundation, Cambridge, Mass.

Claude Sitton, *The Raleigh Times* and *News & Observer.*

Richard D. Smyser, *The Oak Ridger,* Oak Ridge, Tenn.

Joseph Stern, *The Sun,* Baltimore, Md.

Frederick Taylor, *The Wall Street Journal.*

The Institute wishes to thank these judges for their fine work, and to compliment them for their dedication to good writing.

***

Founded in 1975 by the late Nelson Poynter, chairman of the *St. Petersburg Times* and its Washington affiliate, *Congressional Quarterly,* the Institute was bequeathed Poynter's controlling stock in the Times Publishing Company in 1978. It invests its dividends in the educational activities of its four centers: Writing, Graphics, Management, and Ethics. The center faculties teach beginning and mid-career professionals, publish teaching tools such as this book, and conduct educational and research projects, all of which seek the same goal: to raise levels of excellence in newspapers and the communications media generally.

The Institute congratulates the winners and finalists of the ASNE Distinguished Writing Awards.

Robert J. Haiman, President
The Poynter Institute

Acknowledgments

Anchorage Daily News and Craig Medred
The Charleston Gazette and Don Marsh
Chicago Tribune and Cheryl Lavin
Los Angeles Times and Mark Fineman
The Miami Herald, Dave Barry and Belinda Brockman
Philadelphia Daily News and Jim Nicholson
The Philadelphia Inquirer and Steve Twomey
St. Petersburg Times and Thomas French

We wish to thank the following people for their generous assistance in producing this volume: Bobbi Alsina, Jo Cates, Roy Peter Clark, Priscilla Ely, Ed Mehl, and Joyce Olson of the Institute staff; Walter Dorsett, Daryl Frazell, Lisa Schoof, Lesly Stevens, and Adelaide Sullivan; and of course, the authors and their editors.

Book design and production by Billie Keirstead
Illustrations by Raul Alsina
Cover art by Stella Rhodes
Cover photography by Dick Dickinson

Contents

Introduction

Lively newswriting creates the illusion of a real person's voice speaking to us directly from the page. We say, in appreciation, "This really has voice," or "It speaks to me."

This year's ASNE Distinguished Writing Award winners speak in voices as distinctive and varied as their subjects.

Such individual voices do not just happen. They result from combinations of modes of thought, writing techniques, rhetorical devices, characteristic phrasing, and even, in the case of one of our winners, wacky typography.

DAVE BARRY

Probably the most distinctive voice in American journalism belongs to Dave Barry of *The Miami Herald,* one of this year's winners in commentary. Dave speaks as America's favorite wise-ass, who punctures our pomposities, mostly by quoting us verbatim, or perhaps a little beyond verbatim.

Dave describes his adventures in the 1986 Florida senatorial race, as he follows Senator Paula Hawkins and Governor Bob Graham around:

We land in Bartow, which apparently consists of a hangar. Inside the hangar is a smallish agricultural crowd, which Graham, using his oratorical skills, immediately whips into a stupor. He is not a gifted speaker. He is the kind of speaker who, if he were not the governor, people would shoot rubber bands at after a while... During the Bartow speech, I locate, just outside the hangar, an enormous insect of the type that you would never find in a state such as Ohio. I pick it up, using my notebook, which it spits brown glop on, to test a theory I have about Graham, which is that he will comment on anything. I show it to him, and ask: "Governor, would you comment on this insect?"

"This," he says, picking his words very carefully, as he always does, "is an (*here he says a name that sounds like 'Execretius Bolemius,' which he is clearly making up*). It is a Friend to Man. It is a member of the family of Almost-Flying Insects, and one of the many things that it does is that it titillates the toad."

I twitted Dave that the humorist has an advantage over real reporters, because he can make up quotations like that last one. Dave swore that the quotation was not only real but verbatim, and available on tape.

Dave writes famously sprawling sentences, which tend to land on a final thudding word, such as "stupor" or "dull" or "Ohio." He shows us an action, and then tells what we just figured out for ourselves, and then says it a third time, ending with a zinger.

His sentences bump around in fits and starts, very much the way real people talk. He attributes childish actions to adults, such as shooting rubber bands at governors. Dave never loses sight of the brat who lurks inside all of us.

Dave surprised the ASNE judges with a serious piece entitled "Commencement," about his feelings on delivering his son Robby to his first day in kindergarten:

> We're getting near the school, and Robby is trying so hard to be brave that I am about ready to turn around and drive back home and sit down on the living-room floor and play with him and hug him forever and the hell with developing Motor Skills and Language Skills and Math Skills and Socialization and growing up in general.

Here we have the same voice, but speaking in a different tone, one of wistful anxiety. This sentence ambles out to typical Barry length, and pokes fun at Education-Speak with capital letters. He attributes Robby's anxieties and perplexities to himself, and we all remember our own childhood fears and wonder.

DON MARSH

The judges awarded another prize in commentary, to Don Marsh, editor of *The Charleston* (W.Va.) *Gazette.* His voice resembles Dave Barry's in its energy and devastating wit, but with an entirely different world view. Don speaks in an old-fashioned voice, that of the curmudgeon fed up with the stupidities of politicians.

This passage from a piece headlined "Solitary, poor, nasty, brutish, and short" reacts to remarks before the West Virginia supreme court to the effect that thin-seam mines present little hazard to miners:

My vision of a Wilcox machine in operation is more lurid.

It is based on a description I read in the paper. The story said the machine has two four-foot augers that swing back and forth, boring coal and dumping it on conveyor belts. As the machine sweeps back and forth, miners must continuously knock down roof-supporting timbers on one side of the machine while replacing timbers on the other side.

The top is so low that men work on their backs or from a crouch. They can't straighten up to eat a sandwich, drink water, or urinate. One can only imagine the noise, the dust, the darkness.

Don tips us to his attitude with the adjective "lurid," and treats us to his vision of a monster machine flailing madly, tended by miners caught in a claustrophobic nightmare. He speaks in the simple language of miners.

MARK FINEMAN

Mark Fineman, Manila bureau chief for the *Los Angeles Times,* won the prize in spot news for his coverage of the fall of Ferdinand Marcos. Mark had arrived in the Philippines just six weeks before the coup, with no time even to establish his bureau office.

In hard news, we tend to prefer voices that subordinate style to the rapid presentation of breaking events. Mark combines this neutral voice we associate with the AP style with long but quick sentences, as in this opening from his retrospective on the crisis:

MANILA—At 3 p.m. Saturday, the telephone rang at Villa San Miguel, the modest, Spanish-style residence of Manila's Roman Catholic archbishop, Cardinal Jaime Sin.

It was Defense Minister Juan Ponce Enrile, the powerful and once deeply loyal lieutenant of Philippine President Ferdinand E. Marcos. But today, Enrile's voice was trembling.

"Your Eminence, please help us," Enrile pleaded. "In one hour's time, we are going to die. The president's men are coming to arrest us."

Moments later, the phone rang again. This time it was Lt. Gen. Fidel V. Ramos, Marcos's armed forces deputy chief of staff.

Ramos said that both he and Enrile were in grave danger because Marcos suspected them of plotting against him. If the cardinal would help them to make a stand against the authoritarian leader, Ramos said, he could guarantee support from key areas of the military.

Within minutes, Cardinal Sin, an unusually influential man in a nation that is 85 percent Catholic, decided that, with his help, Enrile and Ramos had a good chance of ousting a man who had ruled this nation with impunity and self-interest for two decades. Quietly, he went to work summoning the faithful to rebellion.

Mark manages to spread out a lot of information in long but clear sentences. Some of his sentences equal Dave Barry's in length. But Mark keeps his clauses under tight control, while Dave deliberately creates the comic illusion of sentences about to topple off the page.

Mark lets the reader see his thought as he pairs his observations with light explanation, usually of human character. In the following passage, Mark describes what he saw in the private apartments of the Marcoses shortly after they fled:

Touring the most intimate corners of a palace that many Filipinos had come to view as a symbol of their oppression, a *Times* correspondent found that the Marcoses had fled so hastily that they abandoned scores of precious family mementos—a six-foot oil painting of Marcos half nude in a Philippine jungle, photographs of Marcos and the first lady embracing, videotapes of Marcos family gatherings and of a private visit between Imelda Marcos and Nancy Reagan....

Beside Imelda Marcos's 12-foot-wide bed was a half-eaten banana.

Mark leads us through a series of sharply observed details before landing us with a thud on that half-eaten banana, a sequence worthy of Dave Barry. Mark's voice speaks with great authority, the product of clarity and inclusive vision.

CRAIG MEDRED

Craig Medred, a reporter for the *Anchorage* (Alaska) *Daily News,* also won the prize in deadline writing for his marathon coverage of the Iditarod sled dog race from Anchorage to Nome, 1,100 miles of malevolent nature. Craig writes in a transparent voice that never calls attention to itself, letting the colorful characters of the mushers shine through unimpeded by his style.

This passage describes a terrifying descent down an icy hill:

The team pulling Frank Torres of McGrath was screaming down the hill when disaster struck Monday morning.

"The team went on one side of a tree and the sled went on the other," he said. The towline popped and Torres's dogs were off and running on their own.

Other mushers resting at the bottom of the hill after their terrifying ride down helped catch Torres's team. He muscled his sled back onto the trail and rode it down.

"It's easy coming down without a dog team," he said.

The story "that Frank cut 'em loose to get down the hill" would spread fast among the mushers, Steve Bush of Aniak predicted.

"A little damaged pride is all," Torres countered. "I'm lucky. It could have tore the whole front of my sled off."

"Ya," said Bush, "somebody said it's the kind of hill where when you go over the edge you start to scream, but before you can get it out, you're too busy."

Like Dave Barry, Craig deliberately leaves quotations verbatim ("It could have tore..."), letting the deep country grammar help characterize the mushers. The last quotation by Steve Bush somehow makes perfect sense as you picture the racer flying through space, but the sentence itself defies analysis or paraphrase.

JIM NICHOLSON

Jim Nicholson of the *Philadelphia Daily News* won in a new category, obituary writing. Each day, Jim and the obituary writer of his rival, *The Philadelphia Inquirer,* divvy up the newly dead, and Jim deliberately chooses the ordinary folk of the blue-collar community served by his paper. He writes in a simple voice perfectly tuned to his readers, as in this anecdote about Vincent "Cous" Pilla, the favorite pizza chef of the Philadelphia underworld:

Customers included actor Sylvester Stallone and ex-Eagles coach Dick Vermeil. City Councilwoman Joan Specter invited him to teach a class at her cooking school. The "boys" also came to eat.

Of course, this attracted the people who follow and keep tabs on the "boys." As *Daily News* columnist Larry Fields pointed out once,

"Cous' only crime is making the best pasta in town."

One story goes that federal agents came in one day to question Pilla about some of his diners. Now it is in the mob manual somewhere that the first item a connected guy buys is the most expensive hand-tooled, imported shoes he can find.

As one agent started in on Cous, he was cut short by the exasperated chef who said, "Hey, look at these," pointing to a scuffed, obviously cheap pair of Buster Browns. "Do these shoes look like I'm a gangster?"

We sense a real person sharing with us a wry tale about an equally real person, who, because of a valued skill, can hold his own in a list of celebrities. Jim salts his stories with convincing lingo, such as "mob manual" and "connected guy." Again, like Dave Barry and Craig Medred, he lets elliptical quotations stand. I couldn't paraphrase Cous's last sentence in less than a paragraph, and I wouldn't even try.

Jim uses a feature approach to obituaries, letting family and pals share their appreciation of the quirks and virtues of the dead. In this passage, he describes the ongoing party atmosphere at the house of a bon vivant janitor:

But beyond his outstanding record as a custodian, Hodges is remembered as the man who for some 20 years operated and hosted the greatest after-hours spot in neighborhood memory.

He liked to think of it as an "open house." It didn't have a name—other than being referred to as "Richard's Spot" or "Cafe Richard"—but the house on Brandywine Street was where the action was. It was a house that Hodges owned, located two blocks from his own home.

Friday and Saturday nights and all day Sunday people gathered there who had two things in common: they wanted a good time and they were personal friends of Hodges, the smiling man in the sharp slacks and sport shirt.

Jim writes long conversational sentences in simple wording, and he can invest a phrase like "beyond his outstanding record as a custodian" with real appreciation for real work, without a hint of condescension.

STEVE TWOMEY

Steve Twomey won the prize in non-deadline writing for a long magazine piece debating the viability of aircraft carriers in an age of missiles. Steve's voice often resembles Mark Fineman's in its graphic detail and explanatory power, but he writes with hotter rhythms. In this passage, the officer in charge of deck operations and his assistant (Air Boss and Mini Boss) worry whether their crews can clear away an A-7 bomber before an F-14 fighter plane lands:

"We're not going to make it!" Air Boss said again.

"We'll make it!" said Mini.

Catapult crews had almost finished. The F-14 was just off the stern and plunging, a long hook dangling from its belly that would, it was hoped, catch one of four cables laid across·the rear flight deck to stop the plane cold. It was time to decide: Wave it off or land it. The last of the crew was scampering out of the landing area.

"They made it!" said Mini.

Over the stern, down, down.

Bam.

Fifty-six thousand pounds of F-14 slammed home. Simultaneously, the pilot pushed to full throttle. Heat blasted down the aft flight deck. If the hook missed all the cables, the pilot would simply keep going, over the now-dormant site of the No. 4 catapult, flying off and coming around again. But he was no "bolter." He snagged a wire for a clean trap. Time from the last launch to the first landing: 45 seconds.

Air Boss grinned.

Mini Boss grinned.

Hubba, hubba.

Twomey makes no effort to conceal his awe at the precision and hazard of this complex operation. He rushes us through technical terms so fast that we have no time to wonder what they mean.

But the vividness of that passage illustrates his dilemma in writing this story: balancing his awe at these amazing machines and their highly skilled crews against his need for objectivity in presenting both sides of the debate on the validity of carriers. He can also use the same voice in a calmer tone to lay out the issues:

No one doubts that the United States ought to have carriers. They have uses. The answer to vulnerability, critics say, is to have more of them, to spread the risk. The big ones, however, cost big bucks. *Roosevelt* and two other new, huge, nuclear-powered carriers authorized by Congress, the *Abraham Lincoln* and the *George Washington,* will cost $3.5 billion apiece. Without planes. Add those and add the cruisers and frigates that must escort any carrier—the Navy concedes they need protection—and it costs $17 billion to put a carrier group to sea. That is 10 times the 1986 Philadelphia city budget. The cost of the three carrier groups combined would be enough to pay for all city services—police, fire, sanitation, everything— for 30 years without any resident paying any taxes.

Steve's voice conveys the same easy confidence he used in the graphic carrier landing. He alternates simple sentences with complex ones. Steve uses asides inside his complex sentences to capture the sound of balanced thinking and qualifications.

The ASNE Distinguished Writing Awards celebrate these six remarkable storytellers, and their voices remind us of the rich diversity of our profession.

Don Fry
August 1987

Best Newspaper Writing 1987

Steve Twomey
Non-Deadline Writing

STEVE TWOMEY, 35, was born in Niles, Michigan, and grew up in the Chicago suburbs. Upon graduation in journalism from Northwestern in 1973, he joined *The Philadelphia Inquirer* as an intern, and Gene Roberts talked him into staying on as a general assignment reporter. He became the education writer for three years, and then a labor reporter for three years more, both great Philadelphia beats. He spent two years covering the West from Los Angeles before becoming a foreign correspondent in the Paris bureau. There he wrote the super-carrier story, which also won the Pulitzer Prize for feature writing.

How super are our supercarriers?

OCTOBER 5, 1986

Air Boss looked aft. Through the haze of a June morning off Sicily, an F-14A Tomcat fighter was already banking in low over *America*'s wake, a couple of miles out and coming home to the Bird Farm. Air Boss looked down. Damn. Still no place to put the thing.

On the flight deck below, opposite Air Boss's perch in the control tower, an A-7E Corsair II bomber sat astride the No. 4 steam catapult amidships. By now, the A-7 should have been flying with the rest of the day's second mission. Nobody would be landing while it straddled *America*'s only available runway.

"What's taking 'em so long down there?" Air Boss growled. He had left his leather armchair in his glass booth in *America*'s superstructure. He was standing up for a better look, which he always does when the flight deck crunch is on.

The ship's 79,724 tons suddenly shuddered. Steam billowed from No. 4. The A-7 had vanished, rudely flung out over the Mediterranean by the "cat stroke," like a rock from a slingshot. Finally.

"Launch complete, sir!" said Mini Boss, his assistant.

"Clear decks!" Air Boss boomed into the radio to his launch crews. It would be close, maybe too close. "Secure the waist cat! Prepare to recover aircraft! Hubba, hubba!"

The F-14 was closing at 150 miles per hour. A mile out now. On the deck, crews were frantically stowing launch gear. They had to seal the long slit down which the catapult arm—the "shuttle"—races as it yanks a plane along the deck and flips it heavenward. They had to shut hatches and make them flush with the deck. *America* had to become seamless for its bird.

"Commmme on, commmme on," said Air
Boss. His eyes flitted from the looming F-14 to
his crews working below. The plane's variable
wings were swept wide for landing, 64 feet tip
to tip. Its wheels were down, its twin tailjets were
spewing heat waves. It was a pterodactyl about
to prey on the carrier.

"We're not going to make it!" said Air Boss.

"We'll make it!" said Mini Boss.

Unless they made it, the F-14 would have to
be waved off, sent around for another approach.
In peacetime, that is not fatal. It costs fuel—266
gallons a minute for an F-14, $1,100 an hour—
but no more. In war, a carrier's ability to cycle
its jets in seconds—to launch them, land them,
rearm them, refuel them, launch them again—
could mean victory or defeat. *America* is not at
war now. But *America* trains as if it is.

"We're not going to make it!" Air Boss said
again.

"We'll make it!" said Mini.

Catapult crews had almost finished. The F-14
was just off the stern and plunging, a long hook
dangling from its belly that would, it was hoped,
catch one of four cables laid across the rear flight
deck to stop the plane cold. It was time to decide:
Wave it off or land it. The last of the crew was
scampering out of the landing area.

"They made it!" said Mini.

Over the stern, down, down.

Bam.

Fifty-six thousand pounds of F-14 slammed
home. Simultaneously, the pilot pushed to full
throttle. Heat blasted down the aft flight deck.
If the hook missed all the cables, the pilot would
simply keep going, over the now-dormant site of
the No. 4 catapult, flying off and coming around
again. But he was no "bolter." He snagged a wire
for a clean trap. Time from the last launch to the
first landing: 45 seconds.

Air Boss grinned.

Mini Boss grinned.

Hubba, hubba.

***

It is hard not to love the dance of the carrier deck—the skill, beauty, and sheer guts of men launching and landing warplanes on a 1,000-foot slab on the sea.

Seventy-five times on an average day, up to 400 times during crises such as Libya, *America*'s crew members dodge sucking jet intakes and whirring props to hitch aircraft to the catapults and send them flying. That many times, they help them home and snare them and park them. They can launch planes a minute apart. They can launch and land at the same time. They can do it in the dark or in the rain. Their average age is 19½.

Engines whine, then race—and a plane disappears from the deck in 2.5 seconds. Its exhaust heat bathes launch crews. The air reeks of jet fuel. Steam seeps from the catapult track. The next plane is already moving forward to take the "cat stroke," and there's another behind it. Noise overwhelms the deck. All the while, the carrier slices through the blue.

"There's no way to describe it," said an A-7 pilot aboard *America*. "There's no way to see it in a movie. You've got to come out here and smell it and see it. It's too dynamic. The whole thing's like a ballet."

In all, the United States' carriers number 14; no other nation has more than four. They are the largest engines of war; no one else's are half as big. They bear the names of battles won, Coral Sea, Midway, and Saratoga; of leaders gone, Eisenhower, Forrestal, Kennedy, Nimitz, and Vinson; and of Revolutionary War vessels, *Constellation, Enterprise, Independence,* and *Ranger*. One evokes the place where man first flew, Kitty Hawk. And one is called *America*.

With their pride of escorts, the 14 carriers and 878 carrier-based fighters and bombers are the most tangible sign of U.S. power that most people around the world ever see. They are the heart of the nation's maritime defense, its glamour boys. They are the costliest items in the military budget, the price of one carrier and its escorts equaling the bill for 250 MX ballistic missiles.

Yet, for all their impressiveness and for all the importance the Pentagon attaches to the vessels, many congressmen and defense analysts argue that the supercarriers' day is history. The critics fear they are now unnecessary, too expensive, and, worse, easy marks. Some of the doubters are even Navy men: Stansfield Turner, a retired admiral and the former director of the Central Intelligence Agency; Elmo Zumwalt, the retired chief of naval operations; and Eugene J. Carroll Jr., a retired admiral who once commanded *Nimitz.*

"Like the battleship the carrier replaced, its magnificence cannot nullify basic changes in the nature of war at sea," Sen. Gary Hart, the Colorado Democrat, writes in a new book on U.S. defense, *America Can Win.* "The day of the large aircraft carrier...has passed."

Today, all surface ships are highly vulnerable to two things—missiles and submarines. A British frigate was sunk in the 1982 Falklands War by a single Exocet missile fired from an Argentine jet it never saw. The Soviet Union has 304 attack submarines, enough to dispatch 21 to hunt each U.S. aircraft carrier. By opting for 14 big carriers—a 15th, the 91,487-ton *Theodore Roosevelt*, will join the fleet soon—the United States could lose, perhaps fatally, a very large portion of naval power in a very short time from a very few Soviet missile and torpedo hits.

In short, it might have the wrong navy for the late 20th century. "When you concentrate your total offensive capability into 15 platforms, the targeting system of the adversary becomes very focused," said Carroll, the ex-carrier captain, who is now deputy director of the Center for Defense Information, a private Washington research group.

No one doubts that the United States ought to have carriers. They have uses. The answer to vulnerability, critics say, is to have more of them, to spread the risk. The big ones, however, cost big bucks. *Roosevelt* and two other new, huge, nuclear-powered carriers authorized by Congress, the *Abraham Lincoln* and the *George Washington*, will cost $3.5 billion apiece. Without planes. Add those and add the cruisers and frigates that must escort any carrier—the Navy concedes they need protection—and it costs $17 billion to put a carrier group to sea. That is 10 times the 1986 Philadelphia city budget. The cost of the three carrier groups combined would be enough to pay for all city services—police, fire, sanitation, everything—for 30 years without any resident paying any taxes.

That is money that cannot be spent on other military items. And most of that money goes for "the purpose of protecting this goddamn carrier," said Robert Komer, who was an undersecretary of defense for policy during the Carter administration. Even most of the carrier's planes are there to protect it.

Instead, many critics say, it's time to think small. Overhauling the big carriers at the Philadelphia Naval Shipyard—*Independence* is there now under the Service Life Extension Program—is merely fixing up the past. The nation should have smaller, cheaper carriers. They can do the job. And the nation could then afford more carriers, and more would cut the impact of losing any given one if war comes.

Of course, to speak of cutting losses in any war seems surreal. Only the Soviet Union could really challenge the U.S. Navy. But any sea battle with the Soviets would trigger nuclear war, many analysts say. In that case, it wouldn't much matter if the United States had 15 supercarriers or 30 medium ones. The game would be over. Still, the Pentagon plans for old-fashioned conflict. Its theory is that because nuclear war is final no nation would start one.

But the Soviets might be willing to start a
regular war, so it's vital to have good
conventional armed forces. In that context,
debating what kind of navy to have does make
sense.

And the U.S. Navy has no doubt that it wants
big carriers. It would even like seven or eight
more, up to 22 or 23. In fact, the Reagan
administration, under Navy Secretary John F.
Lehman Jr., has made big carriers the key to a
strategy that would take them right into the
teeth of Soviet defenses in wartime. That is how
much confidence it has in carriers' ability to
survive today. Critics, said Adm. Henry H. Mauz,
commander of *America*'s battle group, "are well-
meaning people, I'm sure. But they're wrong."

Lehman even said in testimony before
Congress last fall that to build small is
communistic, to build big is American. "Should
carriers be bigger or smaller? There is no
absolute answer to that question," he said.
"...[But] our tremendous edge in technology is a
permanent edge built into the nature of our
culture and economic system, compared to the
Soviets. It is to that advantage we must always
build, not to go to cheaper, smaller, less capable
ships in large numbers. That is an area in which
a totalitarian, centralized, planned economy
excels."

Big is beautiful.

***

America's crew sometimes gets lost. There
are so many decks and passageways that sailors
don't know where they are. "I get fouled-up all
the time," said an officer who was consulting a
deck plan on a bulkhead.

Crew members can ask someone for help,
though it'll often be a stranger. With 4,950
men—there is not one woman—who work
different hours on different decks, most don't
know each other, even after spending six months
at sea on the same ship. Usually they learn about
a fellow crew member by reading about him in
the ship's daily newspaper or seeing him on one
of two television stations that beam live news and

old movies and TV shows. (The most popular fare is a raunchy movie about a riot in a women's prison, one aired repeatedly and so bad that the crew says it's great.)

Many days, there is no sensation of being at sea. Unless they stand on the flight deck or work in the "island"—the starboard-side command structure that rises above the flight deck—crew members cannot see the ocean. There are no port-holes. And *America* is so massive, it is often unaffected by the water's roll. Being below decks can feel like being in a building.

When it left Norfolk, Va., on March 10 for a Mediterranean patrol, *America* took $9 million in cash because at sea it becomes its own economy. The crew gets paid. The crew buys things at the ship's stores. The proceeds are then used to pay the crew. Eighteen thousand meals are fixed a day, 280,000 gallons of sea water are distilled. The Navy loves to boast that there is a barber shop, a bakery, a photo lab, a post office, a printing plant, a tailor, and a public relations staff. In other words, much of the crew has nothing to do with weapons or war. They are service-sector Navy.

The bigness does have an objective, of course: to fly a lot of planes and carry fuel and bombs for them. A U.S. carrier has 80 to 90 planes, more than all four Soviet mini-carriers combined. *America* has eight types of planes, more types than either the three British or two French carriers can hold.

Besides 24 F-14s and 34 A-6 and A-7 bombers, *America* has four planes to refuel its planes in the air, four to detect enemy planes, four to jam enemy electronic equipment, 10 to hunt for submarines, and six helicopters to find downed pilots and to hunt for submarines. All told, there are 86 aircraft, which together can deliver 480,000 pounds of bombs, as much as 10 World War II-era aircraft carriers. When they're not flying, the planes can be stored and repaired on the hangar deck, which runs almost from bow to stern below the flight deck.

The aircraft fly off a deck that is 1,047.5 feet long, not the biggest in the Navy, an honor that belongs to *Enterprise* at about 1,100 feet. But if stood on end, *America*'s flight deck would be almost twice as high as Willam Penn's hat on City Hall. It is 252 feet wide. All told, the deck covers 4.6 acres, an expanse coated with black, coarse, non-skid paint. The crew has plenty of straight-away to jog in the hot sun when the planes aren't flying. Five lengths is a mile.

The flight deck is so big, *America* can launch four planes almost at once, two from bow catapults and two from catapults amidships, on an extension of the flight deck that angles left. That angle enables the ship to launch and land simultaneously in some cases. While a plane is launched forward, another lands on the angle. If it misses all the arresting cables, it keeps going left, thereby avoiding the bow catapults.

Despite its weight, *America*, which is 22 years old, can glide through the water at 30 knots. The power is not nuclear but conventional boilers that drive four 22-foot-high propellers. In fuel for the ship and planes, in crew pay, and in food and supplies, each hour of patrol costs taxpayers $22,917. That is $550,000 a day. That is $99 million for the normal six-month cruise— not counting the bills that its escorts run up.

Overall, *America* exudes seductive and expensive power, a sense magnified by the stateroom of Capt. Richard C. Allen. There, in the bowels of a ship designed for war, is an elegant living room with coffee table, sofa, and wing chairs. The carpeting is bulkhead-to-bulkhead. The dining table can seat at least 10. Several lamps lend a soft light to the room.

Its occupant is a serious man who was born 46 years ago in Wisconsin and flew carrier jets until his eyes went bad. He wears wire-rims now; they give his soft and narrow face the look of a teacher. Allen, who has commanded *America* since July 1985, seemed perplexed by a suggestion that his ship might be at risk or should be anything but the size it is.

Two carriers half as big, for example, would mean two of everything, Allen said—two engine rooms, two sets of catapults, two bridges. Thus, two small carriers would be more than the cost of one big one. But neither would be as stable in rough seas, hampering flight operations, and neither would have so many planes able to do so many things. Even with the advances in missile and submarine warfare, he would much rather command a carrier now than during World War II. Besides, because *America* is big, it can take many bomb hits. And it is much harder to find than an airfield ashore.

"It's mobile, it's moving, it's never in the same place," the captain said. "Like right now. You're on it. Do you know exactly where we are? I'll share with you. We're southwest of Sicily. Tonight, we'll go north of Malta. This morning we were east of Sardinia. The carrier moves. As a result, the targeting problem against a carrier is very complex....

"It's extremely remote a carrier would ever be totally put out of—I mean *sunk*. I think it's just something beyond imagination as I see it, by any threat that we see today or in the near future. This is a very capable piece of machinery."

***

Libya. They were actually going to hit Libya. Night had fallen. It was April 14, 1986. Allen looked down from the bridge at a dimly lighted flight deck jammed with aircraft, bombs, and bullets bound for Benghazi. It was no drill. "I don't believe we're really doing this," he thought. "It's just unbelievable."

The crew had manned battle stations in record time. "All you have to do is tell somebody, 'We're going to go kill something,' and the level of interest goes up logarithmically. I mean, people become—they're *motivated*."

Thirty-eight planes from *America* would go. Somewhere in the darkness of the Mediterranean, the scene was being repeated on the *Coral Sea.* One by one, planes roared away. The most beautiful were the F-14s because, in order to get extra lift, they always flipped on their afterburners just before the "cat stroke," sending twin cones of flame 20 feet down the flight deck and lighting up the dark sea.

He was proud, Allen said, "to watch the complexity of the carrier pull together and to watch the thing take shape, until *boom*, there you are at night, and the cats start firing, and things happen just as they were planned."

And in the early hours of April 15, as the planes began coming back, crew members below decks watched the closed-circuit television shot of the flight deck to see whether the bombers had bombs under their wings. They didn't. And all 38 planes returned. The crew cheered wildly. (Fearing terrorist reprisals against the crew's families in the United States because of the carrier's role in the raid, the Navy requested that no crew member's name be used in this article, except Allen's, and it told crew members not to discuss Libya.)

"I just never thought the national decision would be to engage," Allen said. "I'm extremely proud of the president for having had the guts to do what he did."

Whatever its merit or morality, the U.S. raid on Libya to counter terrorism showed what carriers do best. They can sail to remote places and deal with Third World crises. They can, as the Navy puts it, "project power." Virtually every day of 1985, four U.S carriers were somewhere at sea on patrol. Not the same four, of course, but a rotation that enables crews to avoid prolonged periods away from home. No other nation can deliver so much air power wherever it wants. It is this ability to pop up anywhere swiftly that even critics of big carriers say makes carriers worth having.

It was carrier planes that forced down the civilian jet bearing the four hijackers of the cruise ship *Achille Lauro*. Carriers stood off Grenada and Lebanon during land operations in 1983. It is carriers that would be called on to reopen the Strait of Hormuz should Iran ever carry out its threat to cut oil lanes in its war with Iraq. Often, the mere arrival of the carrier is enough; none of its jets has to fire a shot.

"The carrier is an enormous politico-military capability," said Rear Adm. Jeremy J. Black, assistant chief of the Royal Navy Staff. "It is evident power. As you approach the thing, it emanates power. And wherever it will be, it will be a symbol of American power. That itself is so significant."

"The aircraft carrier," said Norman Polmar, a noted U.S. defense analyst, "has demonstrated that it can move to the troubled area. It can remain offshore, in international waters, for days or weeks or months.... You're going to see many more low-level conflicts and confrontations, and aircraft will be necessary for us to observe, deter, and, if necessary, fight."

Used this way, carriers are not at much risk. Grenada or Libya do not have the military skill to mount a serious threat. Or so the Navy thinks. Carriers stood off North Vietnam for years, launching air strikes, but never taking one in return. The Navy has plans for big carriers, however, that would put them at risk.

Imagine: On May 30, 1987, Soviet tanks and infantry swarm across central Europe. For the moment, the conflict is conventional. The European allies are barely holding on, and they need troops from the United States. Convoys are pieced together, civilian 747s commandeered. And carriers flood the Atlantic to baby these sea and air fleets across to Europe. They are to sink submarines and shoot planes. They are to sweep Soviet surface ships out of the sea lanes linking Old World and New.

That has been part of U.S. strategy for years. Navy Secretary Lehman has added a twist, however. After carriers make the oceans safe for passage, he wants to send them on aggressive forays close to the Soviet Union to finish off the Soviet navy and then bomb land targets. Carriers would sail near the Kola Peninsula off the Soviet Union's far north coast. They would sweep into the Baltic Sea. They would cruise off the Soviets' Pacific coast. By crushing the Soviets on their flanks with carrier power, Lehman argues, the United States would take pressure off the war in central Europe.

This "forward strategy" fuels a push by Lehman for a 600-ship Navy. The number of warships had slipped to 479 after Vietnam, and the Carter administration had decided not to build carriers to succeed the aging *Coral Sea* and *Midway,* which were both due to be retired. It thought big ships were too vulnerable and expensive. The number of carriers was set at 12.

But Lehman sought—and got—congressional approval during the first Reagan term for three giant nuclear-powered carriers and all their escorts, which together will consume 41 percent of Navy construction costs from now to the year 2000—$60 billion. Two of the carriers will replace *Midway* and *Coral Sea*, and the third will represent a net gain. So, the number of big carriers will actually rise to 15.

Lehman says the fleet expansion centered on big carriers is crucial to the "forward strategy." The United States must get the enemy in his lair, and only big carriers can do it. But it's not the same enemy as it used to be.

***

"Captain said to tell you we got a Udaloy coming in."

Churning on an opposite course in the twilight, the sleek visitor whipped past on *America*'s port side, swerved across its wake, and pulled up off the starboard side about 1,000 yards away. Its speed and course now matched the carrier's. From the flight deck, a few crew members gave a look, but they had seen one before.

The Udaloy is a new class of Soviet destroyer. Each has 64 surface-to-air missiles, eight torpedo tubes, eight antisubmarine missiles, and two helicopters. The ships steam at 32 knots. *America*'s crew calls them "tattletales."

Soviet destroyers and frigates routinely weave in and out among U.S. battle groups. The high seas belong to no one; the Soviets have every right to sail wherever they want. The encounters are always courteous. Both sides follow the rules of the road. What the Soviets are doing is taking notes. They watch the pattern of flight operations and the types of exercises. They see how the task force moves. They watch how different planes perform.

"The Soviets? Oh yeah, they'll come right off the quarter, 1,000 yards, 500 yards, follow us around, back and forth," Allen said the next day as the Udaloy hovered. "Whatever we do, they do. If we turn, they turn.... They take pictures. They pick up garbage. They do weird things. Usually they just follow you around."

Such open-ocean presence reflects the new Soviet navy. Russia had never been a sea power, under the czars or under communism. Just 20 years ago, Soviet ships spent a fleet total of 5,700 days at sea, according to U.S. estimates. Last year, they spent 57,000. The Soviets now have the world's largest navy, with 283 major surface ships and 381 submarines, split between 77 ballistic missile-launching submarines (for delivering nuclear warheads to the United States) and 304 attack submarines (for sinking ships, such as U.S. ballistic missile-firing submarines or the carriers). That is 664 warships, compared to the 541 the United States has at the moment. That is three times the total of U.S. attack submarines, the kind needed to find Soviet attack submarines before they find U.S. carriers.

Assigned to the Soviet navy are 1,625 aircraft, mainly operating from land. Their job, too, is to sink U.S. ships. Most formidable, perhaps, is the new Backfire bomber, which can fly at 1,100 knots for 3,400 miles without refueling, bearing big air-to-surface missiles. At the end of 1985, there were 120 Backfires, with more being added each year.

Some Soviet planes are even at sea. Four modest aircraft carriers have been built, and each has 13 planes and 19 helicopters. Like British "jump jets," the planes take off and land by moving vertically. Last year, the Soviet Union launched an American-size carrier of at least 65,000 tons and designed for 60 planes and helicopters. It will not be operational for several years, however, because the Soviets must first master the dance of launching and landing so many aircraft.

Though the Soviet navy is large, there is disagreement about how much of a threat it is, at least away from its coastal waters. In a study last year, the Center for Defense Information said that 145 of the Soviets' surface ships were too small, less than 2,000 tons, to venture into the open sea for long. It said the Soviets have a limited ability to resupply ships at sea, which *America* does very well. (It has to: A battle group gulps 10,000 barrels of fuel a day.) Nor do the Soviets have as many anchorages in other countries as the United States has. And while the Soviets now have carriers, no one argues that the vessels are any match for U.S. carriers.

Nonetheless, Lehman and other Navy officials tout the Soviets as a huge, aggressive force, plying waters they never did before with power they never had before. They point to the Gulf of Mexico, where major Soviet naval forces sailed twice last year. "In many areas of the world, the Hammer and Sickle now overshadows the Stars and Stripes," the unabashedly pro-Navy magazine *Sea Power* intoned last fall.

Much of this gloom-and-doom, of course, is to justify the need for 600 very expensive ships: The Pentagon must face a worthy foe. And even the

Center for Defense Information, in its study, said the Soviets would be very tough adversaries close to home if Lehman's "forward strategy" were ever tried. And farther out to sea, Soviet attack submarines and Backfire bombers could, indeed, threaten convoys and their carrier escorts.

Yet even while highlighting Soviet power, the Navy says, in effect, no problem. It's got a system.

***

Much of the time, *America* seems alone in the Mediterranean, free of Soviet tattletales and steaming toward an empty horizon. Not even fishermen chug by. But the Small Boys are never far away.

There are 10 sprinkled in a circle around *America*, two cruisers, four destroyers, and four frigates, sometimes moving in close, sometimes sailing out of sight. One or two U.S. attack submarines are often there as well, but because they are underwater, it's hard to be sure; Allen said only that they are not there all the time.

America never leaves home without the Small Boys, whose crews say that they are the true sailors and that the carrier is just the Bird Farm. Battle groups are the key to what the Navy calls defense-in-depth. The idea is to keep the $3.5 billion airfield at the center from being sunk.

The first sentry is not a ship, however. It is a plane, one that does not carry any weapons and cannot fly fast. The E-2C Hawkeye looks like a small AWACs plane, the Air Force's Airborne Warning and Control aircraft that seem to have a giant mushroom on their backs. The mushroom has radar.

Often the first plane to leave the carrier during launches, the E-2's job is to park in the sky and see what else is up there. Its radar can scan 100,000 feet up and in an arc 250 miles around *America*. If it identified enemy planes, the E-2 would call in what deck crews call the Super Hot Fighter Pilots, only they use a more descriptive word than *super*.

The men who fly the $38.7 million F-14 fighters are just about as smug and smooth as *Top Gun* portrays them. *America*'s pilots haven't seen the movie because they have been at sea. But they've seen the Kenny Loggins video clip, featuring shots of twisting, blasting F-14s. It was flown out to the ship. They love it.

"Yeah, that's us," said a 28-year-old pilot from Drexel Hill. "We're *cool*. We're *fighter pilots*."

Most are in their late 20s or early 30s. Handsomeness seems to be a job requirement. Catapulting off a carrier, which subjects them to a jolt seven or eight times the force of gravity, "is a lifetime E-ticket at Disneyland," said the Drexel Hill pilot.

"To be sitting in that machine and know that 300 feet later you'll be going 200 miles an hour and the whole thing takes 2½ seconds—well, the level of concentration in sports or whatever has never reached *that* adrenaline high," said a 42-year-old pilot from Philadelphia who has done it 1,250 times.

Their job is to hunt down enemy planes and destroy them before they can launch missiles at *America*. Or, as Adm. Mauz, the battle group commander, put it, "We want to shoot the archer rather than the arrow."

F-14s, which can fly at more than twice the speed of sound, have Phoenix missiles with a range of 120 miles, as well as shorter-range Sidewinder and Sparrow missiles. The F-14s would be helped by four EA-6B Prowlers from the carrier, planes whose task is to scramble the radar of attacking enemy planes and baffle their missile guidance systems. Needless to say, the fighter pilots don't think anyone will get past them. What a silly suggestion; without the carrier, they would get wet.

"This is home," said the air wing commander, 40, who is in charge of all the pilots of all the various types of planes. "This is where dinner is. This is where the stereo is."

If the attacking planes did skirt the F-14s and fire missiles, the next line would take over, the Small Boys. They would rely on Aegis, a defensive system just entering service aboard a new line of cruisers and destroyers; *America*'s battle group has one of the new ships, the cruiser *Ticonderoga*. The Aegis is designed to find and track dozens of hostile missiles at once—the exact number is classified—and launch shipboard missiles to destroy them. It can coordinate not only the cruiser's reply missiles, but also those of all the ships in the battle group, automatically. An attack would be swatted out of the skies. In theory.

If that fails, and missiles are still boring in, *America* has a modern Gatling gun called Phalanx. Mounted at three points on the edge of the flight deck, the computer-directed gun has six barrels that together fire 3,000 rounds a minute. That is supposed to shred any missiles. Judging by a test one day on *America*, the gun's noise alone might destroy them.

Soviet submarines would be found by *America*'s 10 S-3A Viking planes. Their electronics can look down through the water and spot a submarine. The plane then drops a depth charge or torpedo. The battle group also scours with sonar and can fire an array of weapons at submarines.

Actually, Navy officials hate to talk about all this defense. They say outsiders spend too much time worrying about how vulnerable carriers are. The ships are for offense, first. "It's sort of like your house," said the air wing commander. "You take steps to protect it, but you don't go around protecting it all the time. I'm not worried every day my stereo's going to be stolen. I'd rather go bomb something."

***

It came out of the west just after lunch, skimming 10 feet above the South Atlantic at 680 miles per hour. On the bridge of *Sheffield*, a British frigate, Lts. Peter Walpole and Brian

Leyshon had seen a puff of smoke on the horizon but didn't know what it meant and hadn't seen the Argentine Super Etendard fighter. One mile out, they both recognized what was coming their way.

"My God," they said simultaneously, "it's a missile."

Four seconds later, the Exocet hit starboard amidships, above the water line, and veered down into the engine room, where its 363 pounds of high explosive detonated. In an instant, *Sheffield* lost electrical power and communications. Fires broke out. The edge of the hole in the ship's side glowed red from the blazes, but there was no water pressure to put them out. As flames crept toward the magazine, where ammunition is stored, the crew abandoned *Sheffield*.

A new, $50 million ship had been destroyed—and 20 of its crew killed—by a single, small, computer-guided missile costing one-hundredth as much.

What happened that Tuesday, May 4, 1982, during the Falklands War was one of the most stunning examples in history of the power of the anti-ship missile. These weapons can strike from much greater distances than naval guns and, unlike shells, can be guided to their targets. Photos of *Sheffield*, listing and burning, depict the critics' nightmare of what will happen to carriers.

There is little chance, certainly, that one, two, or even three Exocets could sink a U.S. carrier. It is just too big. And the Navy accurately says that the British had less ability to detect, track, and destroy enemy planes than a U.S. battle group has. Britain's two Falklands carriers had no planes like Hawkeyes to spot the Super Etendards. They had far fewer fighters to attack them. No British ship had Aegis. Polmar, the military analyst, says a U.S. carrier force would have destroyed the Argentine air force "in two days."

But there are missiles that could threaten a carrier—cruise missiles. They are flying torpedoes with large warheads launched up to 350 miles away from their targets and often moving at supersonic speed. Backfire bombers can carry them. About 30 Soviet surface ships carry them. And so do 62 Soviet submarines, including the new Oscar class. Each Oscar has 24 cruise missiles. Two are at sea now, with another joining the fleet every two years.

"We do not have an adequate defense for cruise missiles," said Adm. Carroll of the Center for Defense Information. "It's been the *bete noire* of naval strategy for some time now. We've made some progress. We've got Phalanx and such. But I'll guarantee you that if you take those carriers in range of Soviet land-based aircraft and cruise missiles, there will be enough cruise missiles coming through the defense to hit the ships. I don't know how many will get through, but say it's one out of five. And if one out of five hits our ships? It's all over."

Aegis is supposed to deal with cruise missiles, but its performance has not been flawless. Initially, it knocked down only four of 15 attacking missiles in tests. Later, that rose to 10 out of 11, but doubts remain. Moreover, a missile doesn't have to sink a carrier to render it useless. Each carrier has four very weak points—its catapults. Without them, planes don't fly. The Navy thinks it is highly unlikely that any enemy will get so lucky as to put all four out of action at once. But then, naval history is replete with lucky moments.

A carrier's greatest foe, however, is not in the air. It is the enemy it never sees. Gary Hart calls them the kings of the sea. And the Soviets have more of them than anyone. In March 1984, a Soviet nuclear-powered attack submarine rose up under *Kitty Hawk* in the Sea of Japan, bumping it and damaging both ships. It was an accident, not an attack. But the battle group had not detected the sub, even though at least five Small Boys were around *Kitty Hawk*.

Because it was peacetime, it was possible the escorts weren't "pinging" with sonar to find subs. The incident, however, illustrates how stealthy subs can be. They are a threat not only from their cruise missiles, but from their torpedoes. While the Navy believes its detection skills are good, they are not perfect. "We don't always know where they are," said Capt. Allen, "so we don't know whether we're being followed or not all the time."

Oddly, Allen has never been on a submarine at sea, despite being in the Navy for 27 years. Critics say that would be an excellent way for carrier captains to learn how their underwater adversaries work and think.

Given the air and sea threats to carriers, Lehman's "forward strategy" could end in the destruction of the heart of the Navy. It would be going right where the defenses are thickest. Stripped of even a few of its carriers, the Navy might then be unable to do its most important job, protecting the sea lanes. That, in turn, would jeopardize a war in Central Europe.

"If we sail into battle against the Soviets depending on just 15 ships, we will, like the Spanish Armada, sail in expectation of a miracle," Hart writes in *America Can Win.* "Perhaps we will get one, although the precedent is not encouraging. Perhaps the opponent, despite numerous submarines and aircraft, will prove incompetent. But our survival, as a navy and a nation, would depend...on massive incompetence, not on our strength."

Even if the strategy worked and the carriers sank huge portions of the Soviet navy, the cornered Soviets might shift first to tactical and then to strategic nuclear weapons to stave off surrender. In that case, the carriers' size wouldn't matter.

***

Astern of *America*, they formed a necklace of lights in the night sky, 15 planes strung out in a row. They had lined up to take their turns coming home. It was 11:30 p.m.

On a catwalk hanging over the side of the flight deck, four landing-signals officers stood peering into the dark. LSOs can tell, just by looking at wing lights, if a returning pilot is on the right glide path, dropping 100 feet for each quarter mile to the ship.

"You're high, high," an LSO said softly into his radio to the first inbound plane. It was too dark to see what kind it was.

No task in all of aviation is more difficult than landing on a carrier at night. While modern jets can all but fly themselves and the carrier has runway lights, pilots have none of the usual reference points, such as the lights of a city. The sky is black, the water is black. They cannot tell where one stops and the other starts. All they can see is a short line of light. They cannot even see the ship, let alone the deck. No matter what instruments can say and computers can do, that is frightening.

The first plane drew nearer. It crossed the stern. Sparks shot from the flight deck as the arresting hook hit first, searching for one of the four cables. It found one, yanking an A-7 to a halt in 350 feet, one-tenth of the distance a plane needs on land. The lights of the next plane grew larger.

"Foul deck! Foul deck!" said two LSOs.

Until the A-7 could be unhooked and moved aside, until the arresting cables were back in position, until deck crews had moved, the LSOs would keep telling the next pilot his runway was blocked. If necessary, they would wave him off. On this night, they would not have to; the crews were perfect.

Sparks flew, engines roared. In 16 minutes, all the planes were down. The ship grew quiet for the night, sailing on.

"Sometimes," said an LSO, "I can't believe what we do out here."

Observations and questions

1) Twomey says that long magazine pieces tend to have introductions rather than traditional leads. Do we pay a price in giving up the concentrated beginning afforded by good lead-writing? A leisurely introduction teaches the reader to have leisurely expectations of a story.

2) Twomey considered no other beginnings for this story. What alternative openings could you imagine for it, and how would each affect the pace and structure of the piece?

3) I asked Twomey about this sentence in the lead, describing an F-14 landing: "It was a pterodactyl about to prey on the carrier." He told me, "The F-14 just sitting was the most menacing thing I'd ever seen in my life. When its wings were swept out for landing, it looked like something about to pick the carrier up and carry it off to a roost and eat it." Do you find the metaphor effective or overdone? Why?

4) In the paragraph beginning, "It is hard not to love the dance of the carrier deck," Twomey uses repetitive sentence structures, repeated pronouns *they* and *them*, and a climactic change in rhythm: "Their average age is 19½." List all the writing "rules" he breaks here and study the resulting effects.

5) Twomey rejected a structure based "around five or six individuals by job function" tied to the question: "Are these carriers worth anything?" Can you think of ways to make such a structure work?

6) Twomey says, "In each of the sections, I wanted to begin specific and small, and expand to general and large." Yet we generally think of explanatory prose as moving from general principles to specific applications. Think about the trade-offs for the reader between catchy specific section openers and explanations that begin with generalities.

7) I suggest that reporters should write their own subheads to improve the shape of the story. Write subheads for Twomey's story and study how they improve clarity and ease of reading. In my opinion, *we should never print stories this long without subheads*.

8) After he arrived on the carrier, the Navy forbade Twomey from using any names of crew members except the captain's. At that point, he had no choice but to agree, and he kept his promise, at some cost to the precision of his story. How can we anticipate such restrictions, especially in military and government stories, and negotiate them ahead of time?

9) Twomey often organizes complex materials by listing them, though he conceals the list form rather well. See how many lists you can find in this story. Hint: one of them is 16 paragraphs long.

10) About the only thing not moving in this whole story is a Corsair sitting on a catapult. Study how Twomey conveys a sense of action by vigorous verbs and imagery.

11) On page nine, we read: "...if stood on end, *America*'s flight deck would be almost twice as high as William Penn's hat on City Hall." Twomey explains: "That would only mean something to a Philadelphian. On the top of City Hall is a giant statue of William Penn, who is wearing a colonial hat, and it has always been

a local measure of comparison to refer to
something by 'Billy Penn's hat.' " Think about
the graphic effect of such localized references.
What local measures of comparison can you use
in your community?

12)   Twomey devotes almost no space to the hot-
shot pilots until about three-quarters of the way
through, because he "empathized more with the
guys who were doing the grunt work." Would you
be tempted to introduce the fighter jocks earlier
and give them more space? What would you gain
and lose?

13)   In the writing session of the 1987 ASNE
national convention, Twomey was asked if he had
attributed the borrowed material about the
Falklands. He replied, "There was no reference
to the book. Perhaps there should have been."
He could have started with a phrase such as,
"According to two British journalists, etc.," or
added a sentence, a note outside the text, or a
sidebar list of sources. In what circumstances
must we attribute paraphrased material, and
how can we integrate the attribution into the
flow of stories?

14)   In some of the debate sections, Twomey uses
vague plural attributions, such as "critics say"
or "many analysts say." Do such generic
attributions help or hinder the credibility of the
argument?

15)   Twomey says that he personally believes
"these are the wrong machines for this era." Yet
he ends the story with another graphic landing,
which he found "stunning in the combination of
beauty and power and terror." What effects
would we achieve by cutting from the bottom and
ending nine paragraphs earlier: "In that case,
the carriers' size wouldn't matter"?

A conversation with
Steve Twomey

DON FRY: Well, Steve, who reads you?

STEVE TWOMEY: Philadelphia is a difficult city for a foreign correspondent to write for, because it's kind of a Jekyll-and-Hyde city, although that casts aspersions on at least half the population.

Which half? [Laughter]

In one sense, it's a very blue-collar community, very working-class, very sports-oriented, probably the best sports town in America. On the other hand, it has remnants of Katharine Hepburn and Cary Grant and *The Philadelphia Story.*

Which half do you write for?

I think I can write a story that can appeal to the blue-collar guy in South Philadelphia, but I can't say that I'm conscious every time I sit down at a VDT that I've got to make sure that somebody in Fishtown or Kensington understands this. I think foreign news is so remote for most Americans that you have to go back to square one for almost everybody.

You have to explain things.

Yeah. Everyone talks about "writing for their mother," and I like to think my mother is a fairly

---

I have edited these six telephone interviews very heavily for clarity and brevity; in some cases, I have rearranged passages and recomposed questions.

sophisticated individual. But even when I was telling editors on the phone about stories, it was surprising to me how often what I assumed to be fairly obvious, came as startling news to them. And that always told me, "Boy, you've really got to explain it well this time, and be very simple and very basic."

When you're ready to write a story, do you call your editor to talk about space and to plan coverage?

Sure. Most of the ideas come from the correspondents. And having worked with the paper a very long time, I think I know what it wants and what it likes, so I didn't have too much of a problem determining whether something was worth a story or not. We would talk about how much a story was worth, and about length. The paper has had a policy of writing shorter and tighter for about the last four or five years, and so the debate usually tended to be, "Can't you write it shorter than that?" or "Surely, don't write it longer than that." I would almost never write a feature story and then say, "Here it is. Do with it what you will."

I don't know that we would discuss in great detail the organization of a story; we might discuss the lead. Particularly in France, I would be telling them what had happened in a given situation, and I could pretty well tell by their reaction what interested them.

Using them as test readers, right?

Sort of. Up until the last six months, none of our editors had ever been a foreign correspondent. So when it came to foreign news, they were "Joe Average," and just as good as anyone else at discerning whether something was new and different or hard to understand.

Does your stuff get edited very much?

No. There was almost nothing done to this piece, aside from two or three little things. When you're a part of the furniture, as I think I am after 14 years, they tend to leave the furniture in place. Maybe having been here so long, I know what works and what doesn't, and what they're going to like and what approach to take.

Tell me about your writing techniques. After you've done the reporting on a big story, how do you organize the material?

I have, quite subconsciously, developed a two-step process. I'll go through all the notebooks or the yellow pads, and I find all the quotes that ought to appear in the story, and type those on a separate sheet of paper.

Do you mark up the notebook?

I do all the usual: underline, star, circle. But that's only for the purpose of going through and typing into the machine what I want to take out of the notebook. The purpose is twofold. One, to make sure that I haven't forgotten some great quote. And two, so I can find things faster than thumbing through two or three or five notebooks.

Then I go through the notebooks, not for quotes, but just for the salient points, things I want to make sure appear in the story: facts, major ideas, and anecdotes. And I write each of those in a one- or two-word code or synopsis on separate lines on a legal pad. And as I write the article, it's a process of crossing off the quotes and the points. As the quotes get into the story, they disappear from the typed sheet. And as the points, the issues, and the anecdotes are put in the story, they get crossed off. And I know I'm done when there's nothing left on either page.

How do you structure the piece? Do you write an outline?

I normally don't write an outline. The placement of the points on the yellow pad tends to be a kind of outline. It would not pass Mrs. Smith's Grammar 101 in terms of following the rules of outlining, but it tends to serve that purpose. I don't do anything as formal as saying, "This is the lead. This is the nut graph. These are the points that will come in order." It never gets that formal, except in the case of this carrier piece.

Did you write an outline on this one?

I did. I did not write a word for a week. I just sat there and contemplated this mass of material, and finally reduced it to an outline.

How much material did you have? Ten notebooks?

Actually, I think it was only three, but I also had some tapes that I had made of various interviews. A lot of material for the piece came in the form of records of congressional hearings, magazines, and books, written material, in other words, that I had not generated myself. A great amount of the information came from other publications, most of them technical, lots of Navy and congressional publications. The number of live interviews for this piece was probably smaller than you'd expect.

How long did it take you to write it?

Coming to grips with how I was going to write it took a week, and writing it took another week. Even as I was writing it according to my outline, I kept thinking, "This is all wrong; this isn't going to work."

What bothered you?

Well, there was no direct correlation, at least not immediately, between what I had seen by going out to the aircraft carrier and the issue of whether these carriers make military sense. The connection was not immediately apparent from being there, but I wanted to be there in order to get color to write the piece.

Had you done all of the background reading before you went out?

I had done a lot of it. I had gone to London from Paris to interview the commander of the British naval fleet in the Falklands. They had two carriers that had come under air assault. I talked to somebody from *Jane's Defense Weekly* and somebody from the Institute for Strategic Studies about the theoretical aspects of aircraft carriers. I had done quite a bit of reading, although not as much as I did after I came back from being on the ship itself.

Let me tell you what struck me as the hardest thing about this story. The issue is very large, and the carrier visit can be seductive.

Absolutely right. I've never had an experience like that as a reporter. I've never had so much fun. I found watching this thing in operation mesmerizing. We were flown out to the carrier from Sicily and did an arrested landing, and then we were catapulted off when we left. And I wanted to stay for a week and watch these things, but I was actually there two nights.

Let's talk about your lead. It extends all the way down to the second "Hubba, hubba," right?

Right. In a magazine article like this, it's almost a misnomer to call it a lead. I think the conventional rules change a lot when you're writing something this long. I wouldn't call this a lead as much as an introduction.

Do you always write the lead or introduction before you write the rest of the story?

Yeah. I am incapable of going one word further with a story unless I'm happy with everything that's in front of it. I cannot do the end part before the second-to-last part or any other segment. It has to go absolutely word after word.

You witnessed the opening scene?

Why would you ask?

I learned to ask from dealing with your former colleague, Richard Ben Cramer. When you read his stuff, you always assume he was present, because, like you, he's a very graphic writer. And sometimes you learn, to your surprise, that he wasn't there.

I was in the control tower standing next to the Air Boss when this whole thing occurred, and I realized pretty quickly, as this was happening, that this was the most exciting moment, because it really was a touch-and-go situation.

I'm struck by the blur of technical terms and jargon. Do you worry about losing your readers?

All the time, but if you're trying to put them there on the deck of this carrier, jargon is part of the scene. Within certain limits, it enhances the story to think the way the Navy does and see it with their eyes.

You punctuate these descriptions with slangy conversations between Air Boss and Mini Boss.

In this introduction, I was not only trying to put you on the ship, but also weave in Amazing Facts. As you've noted, jargon can overwhelm a

reader, and I wanted to give it in small doses.
I wanted to break it up visually.

"Amazing Facts," indeed. Take a look at this paragraph: "Engines whine, then race— and a plane disappears from the deck in 2.5 seconds. Its exhaust heat bathes launch crews. The air reeks of jet fuel. Steam seeps from the catapult rack. The next plane is already moving forward to take the 'cat stroke,' and there's another behind it. Noise overwhelms the deck. All the while, the carrier slices through the blue."
I like those simple sentences and simple imagery, and what a sense of energy.

Well, they let us go out and stand on the flight deck between the bow catapults during launches. It was like a dream. And I wanted somehow to convey what it was like to be out there. And when I finished writing this, I thought I hadn't done it, and maybe it can't be done.

For example, I hadn't expected the smell, the overpowering smell of jet fuel whenever you're on the flight deck. I was prepared for airplanes being launched with great power, but I didn't think it would be that noisy. And I didn't expect that when the planes blow by you on the catapult, headed down the deck, you almost get knocked over by the jet wash. There's no experience that you can have walking around in daily life that prepares you for something like that.

That's what your next speaker says. You pull off this exciting piece of description, and then you have a pilot step up and say, "There's no way to describe it." [Laughter]

Well, I didn't plan that. But it reflects my latent anxiety that I hadn't done it, and this was my way of getting out of it. That, well, I tried it and failed at it, and the reason I failed is here's this guy saying, "Well, you just can't do it." Maybe I was letting myself off the hook.

I think it's a wonderful passage. Here's your problem in a nutshell: how can you reconcile what you see out there on the carrier with the debate? And here's your turning point, two paragraphs later: "Yet, for all their impressiveness and for all the importance the Pentagon attaches to the vessels, many congressmen and defense analysts argue that the supercarriers' day is history." And you're into the debate.

I was concerned that the reader would go on too long without knowing that this is a piece not just about how aircraft carriers are wonderful machines, but also about whether they are wonderful machines that are worth having. In the original version of this story, I wrote something like, "It is hard not to love the dance of the carrier deck. Even those who now argue that their day is history say they cannot help but admire the skill, beauty, and sheer guts, blah, blah, blah."

My editor on this piece, Bill Eddins, talked me out of planting that hint. He said because this is a magazine article, people assume it's going to be more leisurely than a news article. If they begin something like this, they're somewhat committed to finishing it. Bill argued that the beginning was strong enough that I could wait until this point, and turn down a different road, and I thought about it and agreed with him.

Once you turn to the debate, the material mostly comes from your prior reading, right? Did you write any of it before you went out on the carrier?

No. I didn't know how this was going to turn out until I got back. I had planned to organize it around five or six individuals by job function. Then I realized that wouldn't work at all. I thought, "I went out there and reported the wrong damned story."

So how did you get from there to the present structure?

I had to rethink the whole thing. The fundamental question was: "Are big carriers the way to go?" So, number one, I had to get people graphically onto the deck of a big carrier, and that was the introduction. And then logically came the section that an editor named John Katz once described as the "why you're invited to this party paragraph."

Great term: I'll steal that.

And that section begins, "It is hard not to love the dance of the carrier deck...." I had to give the pros and cons. And next, since we're debating big carriers, we have to ask, "Well, just how big are these carriers?" And that's chapter three, as I started calling them in my outline.

Then came, "What are the big carriers good for?" That became chapter four, which starts, "Libya. They were actually going to hit Libya." That section argues from the Navy's point of view and from its supporters' point of view, why big carriers are advantageous. In going through my notes, I realized that this particular carrier had given me a graphic example of one of the things the Navy says they're good for, and that was the attack on Libya.

What's next in the structure?

The next thing was, "What is the threat to what carriers can do?" Then came the discussion of the Soviet navy.

The next part asks, "If that's the Soviet navy, how does the U.S. Navy propose to deal with it?" That section begins, "Much of the time, *America* seems alone in the Mediterranean...." And the next section starting "It came out of the West" asks, "What could overcome those defenses?"

In each of the sections, I wanted to begin specific and small, and expand to general and

large. So each section begins with some sort of...I
don't necessarily want to say "anecdote," because
they're not little stories...

Little vignettes.

...vignettes, or something specific that happened out there on the ship, or in the case of the
Falklands, on somebody else's ship. And from
there, I blossom into a discussion of the more
general points. So in effect, there are nine stories,
and each has a nut graph, and a beginning, a
middle, and an end.

**That's why it reads so well. I believe readers
can follow a complex story better if they
have a sense of discernible shape. I tell
reporters to write sub-leads and sub-kickers
in each part, to show the readers where the
breaks fall. You use a nice alternating
structure, and you let it show.**

Frankly, I thought the story started strong and
steadily tapered off, and the sections became
more technical and less colorful as the story went
on.

**I don't think that at all. I like the alternation
of complex explanation with action, and I
never got to the point where I said to myself,
"I'm getting tired of this part." That's a
matter of selection. Anybody who's done the
kind of reporting you do has tons of stuff to
put in, and you leave tons of it out.**

Well, there were some pretty rigid rules on how
long this piece could be. So I threw out a lot of
stuff. Even though I spent two days in London
and conducted about six hours of interviews,
there's only one quote in this piece from all the
people I interviewed in London. So almost all that
stuff did not get into print. However, it enabled
me to write a little bit more confidently, knowing
what these people had to say.

Do you write subheads?

No. When I wrote my first magazine piece about four years ago, it was virtually seamless, with no natural breaks. And being used to writing news stories, I tried to keep readers going with transitions through the entire story. That's because I was writing stories that were 30 inches long, and this one was nearly 200. And the magazine editor I mentioned earlier said, "The reader's choking to death. You've got to let him come up for air. Think of it in chapters."

Good advice.

Think of it as a story that needs to be told sequentially from point to point with abrupt breaks between sections, no, *abrupt* is too strong, but...

Noticeable?

...noticeable breaks in which the reader can see that we are moving on to something else. And she had me redo the piece, and she was absolutely right. I don't think these are original thoughts. Every reporter doing a piece like this probably thinks in these terms.

As a matter of fact, most reporters don't think that way at all, and neither do editors. In our teaching at Poynter, we urge writers to break stories up into sections. And we even suggest that reporters write their own subheads.

Really?

Now, you have to come to an understanding with the desk, so they don't think you're stepping on their turf. But we find that reporters who write their own subheads do structure stories better, and their editors understand them better when they edit them.

I put a center bullet to delineate the section break, but I don't write a subhead. But I let them know that this is a different section, and they exactly followed the suggested structure on this piece.

You've got an interesting quotation on page seven from Secretary Lehman. "Lehman even said in testimony before Congress last fall that to build small is communistic, to build big is American. 'Should carriers be bigger or smaller? There is no absolute answer to that question,' he said. '...[But] our tremendous edge in technology is a permanent edge built into the nature of our culture and economic system, compared to the Soviets. It is to that advantage we must always build, not to go to cheaper, smaller, less capable ships in large numbers. That is an area in which a totalitarian, centralized, planned economy excels.' "

"Big is beautiful."

What did you think of Lehman's statement?

That's a good question. In the first draft, that quote appeared near the end of the story, where I was summarizing many of the arguments. And my editor said, "You've told people that. You're going around and around. Just ease out, put us back on the carrier, and be done with it. You don't have to bash people." And I said, "But I love this Lehman quote. This has got to appear somewhere in the story."

You're hinting that he's a demagogue, aren't you?

Maybe. I think to argue that a type of ship reflects the value of a political system is a little absurd. Or to argue that another type of ship shows the failure of the system is also ridiculous. And to argue that aircraft carriers reflect the in-

herent goodness of America, I thought was pretty
crazy. But what was important is not so much
whether he was right, but that he believed it, and
that it exemplified the thinking at the top of the
Navy hierarchy.

I tried not to make an editorial comment
along the lines that I just have given you.
Intuitive readers will come away with their own
assessments of these quotes. It's not necessary
to bash them over the head with it, even in a
magazine article where you're allowed to be more
opinionated, at least around here.

**You undercut the quotation with the adverb
"even" in the attribution: "Lehman even
said...." You're telegraphing there.**

Probably true. I plead guilty. Words like "even"
are loaded words, just as using "buts" and
"howevers" can be loaded decisions, too.

**Tell me about your interview with Captain
Allen.**

Navy men assume you don't know anything
about what they do and that you never really will
understand what they do.

Like cops.

Or newspaper people.

Exactly.

The captain gave quite willingly of his time, but
his demeanor was, at the beginning, more
pedantic than I would normally encounter in an
interview, a kind of quiet superiority. His tone
at the beginning was very condescending. Things
warmed up after about an hour, and it was quite
clear that he didn't want to stop. I had been told
not to talk about Libya, but he brought it up, and
that was when he started being his most graphic.

Is he the only source for the next part, about Libya?

No. In terms of the number of planes and what they were doing, that was all public record. We were on the carrier in the first week of June 1986, and they had bombed Libya in April, so it was about six weeks earlier. And everybody was still glowing. The account he gave is not particularly controversial. I thought it was important for his description of his pride in what this carrier could do.

In the Libya section, there's a disclaimer in parentheses: "(Fearing terrorist reprisals against the crew's families in the United States because of the carrier's role in the raid, the Navy requested that no crew member's name be used in this article, except Allen's, and it told crew members not to discuss Libya.)"
     Did the desk add that, or did you put it in?

I added that, because I wanted an explanation in the article somewhere as to why I wasn't using personal names.

Why did you put it *there*?

It fit there. I write stories by ear as much as by anything else, and to put it in anywhere else would have clanged so badly that I would have cringed. If I had put it in the introduction, where we're talking about Air Boss, or told the reader, "The reason we're not giving you their names is due to this raid on Libya, which we haven't yet told you this ship was involved in," it would have disrupted the whole flow of that introduction. The pace, the momentum, the immediacy, and the drama would have disappeared.

If it were an editor's note, I was surprised that they didn't put it outside the body of the

text. But if you wrote it, I see why it goes there.

Do you think it was necessary?

Oh, yes. I kept wondering, until I got to the disclaimer, why there were no names, except Captain Allen's.

It really irritated me. I wish they had told me before I left, because I would have tried to argue them out of it. But once I got onto the ship, there was no one who had the authority to overrule the order they had been given by the office in London.

Let's go to your description of the attack in the Falklands. By the way, what was your source for this scene?

There was a book put out by two or three reporters for the *Times* of London about the Falklands War, one of those six-months-after-the-end-of-hostilities-instant-paperback-successes. And they had an entire chapter devoted to the attack on the *Sheffield*, including interviews with these two officers as to what they had seen and what they had said. And, as the article says, they both had said the same thing at the same time. All the detail comes from that particular book, and much of that was in the public domain.

And you had that before you went out?

No, I had that when I came back. I knew before I went out that in naval circles, the Falklands War had become a major topic of discussion, because it really was the first war in history to pit airborne missiles against surface ships. But it was only after I came back that I decided I had better bone up on this to know exactly what had happened, and how it would apply to an attack on an American battle group.

You're dangling the reader. You tell us above: "It came out of the west just after lunch...," and we read two paragraphs before we discover that "it" refers to a missile. You introduce transitions very indirectly, and then several paragraphs down, you bring in what you're talking about.

I've had a lot of discussions with editors about whether we were holding off too long. I probably do it less now than I used to, but it still works its way in. It seems to add punch and a little drama and a little mystery.

Only experience can tell you how long you can dangle a reader. Let's go to the ending. You get out the way you got in, with carrier landings. Talk about that.

Right. I spent a good two hours on the catwalk with the LSOs, landing signal officers, as they went through two landing cycles. As with the launches, I found it stunning in the combination of beauty and power and terror. The next-to-last section discusses how carriers are vulnerable, and how we may have bet on the wrong horse. And I wanted to finish by saying, "That may be so, but they're fun to watch." And that brought me back to the beginning, and in a sense, a landing, a coming home, is a nice, obvious way to end the story.

I like the way you end it. " 'Sometimes,' said an LSO, 'I can't believe what we do out here.' " You were talking earlier about your conflict between awe and the debate, and there's the awe. It's a great kicker.
Did you have an opinion on this issue of carriers, and did you have trouble keeping it out?

Yes. My opinion before I left to go out on the carrier was that these are the wrong machines for this era, and that's still my opinion. I had to work to minimize this dilemma of being so utterly fascinated by the show that I let it color my judgment. I was conscious of trying to be fair to the Navy in this piece, and that's why I went to London to talk to those experts, all of whom agreed with the Navy, by the way, in its assessment of the value of these carriers. And by telephone from Paris, I must have talked to a dozen defense analysts to try to ferret out whether people agree with the Navy, and some of them do.

Well, I found it a balanced story.

Well, I thought it was. I sent copies off to the Navy in London and never heard a word from them, which I assume is probably a passive sign of acquiescence.

You'll find out if you apply to go out on a carrier again. [Laughter] Well, that's the end of my questions. Do you have anything you wish I would ask so you could answer it? [Laughter]

No, I can't think of anything, except my only apprehensions in doing this story were landing and taking off! [Laughter]

Thank you, sir.

You're welcome.

Mark Fineman
Deadline Writing

MARK FINEMAN, 34, was born in Chicago and was graduated from Syracuse University in 1974 with bachelor's degrees in journalism and philosophy. He started on the suburban section of the Chicago *Sun-Times*, and after four years moved to the Allentown *Morning Call* in 1978. He then worked at *The Philadelphia Inquirer* for a year on the suburban beat, until he opened their New Delhi Bureau, which he headed until 1986. He moved to Manila as bureau chief for the *Los Angeles Times,* arriving on January 10, 1986, just six weeks before the fall of Marcos. Earlier he won first and second prizes in the Amos Tuck Awards, as well as the George Polk Award in 1985.

Two leaders renounce Marcos, seize bases

FEBRUARY 23, 1986

MANILA—In an act of open mutiny, the Philippines' defense minister and the deputy armed forces chief seized control of the nation's military headquarters Saturday night, demanded that President Ferdinand E. Marcos resign because his Feb. 7 election victory was fraudulent, and pledged their support to opposition leader Corazon Aquino.

Backed by hundreds of heavily armed soldiers, Defense Minister Juan Ponce Enrile and Lt. Gen. Fidel V. Ramos, deputy chief of staff, sealed off the Defense Ministry building inside Camp Aguinaldo, one of the capital's three large military bases, and called on the remainder of the president's Cabinet and the nation's 200,000-man armed forces to support them. The rebels also seized nearby Camp Crame.

SUPPORT THIS MOVEMENT

"I cannot in good conscience recognize Marcos as commander in chief," Enrile told reporters inside the heavily fortified Defense Ministry, and urged "all decent elements in the Cabinet...to wake up and support this movement." Marcos should resign, the defense minister said, "while there's still time."

During an hour-long press conference at noon today, Marcos said he had deployed two battalions of troops around the bases, but he pledged several times to seek a non-violent solution to the crisis.

"We can settle this matter without any bloodshed," Marcos said. "...I want to talk to them."

While not ruling out "accidental firing," he said, "I am not giving up my position of non-volatile settlement of this matter very easily." He called the crisis "an awkward situation."

INCREASING HIS OPTIONS

The rebel officers at Camp Aguinaldo saw Marcos's statements as an attempt to avoid forcing his former aides into a corner, thus increasing his options and buying time. They took this as evidence that he lacked the power to quash the rebellion.

Marcos also said that if Aquino were to proclaim a provisional government, he would consider that "another act of rebellion."

Saturday night, a few hours after the seizure of military headquarters, the 68-year-old Marcos appeared on national television to charge that Enrile, his long-time friend, and Ramos, his first cousin, had been plotting to attack the presidential palace, assassinate him and his wife, and topple the government in a *coup d'etat.*

At today's press conference, however, he backed off the charge that Enrile and Ramos were directly involved in the coup and assassination plot, saying, "These actions were taken separately."

Marcos claimed in the Saturday night broadcast that he aborted the attempted coup when troops loyal to him captured the attack force of three military battalions and "neutralized without bloodshed three-fourths of the force."

As troops apparently loyal to Marcos manned 10-foot-high walls of barbed wire at every entrance to Malacanang Palace, Marcos appealed for calm, declared that his government was completely in control of the situation, and claimed "the armed forces are still unified in support of the president."

Calling the rebellion "the height of treason and rebellion," Marcos demanded that the two officials "stop this stupidity and surrender so that we may negotiate...what will be done with them and their men."

Marcos presented a man, identified as an Army Capt. Edgardo Morales, a personal guard of first lady Imelda Marcos, who read a confession that he had participated in a plot against the Marcoses. Early today, Marcos presented a second man who also implicated himself in the plot.

MILITARY DEEPLY SPLIT

Marcos said he could put down the mutiny with force but that "would mean the elimination of all the men who are in that corner of Camp Aguinaldo." Marcos said he believed there were 1,000 soldiers inside the military camp about three miles from the palace, although Enrile said he did not know how many supporters he had and acknowledged that the armed forces were deeply split.

After the announcement of the mutiny, several other Philippine leaders resigned, including Supreme Court Associate Justice Nestor Alampay and Navy Capt. Jose Roilo Golez, the postmaster general.

Besides Aguinaldo, the rebel officials controlled an adjacent base, Camp Crame, headquarters of the national police, and the mutiny became a tense stalemate today between rebel reformist factions and Marcos loyalists in the Philippines military.

Ramos said on the Roman Catholic Church-operated Radio Veritas this morning that he has been receiving expressions of support from military units around the country and that he has the backing of at least five of the 12 regional commanders.

TROOPS REPORTED MOVING

But Col. Tiaso Godor, a battle group commander at Camp Aguinaldo, said that two battalions of troops loyal to Marcos were converging on Aguinaldo and Crame and were expected to be outside the installations by midafternoon.

Outside telephone connections to Crame were cut off this morning, and Marcos's forces were also expected to cut the lines to Aguinaldo, Godor said. He added that there are about 1,000 rebel troops within the two camps.

"We are not in a tactically sound position," he admitted. "We may lose the game but win our political objective."

Marcos said that the military remains under the command of controversial Chief of Staff Gen. Fabian C. Ver, although the president had announced a week ago that Ver was retiring immediately. It was not clear today whether Ver or Marcos himself was in charge of the nation's powerful military.

MAJOR POLITICAL CRISIS

The rebellion plunged the nation into one of the worst political crises in its history and raised the prospect of a military showdown between Marcos and two of his closest aides, but Manila was calm this morning. A marathon was run along the shore of Manila Bay, millions attended Mass, and thousands of schoolchildren marched in a parade down Roxas Boulevard with floats honoring "Dental Week."

At Camp Aguinaldo, Enrile stood beside soldiers carrying rifles at a Mass conducted by Father Nico Bautista. "This may be the darkest hour in the history of our country, but this is also our finest hour," said Bautista, praising Enrile and Ramos for their action.

The Catholic archbishop of Manila, Cardinal Jaime Sin, offered to mediate to avoid bloodshed, but he also broadcast a statement calling on the Filipino people to protect Enrile and Ramos.

"I am in deep concern about the situation of Minister Enrile and Gen. Ramos," Sin said. "I am calling our people to support our two good friends."

CROWDS GATHER

By midnight Saturday, eight hours after the mutiny began, thousands of Filipinos heeding Sin's appeal over Radio Veritas surrounded military headquarters. They chanted, "Marcos concede!" and "Cory, Cory!"—Aquino's nickname—and threw bags of food over the fence.

Aquino was holding a rally in the southern city of Cebu when the revolt occurred, and a spokesman for her later said she was "secure in a safe place." An aide, Aquilino Pimentel, told United Press International that the rebellion was "totally unexpected" and that Aquino had briefly spoken with Enrile by telephone to inquire about the situation.

"I told her we are all right," Enrile said later. "She asked what she can do and I said, 'Pray for us.'"

At a press conference in Cebu today, Aquino said: "I am asking the military all over the country to support Enrile and Ramos. I think we are seeing Filipino people power at its best."

Enrile, in an emotional press conference, blasted Marcos for using blatant fraud to win the presidential election. Enrile, a Harvard-educated lawyer who had supported Marcos without question for two decades, said the president had personally asked him to cheat in his home province of Cagayan. Ultimately, Enrile said, Marcos forces invented 230,000 nonexistent votes in that area for the government's final tally.

Enrile, 62, and Ramos, 57, both denied that they were leading a coup and said they believed Aquino was the legitimate victor in the hotly disputed election.

"I believe that the mandate of the people does not belong to the present regime," Enrile declared. "I am morally convinced that it was Mrs. Aquino who was duly elected by the people. We have to support her and work for her.... That is why we are withdrawing our allegiance from Marcos."

The rampant election fraud "bothered my conscience," Enrile declared, as his troops, all of them members of a recently formed reform movement within the military, embraced, exchanged handshakes, and tearfully proclaimed victory. The troops were armed with Uzi submachine guns, grenades, rockets, mounted machine guns, and a huge stockpile of ammunition.

Junior officers vowed never to surrender, but there were signs that Enrile was willing to negotiate with Marcos. He suggested early today that Gen. Rafael (Rocky) Ileto, currently the Philippine ambassador to Thailand, might serve as an intermediary. Ileto is now in Manila.

Enrile said he made his sudden decision Saturday afternoon to mobilize his forces and hole up in the Defense Ministry after receiving reports that Marcos had ordered that he and all the senior military officers involved in his reform movement were to be arrested.

WILLINGNESS TO DIE

Describing his troops at the camp as "defensive only," Enrile said he took the action for "survival," but quickly added he is willing to die if Marcos attacks.

"He can have me shot, but if he will shed the blood of these young officers who are here with us, I do not think he will be able to live through it," Enrile said.

Soon after Enrile arrived at the ministry compound, two helicopters landed, packed with small arms, crates of ammunition, grenades, rockets, and food rations, indicating that he and his men expect a prolonged stay.

The first telephone call Enrile said he made after his troops took up positions was to U.S. Ambassador Stephen W. Bosworth, who told him he would relay the information to Washington. Enrile added that he had met with President Reagan's special envoy, Philip C. Habib, who left Manila just hours before the mutiny, but Enrile stressed that his actions were unknown to Habib when he left.

Enrile said that he did not know what percentage of the armed forces support him and Ramos and how many remain loyal to Marcos and Ver. But the defense minister said, "We are many," and the top colonels holed up with him at the ministry building said their supporters were spread throughout the nation.

"We are not acting at the behest or under the influence of anyone," said Enrile, who appeared to have dressed hurriedly in blue jeans, sneakers, a fatigue jacket, and a bulletproof vest. "We are not involved with any foreign power."

Asked how he thought Marcos would react to their mutiny, Ramos, a reform-minded career soldier who came up through the ranks in his 39-year career, said he believes that Marcos would put more military battalions around his palace "to make sure he has all the cards before he makes his move."

SCENE AT PALACE

"The best thing would be for him to come out and die along with us in a neutral venue," Enrile said.

The handful of reporters invited to the presidential palace Saturday night to witness Marcos's television statement saw no unusual troop deployments within the palace grounds. Instead, workers were uprooting the palace vegetable garden and erecting a stage for Marcos's inauguration ceremony, which he said was still scheduled for "high noon" on Tuesday.

Ramos, who met the press with another relative of the president who heads the national customs bureau at his side, said that he is resigning because Marcos "no longer is able and capable as commander in chief. He has put his personal interests, his family interests, above the interests of the people."

Ramos served for 15 months as acting chief of staff while Ver was being tried for the August 1983 assassination of Aquino's husband, Benigno S. Aquino Jr., as he returned to the Philippines from the United States. Ver and 24 others on trial were acquitted.

A West Point graduate, Ramos has been regarded by U.S. officials as a force for reform in the increasingly corrupt military.

At the press conference, Ramos called on all members of the armed forces to remain calm, to

avoid bloodletting, and to "look into their con-
sciences" to see whether they can still support
an "illegitimate government."

"I am only appealing to the troops now to do
what is right under the constitution," said
Ramos, adding that Marcos has refused many of
his attempts to effect reforms in a military
establishment frequently charged with murder,
torture, and other human rights abuses.

Throughout his time as acting chief of staff,
Ramos was constrained by a presidential
directive that all of his orders had to be cleared
first by Marcos.

"There has become an elite armed forces
within the armed forces of the Philippines that
no longer represents the officer and the soldier
corps," Ramos said. He listed three close political
associates of Marcos—including Benjamin
Romauldez, the ambassador to the United States
and brother of the first lady—who, he said, were
authorized large quantities of weapons and
ammunition before the election to coerce voters
to cast ballots for Marcos.

Ramos also warned the nation of a serious
threat from Marcos's tightly knit National
Intelligence Security Agency, a military wing
under the direct control of the president, Gen.
Ver, and Ver's son, Irwin.

The top-secret intelligence agency, which
keeps computerized files on all dissidents and
was implicated in the Aquino assassination, has
been functioning without any checks or balances,
Ramos said.

Ramos also listed several cases in which his
investigators documented corruption and murder
cases against top military commanders close to
Marcos, only to have them thrown out after key
witnesses disappeared or the president
personally intervened.

Ramos added that, despite his call to all
military personnel to disobey "illegal orders"
from Marcos's commanders, he issued orders of
his own for all soldiers and military police to

remain vigilant for attacks by the armed rebels of the Communist New People's Army. He said the rebels were likely "to try to take advantage of this crisis situation."

Like Enrile, Ramos said that he is willing to die during the current struggle, but he did not remain inside the Defense Ministry. Casually dressed in a safari suit and without a bulletproof vest, Ramos strolled out after the press conference, got into a silver Toyota, and sped off, followed by two cars packed with heavily armed soldiers. "I'm going jogging," he said.

Top aides said that Ramos was sequestering himself in his office at the headquarters of the national police, which he commands, in Camp Crame across the street from Camp Aguinaldo. Some reports said that he was protected by a force of about 400 soldiers.

But early today, Ramos came out of Camp Crame in civilian clothing and greeted the crowd, which chanted his name and surged forward to shake his hand. He climbed atop a pickup truck and said he was trying to protect the constitution. "We thank the people for giving us your support," he said.

Enrile, an elected member of the national legislature and long one of Marcos's most articulate supporters, was the more emotional of the two rebel leaders Saturday night.

"What I am doing is an act of contrition," the minister said, "to atone for my participation in the declaration of martial law (in 1972). If I had known martial law would be prostituted...I never would have supported it."

Marcos's declaration of martial law, which ended in 1981, was among his most controversial acts. While welcomed by many in the beginning, it led to rampant corruption and abuse by the military and is now said by most analysts to have marked the beginning of the Philippines' economic and political crisis.

Enrile added that he doubts that Marcos can declare martial law now, despite the crisis in the military, because "the people won't support it. It will cause a civil war."

And one source in the presidential palace, who asked not to be named, said Saturday night that Marcos would be afraid to invoke martial law "because he's afraid to find out just who supports him and who doesn't."

Enrile said Saturday that martial law never really ended. "We do not have any democracy here. It is a democracy of manufactured votes, manufactured tallies," he said, adding that he took his drastic action "so never again will tyranny be let into our country."

Several times, Enrile spoke fatalistically about dying in an assault on his stronghold—an attack that he believed was likely today.

"The hour of reckoning is here and now for me, and I would rather die fighting for my people," he said. "For me, it is now more honorable to die fighting this regime than die fighting for it."

Enrile, who had been mentioned as a possible ruling party candidate for president or vice president and is known to have had strong political ambitions, flatly denied that his motives in the mutiny are political.

"I am not doing this because I want glory or wealth or power," Enrile said. "This is not just our fight. This is the fight of all of the Filipino people."

Observations and questions

1) Fineman's uncharacteristically long and dense lead contains three place names, four personal names (each with titles), and four numbers. Weigh the risks and gains of such a lead in such a story.

2) Fineman assumes that "the readers have watched television for the last 12 hours, and they know what's happening over here in images. But they don't necessarily know what's happening here in context." Should we assume in framing a story that readers have seen pictures of the event on television? How would that assumption affect what we explain and describe?

3) This story consists essentially of a group of public statements by the principals. Study how Fineman spaces his speakers and how he frames each one for clarity and impact.

4) Fineman tells us in the conversation, "This country has a tendency toward the dramatic, and [I] viewed what was happening here almost as a script, where you had key characters and minor supporting actors, whose roles were crucial." Think about his script simile as an organizing tool for complex materials, but keep in mind its potential hazard: over-dramatizing.

5) Fineman and his fellow reporters often knew very little about what was going on, because the principals did not know what was going on either. He says he deliberately admitted his confusion to the reader. How can we do so without destroying our authority and the flow of the story?

6) Fineman keeps his readers oriented by repeating markers of place and time, such as "by midnight Sunday" or "at Camp Aguinaldo." Brevity pressures us not to repeat them, but clarity demands them. We write for readers, not for layout.

7) We do not learn the fate of Corazon Aquino until paragraph 28, and she does not speak until the 30th paragraph. Would you be tempted to move her higher? What would you gain and lose?

8) Study the presentation of Enrile, Ramos, and Marcos separately. Do the characterizations seem consistent? Can you tell Enrile and Ramos apart? Does Marcos seem to suffer from secondhand accounts?

9) Reread the story section by section. At the end of each section, ask if the story seems balanced. Does the story seem balanced at the end?

10) The last six paragraphs contain four quotations. Consider each as a potential ending. How would each one affect the readers' interpretation of the story?

Fall reveals a private world in palace

FEBRUARY 26, 1986

MANILA—The Marcos family's once-private living chambers in the Malacanang presidential palace were testimony Tuesday night to the haste of a fleeing Third World dictator.

The parquet floors of President Ferdinand E. Marcos's quarters were strewn with private papers and decrees. Emptied drawers stood half-open.

The mirrored dressing room of first lady Imelda Marcos was still filled with hundreds of her costly silk dresses and large wicker baskets overflowing with scented soaps from around the world.

Dozens of quart- and gallon-size bottles of the most expensive French perfumes still scented the room more than two hours after their owner, with husband and family, had fled a nation that no longer wanted them after two decades of rule.

Touring the most intimate corners of a palace that many Filipinos had come to view as a symbol of their oppression, a *Times* correspondent found that the Marcoses had fled so hastily that they abandoned scores of precious family mementoes—a six-foot oil painting of Marcos half nude in a Philippine jungle, photographs of Marcos and the first lady embracing, videotapes of Marcos family gatherings and of a private visit between Imelda Marcos and Nancy Reagan.

They also left behind a lavish, half-eaten meal with the family's silver service, a half-dozen wide-screen television sets, costly stereo units, a double freezer stuffed with imported American steaks, and a 10-foot-high closet packed with the first lady's nightgowns.

Beside Imelda Marcos's 12-foot-wide bed was a half-eaten banana.

One thing that the first lady did take with her, though, was her famed jewelry collection. Two large jewelry display cases were empty, and the floors of her bedroom were strewn with empty jewelry boxes.

There were many other signs in the first family's private quarters—which had been off limits to journalists for two decades—of the lavish lifestyle that had so alienated the Marcoses from so many of their countrymen as the nation's economy went from crisis to crisis.

The floors of every room were covered with valuable rugs from Afghanistan, China, Iran, and India. Chinese silk prints graced the walls. Crystal statuettes stood atop rosewood coffee tables, and Marcos's bedroom contained two wide-screen television sets, sophisticated exercise machines, and even a five-foot-long, remote-controlled toy car.

Imelda Marcos's private bathroom was equipped with a 15-foot-square sunken bathtub, mirrored ceilings, gallon bottles of a custom-made French perfume called First Lady, and no fewer than five Italian bathrobes.

And her husband's gymnasium-sized bedroom was a mute statement of a chronic condition of ill health that the president had always denied.

Beside Marcos's king-size bed was a specially fitted hospital bed connected to an oxygen machine and an intravenous bottle containing an unlabeled clear liquid. Elsewhere in the room stood a sophisticated piece of medical equipment called the "Centurion Magnotherapy," which a brochure explained was designed to treat chronic and degenerative illnesses of the heart, lungs, and kidneys.

The president's obsession with illness was obvious elsewhere in the palace. On the ground floor, Marcos had outfitted by far the most sophisticated operating theater and hospital emergency room in all of the Philippines.

There were also many signs in the palace of

the personality traits of Marcos and his wife. Books that Marcos had left lying out included *Operating Manual for Spaceship Earth* by Buckminster Fuller, *The Great Book of Jewels,* and *Self Learning Course on Goat Raising.*

Imelda Marcos had filled every inch of space on the several oversized, imported grand pianos in her chambers with photographs of her, without her husband, greeting leaders from virtually every nation of the world.

Throughout the rooms, though, there were also ample hints of the crisis that forced the exile of a man who had vowed never to leave his palace alive.

On a second-floor balcony, near the spot where Marcos had been sworn in for another six-year term at noon Tuesday, was a large blackboard depicting a detailed map of Manila's military Camp Crame, the revolutionary headquarters of Marcos's former defense minister, Juan Ponce Enrile, and his former deputy armed forces chief of staff, Lt. Gen. Fidel V. Ramos.

Beside the map were notes listing the rebels' possible strength in men and arms.

In a pile of documents stamped "Top Secret and Confidential" near the president's bed was a letter from Ramos to Marcos dated Feb. 19, three days before Ramos joined Enrile in defying the Marcos regime.

The letter warned the president that a recent flurry of "midnight appointments or assignments" within top military ranks by Marcos's chief of staff, Gen. Fabian C. Ver, "is not good for the armed forces of the Philippines."

Near the stack of documents, though, was perhaps the most apt symbol of all for a leader who vowed on national television just 24 hours before he fled that he would never resign, never flee, and would instead stand and fight "like a good soldier."

Beside the two pillows on Marcos's unmade bed was one more souvenir that the president had left behind—his World War II army helmet.

Observations and questions

1) Fineman smudges the fact that he was essentially alone in the private quarters. He modestly explains his discomfort at trumpeting exclusives and scoops. Should print reporters hide their lights under a bushel in a television age?

2) Fineman lists things he saw as signs of the characters of the Marcoses. Write down descriptions of the resultant characters. Which is harder, listing signs or describing character?

3) Do you have any ethical qualms about penetrating the private apartments of fallen dictators and their wives and describing their possessions? Do baddies, even foreign baddies, have a right to privacy?

4) Study the order of things described. What patterns, sequences, and groupings do you see? How else could Fineman have arranged this material?

5) Notice how often Fineman tells us the size, quality, and quantity of objects. Note the lack of any comparisons to normal sizes, quality, or quantities. Readers supply their own "private living chambers" as a norm.

6) Journalistic wisdom tells us to put our best stuff high, but notice the wonderful clang of the last word of this story.

The 3-day revolution: How Marcos was toppled

FEBRUARY 27, 1986

MANILA—At 3 p.m. Saturday, the telephone rang at Villa San Miguel, the modest, Spanish-style residence of Manila's Roman Catholic archbishop, Cardinal Jaime Sin.

It was Defense Minister Juan Ponce Enrile, the powerful and once deeply loyal lieutenant of Philippine President Ferdinand E. Marcos. But today, Enrile's voice was trembling.

"Your Eminence, please help us," Enrile pleaded. "In one hour's time, we are going to die. The president's men are coming to arrest us."

Moments later, the phone rang again. This time it was Lt. Gen. Fidel V. Ramos, Marcos's armed forces deputy chief of staff.

Ramos said that both he and Enrile were in grave danger because Marcos suspected them of plotting against him. If the cardinal would help them to make a stand against the authoritarian leader, Ramos said, he could guarantee support from key areas of the military.

Within minutes, Cardinal Sin, an unusually influential man in a nation that is 85 percent Catholic, decided that, with his help, Enrile and Ramos had a good chance of ousting a man who had ruled this nation with impunity and self-interest for two decades. Quietly, he went to work summoning the faithful to rebellion.

Three days later, a frightened President Marcos and his weeping family were hustled into four U.S. Air Force helicopters on their way out of the country. One of the world's longest-serving dictators had fallen with relatively little bloodshed. An oppressed nation of 55 million rejoiced.

"The force of the Filipino people stormed heaven with prayer, and got answered with a miracle," a happy and smiling Cardinal Sin said Wednesday.

The cardinal's mobilization of the devout Philippine masses was the key to the victory. But the story behind the three-day fall of dictator Ferdinand Edralin Marcos is far more than a demonstration of the power of the Roman Catholic Church in the Philippines.

It is a story of how two powerful and once-aloof national leaders switched loyalties in what they saw as their final hours, using their intimate knowledge of their leader and his army against him to purge themselves and their nation of years of injustice.

And it is a story of how a nation mobilized its most basic force—its people—to rid itself of a man so determined to cling to power that he refused to let go until every institution in his society had turned against him, until his own helicopters strafed and bombed his Malacanang Palace, until the clergy of his own religion had used their spiritual mandate against him, and until the sophisticated television and radio network that he had set up to distance himself from his people while dictating to them was captured and used to destroy him.

Here, based on eyewitness reports and interviews with the principal actors in the drama, is the account of the final days of a dictator.

Cardinal Sin, a shrewd and careful man, has long resisted working actively against Marcos. This time, however, he had picked his spot. It was not until he was convinced that Enrile and Ramos were truly united against the president and behind the standard bearer of the opposition, Corazon Aquino, that he made his move.

After his conversations with Enrile and Ramos, he quietly called on his bishops and nuns and priests to use their "spiritual power" to bring tens of thousands of their parishioners into the streets, where they were to form massive barriers to any counteraction by the regime.

He called on the church's vast radio network to mobilize and coordinate the effort and launch a propaganda campaign against Marcos.

And he called on his household nuns—Carmelites, Franciscans, and Pink Sisters—to expose the Holy Sacrament in the monastery beside his home, to fast for three days and three nights, and to pray for the fall of a dictator.

The alliance between Enrile and Ramos—the cooperation between a politician with intimate knowledge of Marcos's mind and a progressive general who commanded high respect from Marcos's most senior disgruntled officers—had its roots in perceived threats from the palace.

Enrile acted at first out of fear for his life and the lives of about 300 officers in a group that he had organized on another occasion when his life had been in danger.

That had been in 1982 when an attempt was made on his life. After the attack—its perpetrators are still unidentified—the tough defense minister ordered his most loyal officers to form a group called the Reformed Armed Forces of the Philippines Movement, informally known as We Belong.

The group had two goals: to improve professionalism in a corrupt and abusive military under the control of Marcos's unswervingly loyal chief of staff, Gen. Fabian C. Ver, and to keep themselves alive.

Enrile was having coffee when he received a call Saturday morning. "A friend" in military intelligence had intercepted a message saying Enrile and the We Belong group were to be arrested that night by Marcos loyalists in the Presidential Security Command and charged with plotting a coup and Marcos's assassination.

Thoroughly frightened, Enrile called the group's colonels, ordered them to collect their men and a huge cache of arms and ammunition that they had stashed for just such a contingency, and arranged to meet at his Ministry of National Defense building in the Camp Aguinaldo military base near suburban Quezon City. Then he contacted Ramos.

HAD WARNED MARCOS

Just three days before, Ramos had written a confidential letter to Marcos warning him that moves by Ver to dismiss or reassign some of the services' most professional officers and replace them with his own men, many of whom were little more than criminals and thugs, were creating deep dissension within military ranks.

For Ramos, the threats that Enrile conveyed from the palace and Enrile's personal willingness to risk his life in one final stand against Marcos were enough to gain his support.

Finally, Enrile quietly spread the word to the foreign press, whom he later beseeched to remain by his side as some measure of protection, that something was up at Camp Aguinaldo.

When the handful of Western journalists arrived at the sprawling military complex just before sunset Saturday night, Enrile was already sequestered in his office. A dozen officers draped with Uzi submachine guns, pistols, and radio sets stood guard outside.

In every inch of the building, dozens of soldiers in flak vests worked with silent, efficient determination to convert the ministry building in just two hours into a three-story combat bunker.

Corner offices became light machine-gun nests. Decorative flagstones in a center courtyard were stacked into a makeshift launching pad for anti-aircraft rockets and grenades. Snipers took up positions behind TV antennas on the roof.

As the soldiers unloaded crate after crate of rockets, grenades, C-rations, machine-gun ammunition belts, and M-16 assault rifles, reporters were left with answerless questions and a sense that history was about to be made.

In a third-floor conference room just after 6:30 p.m. Saturday, the crush of TV cameramen was so great that as Enrile and Ramos made their

way into the press conference, the cameramen
smashed a glass table and knocked over plants.

SPONTANEOUS DECISION

The way the two men were dressed attested
to the spontaneity of their decision. Ramos wore
a safari suit and running shoes; Enrile wore
baggy blue jeans, sneakers, and a fatigue jacket
over a bulletproof vest.

"There was an order to round up myself and
the members of the reform movement tonight,"
Enrile began cautiously, adding that only Marcos
or Ver could have given such an order. "As far
back as 1982, we've been getting consistent
reports (that) there were efforts to eliminate us....
It seems they chose tonight to do it."

Rather than dying without first making a
statement, Enrile said, he and his men decided:
"We will have to make a stand here, and if we
have to go down, we will go down here."

As the press conference went on, though, the
defense minister gathered momentum. He grew
more confident. He stopped shaking. And though
he continued to chain smoke, he seemed to
undergo a transformation—"an act of contrition,"
Enrile finally said, "to atone for my participation
in the declaration of martial law," a nine-year
suspension of personal liberties and human
rights that was one of the bleakest periods in
Philippine history.

For the next 90 minutes, reporters listened
in awe as Enrile, who had acquired an almost
villainous image as the chief administrator of
martial law between 1972 and 1981, unloaded
on the president, charging that he had blatantly
rigged the Feb. 7 presidential election, that he
had abused the public trust for years, and that
he was no longer fit to rule.

"I searched my conscience," Enrile said in
announcing his resignation, "and I found I could
not serve the president with the present
government any longer."

Then, it was Ramos's turn. The soft-spoken general who has long been viewed as a reformist was equally straightforward.

"The armed forces of the Philippines has ceased to be the real armed forces of the Philippines," he declared angrily. "There has become an elite armed forces within the armed forces that no longer represents the officers and the soldiers corps of the armed forces."

The reputation of the military had been subverted by Marcos, perverted by Ver, and was fast becoming an "immoral" force in society, Ramos said in announcing his own resignation.

Ramos then detailed how Marcos had personally authorized close presidential friends, known as "cronies," to use firearms and force to intimidate voters during the recent election, how he had allowed Ver to promote loyalist friends over qualified officers simply to safeguard the Marcos lust for power and money.

The military had become "practically the servants of political powers in our society rather than servants of the people," Ramos said.

"I think the president of 1986 is not the president we knew before. He is no longer able and capable of being commander in chief. He has put his personal self-interests, his family interests, above the interests of the people.

"I am motivated simply by the urgent desire for a better future for the people."

LAST STAND

This was their final stand against a regime that they once had risked their lives to protect, the two men said. And they insisted, and sources who know them well later agreed, it was nothing more than that—two men who had reached their breaking point. There was no planned conspiracy, they said, no CIA plot to overthrow the government, and no self-interest in gaining personal power.

"I have never had any plans to stage a *coup d'etat*," said Enrile, whose personal political ambition to someday become president was widely known in the Philippines. "All we are doing is defending ourselves...and nation."

Ramos added: "I am only appealing to the troops now to do what is right under the constitution."

And with that, the two leaders and their 300 or so men dug in for the night—Enrile at his ministry building in Camp Aguinaldo; Ramos at the general headquarters building of the national police, a military body, in Camp Crame across the street. Both knew that at any time Marcos could bring the force of his loyalist troops against them, outnumbering them hundreds of times over.

But when the attack came at 10:30 p.m., it was a verbal one.

The president used his powerful government-owned national television network to denounce the two men as traitors who had been conspiring against him for days.

"They were part of an aborted *coup d'etat* and assassination attempt against the president and the first lady—to attack Malacanang and assault and eliminate the president and/or the first lady," a furious Marcos declared.

"But we were able to neutralize without bloodshed three-fourths of the force that was planning to attack."

The remainder, Marcos claimed to the disbelief of the press and even his political supporters, were the men holed up with Enrile. They "would be easy to wipe out," he said.

But Marcos, who top advisers said was trying to change his image as a ruthless dictator to that of a more tolerant ruler so that he could redeem his reputation for posterity, vowed not to take the two defectors' positions with force.

UNDONE BY LENIENCY

In the end, that leniency may have been his undoing. If Marcos had attacked that night or the following night after Enrile had moved all his

men over to Ramos's camp in a dramatic show
of unity, Marcos could have eliminated the
rebellion.

But it was during Saturday night that
politics, religion, and military might fused
together in a movement now known as "People
Power."

Heeding the call of Cardinal Sin, the church-
owned station Radio Veritas began issuing
constant pleas for the Filipino people to pour out
into the main street between the two camps.
Priests, nuns, and seminarians flooded out of
their churches and monasteries. Volunteers
brought boxes of food and crates of soft drinks
to the soldiers holed up inside Camp Crame.
Their cause became a national cause.

By sunrise Sunday, the entire eight-lane
width of Efran de Los Santos Street was choked
with humanity. By the afternoon, when Enrile
strategists intercepted military transmissions
deploying two full battalions of loyalist marines
to the camp perimeter, the civilian crowd
summoned by Radio Veritas's "People Power"
campaign had grown to nearly 100,000 and
stretched for miles down the street.

The human barricade protected Enrile and
his renegade band as they knifed their way
through the crowd to Camp Crame, where Ramos
and his men gave them a hero's welcome.

The two leaders of what was on the brink of
becoming a full-blown rebellion then sequestered
themselves with their aides in Ramos's wood-
paneled office for several hours. They discussed
strategy, theorized about how Marcos might act,
and monitored military radio transmissions.
They began calling in their professional and
personal IOUs, contacting regional, provincial,
and unit commanders and asking them to join
in their last stand.

PLEDGES OF SUPPORT

By midnight, according to aides who were in
the room that night, Enrile and Ramos had

secured pledges from a number of provincial commanders and a few regional commanders, commitments duly reported by Radio Veritas for the morale of the crowd holding vigil outside. But their numbers were too few, and the soldiers involved were at least a day away from Manila— too far to stop the advancing armored column of Marcos's loyalist tanks, recoilless guns, and howitzers that were, by sunset, just a mile and a half away.

Their goal was to reach Camp Aguinaldo, which Enrile had abandoned that afternoon. There, according to dispatches over the loyalists' field radio network, the marine infantry battalions were to establish assault positions and await orders to shell Camp Crame.

But the armored column did not make it that night. It was at sunset Sunday that "People Power" had its first victory in a vacant field more than a mile away from a rebel army they had come out to protect. A human mass of tens of thousands—middle-class businessmen, artists, teachers, students, nuns, priests, and bus drivers—had placed their bodies and lives before Marcos's tanks and artillery.

Gen. A. A. Tadiar, the commander of the Marine Division, was forced to wait in the field with his men and machines. After several hours, he gave up and turned his column around.

Buoyed by that small victory of "People Power," Enrile and Ramos tried to go on the offensive during a press conference also designed to boost the movement's morale.

They warned the government soldiers not to attack. "We will assault you, and we will not spare you," Enrile said. And Ramos praised the men and women, both civilian and military, "who defended this little bastion of Camp Crame."

TOO FEW TROOPS
But the rebel leaders knew their numbers both inside and outside the camp were too few

to repulse an attack, if Marcos and Ver changed their tactics, and they went to sleep in the office knowing that unarmed civilians could not protect them indefinitely.

Just before sunrise Monday, the "People Power" revolution appeared to hit its lowest point. Loyalist riot troops swooped into the civilian crowd, its numbers already depleted by the night's dampness. They fired dozens of tear gas grenades and wielded truncheons to clear a path for Tadiar's tanks and artillery to rumble through to Camp Aguinaldo.

Inside Camp Crame, it looked even bleaker. Enrile's sophisticated tapping equipment picked up a transmission that all six helicopter gunships in the 15th Air Wing had been dispatched to the presidential palace to be ready for an attack on Camp Crame the minute the order came. Against heavy artillery across the street and rocket-armed helicopters in the air, the rebels, with their assault rifles, grenades, and rockets, hardly stood a chance.

"A half-dozen shells and a few good strafing runs and we're all dead," one of Enrile's colonels said with resignation that morning.

Suddenly, at sunrise, a series of unlikely events "turned the tables for us," Ramos said that morning. They changed the face of Philippine history.

AIR WING DEFECTS

First, the 15th Air Wing did not attack. Rather, the six gunships and their pilots under the command of Col. Antonio Sotelo landed in the heart of Camp Crame and announced that they were defecting to Ramos's New Armed Forces of the Philippines. Ramos's men dashed wildly out of the command headquarters, hugging the pilots and gunners, doing high-five handshakes, and weeping with joy. Ramos and Enrile, almost in disbelief, climbed onto the base of a flagpole and declared victory.

Behind the rebel leaders' triumph, though, was a deliberately false message put out on a loyalist military radio frequency that Marcos and Gen. Ver knew the rebels had been monitoring. It said that Marcos had fled the country.

Later, Enrile recalled, they realized that the bogus message was a clever ploy by Marcos, first to draw the rebels out and lure them into revealing the actual size of their force, and second to get them to report the news to Radio Veritas, which immediately began broadcasting that Marcos had fled to Guam. That gave Marcos justification to declare a national state of emergency that would allow him to shut the station down.

When the news blared through radios all over Manila, confusion reigned. Radio Veritas is considered by far the city's most credible station.

It was then that Marcos made his big mistake. He called a press conference to be televised live nationwide just after 9 a.m. Monday. He would show the world that he was still in his Manila palace and declare the state of emergency to shut down the rebels' primary propaganda outlet.

TACTICAL ERROR

"If he had never held that press conference, he would still be president of the Philippines," said Col. Mariano Santiago, a former member of Marcos's feared Presidential Security Command who defected to opposition leader Aquino's campaign before the election.

What Marcos did not know as he put on his powerful front and showed off his wife and children on television Monday morning was that Santiago was outside the government TV station several miles away with an assault rifle, a ragtag team of New Armed Forces commandos, a few thousand civilians to use as a shield, and a megaphone telling the station's employees and armed guards to surrender.

After a brief skirmish, Santiago, with the help of commando reinforcements sent by Enrile

and Ramos, captured the station. The broadcasting switch was flipped off, cutting Marcos off
in mid-sentence as he was authorizing his troops
to use small arms against the rebels in defense
of government installations.

The soft line apparently was triggered by
urgent overnight messages from President
Reagan, who put Marcos on notice that he would
cut off all military aid to his government if he
attacked the rebel stronghold.

But, as it turned out, Marcos had lost his last
real chance to put down the rebellion that
morning.

VER FAVORED SHOOTING

Forty minutes after Marcos had lost his last
real link with the Filipino people—the ailing and
aloof president had spent his last several years
largely in his palace—an angry Gen. Ver did
order the artillery divisions in Camp Aguinaldo
to open fire. Ver had been seen by the entire
nation arguing heatedly on television in favor
of bombarding Camp Crame to destroy the defecting helicopters.

By then, it was too late. According to air force
Col. Manuel Oxales, who was inside Aguinaldo's
general headquarters when the order to fire came
over the secret palace radio frequency, the field
officer in charge decided to disobey it.

"We decided it was all over when we saw the
president on television with only three generals
with him in the palace," Oxales said. "We knew
then his support was gone."

The field officer refused two subsequent
orders, and, when the order finally did reach
commanding Gen. Tadiar, who was about to
implement it, a countermanding order came over
the radio. An American communications expert
sympathetic to the rebels said he had helped the
rebel force tap into the secret frequency to issue
the final order not to fire.

At noon Monday, the loyalist forces were
recalled to their base at Fort Bonafacio, the last
loyalist bastion outside the palace complex.

"He's counting heads," said opposition leader Ernesto Maceda, now an Aquino Cabinet minister, who was eavesdropping on the palace's military radio transmissions that day. "He's trying to see if he still has enough of a force to launch an attack against the revolution."

PROPAGANDA CAMPAIGN

Quickly, Gen. Ramos seized the advantage. Playing off Marcos's declaration that morning that he and his rebel force were "a revolutionary government," Ramos launched a propaganda campaign in behalf of his New Armed Forces of the Philippines, appearing repeatedly on television to announce the names of the latest units and provincial commands to defect.

Ramos also took the offensive in the air. He sent Col. Sotelo and his 15th Air Wing on harassment raids. The thundering gunships moved around Manila's airspace at will, rocketing the presidential air fleet at Villamor air force base and dropping grenades into the president's palace. That attack moved Marcos later that night to tell the nation on the airwaves: "My family here is cowering in terror in Malacanang...."

Few outsiders could understand at the time why the president did not send his air force to shoot down Col. Sotelo's gunships. They did not know what Marcos and his air force commander, Gen. Vicente Piccio, knew. High above the gunships were two F-5 fighters flying cover. The jets were part of the 5th Strike Wing, which also had defected to the side of the revolution Monday. By day's end, after Ramos's show of force in the air, the entire Philippine air force had switched sides too.

When night fell on Camp Crame on Monday, Enrile and Ramos knew they had won. Ramos's claims over the commandeered government TV station that night were not empty boasts. The rebels controlled 85 percent of the nation's military. The only question that remained was how hard Marcos and his dwindling loyalist forces would fight to fulfill the president's repeated pledge that he would never resign and never leave the Phillipines.

MESSAGE FROM REAGAN

Anticipating the inevitable, Reagan sent a message to Marcos and the world through spokesman Larry Speakes, urging Marcos to resign and offering him asylum in America.

But the Philippine ruler remained firm. He had marshaled his forces Monday to set up a hastily rigged microwave link between his palace and the Channel 9 television station, one of four stations controlled by his daughter, Imee Marcos Monotoc. That night, he gave what was to be his last televised address to the nation.

The president went on the air at 8:10 p.m. in a stark and dimly lit room of his palace. He sat at a desk in a denim jacket, a symbol, he said, that after the helicopter bombing that day, "we're ready for anything."

To his right sat his wife, Imelda, bouncing one of his grandsons on her knee. Beside the first lady were two of Marcos's children, Imee and Ferdinand (Bong Bong) Marcos Jr., the latter dressed in combat fatigues.

Marcos did his best to put up a powerful front. He blasted Enrile and Ramos as "a third force" trying to usurp power from both him and Corazon Aquino, who had been leading a nonviolent protest campaign in an effort to claim the victory that she said Marcos had stolen from her in the election.

He launched an attack on the rebel civilian support system of "People Power," calling it "spiritual terrorism," and chided "that renegade Santiago" for that day's successful attack on the government station, Channel 4—"physical terrorism," he called it.

CERTAIN HE MEANT IT

Even now, former Marcos loyalists say they are certain the president meant it Monday night when he pledged in the most sincere tones, "We have no intention of going abroad... We will defend the republic until the last breath of life and until the last drop of blood in our bodies."

But Enrile, Ramos, and others who had come to know every nuance of the president in the decades that they served him saw that he was a beaten man Monday night.

"I was his martial law administrator," Enrile said that night. "I know his capabilities. The war is almost over."

Marcos appealed to his loyalists: "I am calling on all the people to support the legally elected government."

And, almost pathetically, he held up a copy of the day's newspaper, pointing to the date to prove that he was actually in the palace and that the transmission was live. As if it were not enough, the president then declared, "At 8:20 in the evening of the 24th of February, I am here."

Twenty-five hours later, Marcos would be gone.

That last day, however, was to bring the worst of the bloodshed in the near-bloodless coup. At least 15 people were to die in the violence between Marcos die-hards on the one hand and the rebel troops and civilian mobs on the other.

At daybreak Tuesday, small bands of Marcos loyalist troops had taken to the streets in an effort to subvert the rebels by guerrilla attacks.

One group that reportedly had been ordered by Ver to reclaim the government TV station established a base inside a ground station adjacent to a 1,000-foot TV transmitter for Channel 9, the one station to which Marcos still had access.

Two loyalist snipers climbed halfway up the tower and opened fire with rifles on the street below, trying to break up the sprawling human mass that "People Power" had used to surround and protect the rebels' commandeered station.

Again, the plan backfired. After a two-hour firefight that critically injured three civilians in the crowd, Ramos's troops killed both snipers, and a helicopter gunship knocked out the transmitting antenna for Channel 9—Marcos's last link with the world outside his palace.

SHORTEST TERM

The station was blacked out seconds before Marcos was to be sworn in for his fourth term as president of the Philippines, perhaps the shortest presidential term in history.

The crowd that came to his palace for the Tuesday noon event was dwarfed by the legions of supporters who had flooded a suburban clubhouse for a similar presidential inauguration for Aquino just half an hour earlier. Aquino's swearing-in was unconstitutional, but few Filipinos questioned her mandate.

The streets of the sprawling city were jammed with her supporters in yellow, her campaign color. Demonstrations formed spontaneously at intersections throughout Manila. There were no policemen to be seen. The nation seemed on the brink of chaos. It had two presidents and no government.

Unknown to most, though, Marcos already was negotiating on the phone with Enrile.

DECISION ALREADY MADE

The president had made his decision to leave even before he stood on his second-floor balcony with his hand raised and declared: "This is the best day of my life." Beside him, his wife stood in tears. His vice-presidential running mate, Arturo Tolentino, was nowhere to be seen.

By then, Marcos had phoned U.S. Sen. Paul Laxalt (R-Nev.), a close friend of President Reagan.

Reagan had sent Laxalt to see Marcos last October in an effort to persuade the Philippine president to implement reforms. Marcos and Laxalt had hit it off.

Marcos phoned to ask Laxalt about rumors that Reagan was sending the U.S. Navy up the

Pasic River to shell Malacanang. He wanted to know if he really had lost Reagan's support.

Then, after Laxalt had consulted Reagan and phoned back, Marcos asked the senator what Laxalt thought he should do. Laxalt told Marcos that he personally thought that the time had come for Marcos to make a clean break, to leave the Philippines. A defeated Marcos replied, "I am so very, very disappointed."

The president hung up, and, at 11 a.m., called Enrile. First, Marcos asked his former defense minister to form a provisional government that would exclude Aquino—"he wanted to see that the person who handles the transition government is a person who will at least protect some of his people," Enrile recalled Wednesday.

Enrile rejected the idea. "I do not believe in military juntas," he said.

At 4 p.m., Enrile got a second call from the palace. "Please tell your men to stop firing at the palace," a frightened Marcos told him.

"Mr. President," Enrile replied, "I don't have any men in the vicinity of your palace."

"Nonetheless, will you see to it that it stops?" Marcos pleaded.

U.S. ESCORT

Later in the conversation, Marcos finally agreed to leave the palace that night. He asked Enrile to get U.S. Gen. Theodore Allen, commander of the Joint U.S. Military Assistance Group, to provide Marcos and his family and friends a security escort.

Enrile then phoned U.S. Ambassador Stephen W. Bosworth and told him what Marcos had requested. Bosworth took it from there.

It was just after 9 p.m. Tuesday that the first two U.S. Air Force helicopters arrived, followed a few minutes later by two more. The Marcos family had spent their last hours in Malacanang tearing through the few precious belongings that they could bring along—Imelda Marcos's jewelry, some of Marcos's diaries, and just enough clothes to last until they reach one of their many homes in the United States.

The family ate their last meal in the palace: fish, wine, and vegetables served from half a dozen sterling silver buffet trays. Outside the walls of the palace compound, street fights were breaking out between protesters trying to claim the palace for the people and loyalist civilians who had been issued firearms by palace guards that morning.

The helicopters evacuated about 60 people in all from the palace for the 50-mile ride to Clark Air Base.

Two hours later, after the chants of opposition crowds gathering before the palace had replaced the throb of the helicopter blades, a young farmer—one of the loyalist vigilantes who believed that he was defending his president still inside—was beaten to death—mistakenly by someone on his own side.

Police were still trying to identify the victim Wednesday, but, said one police corporal, "One thing's for sure. He's the last of so many to die for President Ferdinand E. Marcos."

Observations and questions

1) Fineman got the account in his lead directly from its subject, Cardinal Sin. Yet he felt compelled to confirm it with aides to Enrile and Ramos, even under the heaviest deadline pressure. Do we need this kind of cross-checking on every anecdote, or only on one this crucial?

2) Notice that Fineman does not attribute the lead account. Should he? How could he do so without losing the flow or cluttering the beginning of his story with reporting apparatus?

3) After the lead, Fineman gives three paragraphs of themes he will develop in this long reconstruction. He risks slowing the flow of the narrative action to orient the reader. But this framing will tie together the three days of confusion and detail to follow. Authors put a table of contents at the front of a book for a reason: to serve the reader.

4) As you read this long account, study how Fineman telegraphs his admiration for Enrile and Ramos while balancing it with efforts to understand the motives of Marcos.

5) For years, Enrile had been depicted in the American press as a villain for his role as "the chief administrator of martial law." How does Fineman evoke and undo that image at the same time?

6) Marcos and Enrile reflect each other's characters, often by describing their opponent. As Enrile rises in our estimation, Marcos declines.

7) Fineman describes in detail the public relations efforts of both sides, but he often undercuts them with immediate asides on how events turned out. For example, see page 70: "It was then that Marcos...before the election.". Marcos makes a tactical error in calling a press conference for Monday morning, and Fineman juxtaposes an assessment from a defecting officer. Does a retrospective story have different rules for fairness? Does it require different techniques for establishing context?

8) Study the placement and wording of the subheads, some of which break the sections inappropriately. Letting reporters segment their own stories and write their own subheads would help solve this problem.

9) Fineman describes the structure of this piece as chronological with contextual framing. Identify the various flashbacks and ask how each contributes to the readers' understanding of events.

10) Fineman ended with the death of a young farmer and the remark of a police corporal. Do you find this ending downbeat or upbeat? Consider other ways of ending this piece, such as returning to Cardinal Sin, the subject of the lead.

11) Fineman tells us that he neither revised nor reread this piece before dictating it over the phone. How is it possible to achieve such polish without revision?

12) Our conversation with Mark Fineman shows he is a natural storyteller, who explains his professional life and techniques by telling anecdotes and reconstructing dialogues. How can we transfer our own conversational skills to make our writing clear and vivid?

Enrile's revolt sparked by his children

MARCH 2, 1986

MANILA—Three days before Defense Minister Juan Ponce Enrile declared war on his president, a letter from his son arrived.

"Dear Dad," began the handwritten message from 27-year-old Juan (Jackie) Ponce Enrile Jr., who campaigned heavily and loyally for President Ferdinand E. Marcos in the recent presidential election. The letter said:

"I will never be able to fathom how such a great man can stoop to such lowness as to cheat all of us out of our right to choose.

"I'm afraid we are reaching a point wherein future generations of Filipinos may emulate such despicable acts and feel justified, simply because we, when we had the chance, did not stand up for the truth."

As Enrile was reading the letter, his daughter, Kristina, came home from school at Manila's Ateneo University. She was crying. Once again, she told her father, the other students had jeered her on her way home because her father was Marcos's loyal defense minister.

"I guess that really was it," Enrile said in an interview Saturday with the *Times*. "If my son and daughter feel like this and see no future for their country, then I thought I had better do something about it."

Enrile threw his Uzi submachine gun over his shoulder and three books on war, revolution, and law into a bag. He went down to his ministry office and led 400 men in a rebellion that in just three days toppled Marcos's 20-year regime.

Sitting in his still-fortified office Saturday night, reflecting on the rare revolution that has made him a national hero, the 62-year-old Enrile said that he launched the revolution both for his

children's generation and for himself. He also
said that Marcos had personally threatened his
life the week before, and that Marcos had made
him experience the same frustrated terror that
he felt while a prisoner of the Japanese in World
War II.

Noting that five tanks and armored
personnel carriers are still deployed outside his
ministry building and that he still sleeps every
night on a couch in his office, surrounded by
armed guards, Enrile added that it will take two
to three weeks more before the revolution is
complete.

But in the wake of the coup led by Enrile and
Lt. Gen. Fidel V. Ramos, now the armed forces
chief of staff, Enrile vowed that he is not seeking
a share of the political power, that he and his
military organization will remain "absolutely
subservient" to the civilian government of
President Corazon Aquino, and that he hopes to
retire from the government entirely when
Aquino's government stabilizes—"probably in
one or two years."

Enrile said that he met Aquino at her
presidential swearing-in ceremony Tuesday for
the first time since the late 1970s, when she came
to him pleading for rights to visit her husband,
Benigno S. Aquino Jr., whom Enrile helped jail
for nearly eight years on charges of trying to
overthrow Marcos's government.

He said that he believes Corazon Aquino is
competent to govern the Philippines and pledged
"to obey each and every order of my commander
in chief."

"You can call me to account if I ever renege
on this: I will always place this ministry and the
military under Mrs. Aquino," Enrile said. "These
are my ideals as a person."

Enrile, who has made his ambition for the
presidency known to the ruling party's inner
circle for several years, added, "I would probably
have tried for it if the president did not run...but
having gone into this kind of experience, all I

want to do is help put the country back together and then leave.

"If I wanted the power or the presidency, it was being handed to me on a silver platter. We had control of 85 percent of the military (at the peak of the uprising against Marcos). Marcos asked me to take over through some sort of junta and forget about Mrs. Aquino. But I think history would have been very harsh on me if I had started such a tradition in the Philippines."

Asked whether history mattered to him, Enrile said: "Yes, yes, very much. I am a student of political theories."

And Enrile is also very much a product of his past—six decades of learning about war, religion, and survival.

At one point in the wide-ranging interview, Enrile said: "I learned how to defend myself. I learned how to survive. Survival. That is something President Marcos never knew."

The lessons started early for Enrile, the impoverished, illegitimate son of a village woman in the northern province of Cagayan. His father was a prominent attorney, Alfonso Ponce Enrile, but the elder Enrile already had a wife and family in Manila, and his illegitimate son grew up walking barefoot to school.

One day in high school, when Enrile was 17, four wealthy students attacked him in an argument over a girl. They stabbed him three times in the arm, stomach, and throat. "I nearly died," Enrile recalled. His family decided to press charges, but when the case came to court, the four boys had high-priced lawyers who paid off the judge and got off, he said.

"Not only that, but I was the one who got expelled from school..." for the incident.

The incident, according to family and friends, scarred Enrile for life—both physically and morally. "I guess he vowed then never to tolerate that kind of injustice," Jackie Enrile said Saturday. "And when he was forced to tolerate it, he vowed to atone for it."

Enrile's second lesson in survival, he said, came Oct. 10, 1944, when he was captured while fighting for the Philippine resistance against Japanese occupation in World War II. Enrile spent the next three months in a prison camp, where, he said, "I learned to cope with danger.

"I heard the cries of the other prisoners being tortured, and I had to kneel before my captors and feel the blade of that samurai (sword) against my neck and listen to the Japanese officers bluffing me that they'd kill me if I didn't tell them what they wanted to know.

"That was the same thing I experienced here Saturday night"—the night more than a week ago that Enrile and Ramos seized two Manila military camps and launched their coup against the dying regime of a man Enrile had served faithfully for two decades.

"I did not have any medals," Enrile said in a comment aimed directly at Marcos's disputed claims about his own war record, "but I went to war."

BEATINGS AND TORTURE

"I was beaten up by the Japanese and tortured for almost a month, and they never got anything out of me. That's why when I came here I said, 'Mr. Marcos is going to get it. He'll either kill me or he is going to get it.' "

Still, it was not an easy decision for Enrile, who had been at Marcos's side since the toppled president's first campaign in 1964. Marcos picked Enrile out of a crowd of young lawyers that year, after Enrile had persuaded his father to finance his law studies at two Philippine universities and Harvard University in the United States.

In the early years, Enrile was part of a dynamic new government, then likened to that of President John F. Kennedy. But when Marcos declared martial law in 1972 to crack down on a Communist insurgency, rural private armies, and rampant street crime, he named Enrile his martial-law administrator.

LINKED TO MARTIAL LAW

Like most Filipinos, Enrile said the strict doctrine was good for the first two years. "It was planned as a noble effort to correct the societal ills and to stabilize the country," he said.

"But it became something else after a time. I could not leave. I became a prisoner of it. I wanted to leave for a long, long time, but there was always something.

"I kept getting threats every now and then."

Enrile recalled that shortly after the 1983 assassination of Benigno Aquino, a man Enrile believes was sent by Marcos visited his barber and asked if the barber wanted to make a lot of money.

"You are the minister's barber," Enrile quoted the man as saying. "Why don't you just slit his throat for us."

THREAT RECALLED

Then, at Marcos's last Cabinet meeting the week before Enrile and Ramos staged their coup, Enrile said that Marcos warned all his Cabinet ministers that their lives might be in danger if they withdrew their support from him.

"I was sitting beside the president, and he leaned over and whispered to me, 'Johnny, you are the prime target.' "

An intelligence report in a similar vein reached Enrile from a meeting that Marcos held with Ramos and other top generals 10 days ago. The report, saying that Enrile and others would be arrested and perhaps killed, forced him to act when he did. While his children's reaction to Marcos's tainted victory in the recent election gave Enrile the cause to act, it was the death threat that gave him the urgency.

Yet Enrile was insistent throughout the historic, three-day drama which brought Marcos down that the president and his family not be harmed physically.

MARCOS ISOLATED

On the final day of the coup, several hours before Marcos asked Enrile to help arrange his departure from the Philippines, Enrile and the thousands of defecting troops had totally isolated Marcos in his presidential palace. The previous day, Enrile had sent a helicopter gunship to strafe the palace, but stressed that no residential areas be targeted.

"If I wanted to hit the president—you know, some of the men under me asked permission to hit the palace and I said, 'No, don't hit the palace.' "

The tactics of the coup, he said, were purely psychological warfare, hitting at what Enrile learned through the years were Marcos's most sensitive points. From the very first day, Enrile worked on Marcos's mind, trying to make him feel more and more isolated.

MESSAGE TO MARCOS

Last Sunday, when Marcos still held the upper hand in the battle for control of the 200,000-member armed forces, he tried to get Enrile on the telephone, but Enrile refused to talk to him. Instead, he sent the president a note telling him to beware, that the men he had around him to protect him might simply imprison him and hold him hostage.

"As far back as July 1983, before the Aquino assassination, I told the president, 'In the end, you will become a prisoner in your own palace,' " Enrile said. "I played on his isolation."

That was the reason, Enrile said, that Marcos, rather than ask his own aides to contact U.S. Ambassador Stephen W. Bosworth to arrange for his hasty departure Tuesday, asked Enrile to do it.

"I tried to use everything I learned about the president in those 21 years against him," Enrile said, adding that he had brought three books with him when he left home to set up his command headquarters last weekend.

Enrile said he took *Revolutionary Change* by Chalmers Johnson "because it tells why a society breaks up." He took *The Idea of Law* because "it tells what is the fabric that brings a country back together," and *The Art of War* by Sun-Tzu, the Chinese general and military theorist, "because it says what is the art of doing something about it."

But Enrile, who has two pictures of Jesus Christ in his office, also relied heavily on religion to pull off what many Filipinos still regard as a miracle.

He and Ramos did not even launch their revolt until they had the blessing—and political assistance—of Cardinal Jaime Sin, archbishop of Manila and Roman Catholic primate of the Philippines. Sin mobilized the church and Radio Veritas, the church-operated radio station, to get tens of thousands of civilians into the streets to act as a buffer for the initially ragtag rebel band.

Sitting outside his father's office in full combat gear on Saturday, Enrile's son Jackie summed up his father's change of heart:

"I guess his conscience was really bothering him—all the lying and all the deception.... I look back on this whole thing, and, really, I think it was all an act of God."

Observations and questions

1) Where does the lead on this story end? Does this story even have a lead? Do we need a lead on every story, especially analysis pieces?

2) In the eighth paragraph ("Sitting in his still-fortified office..."), Fineman places Enrile in a setting, but leaves himself out despite the exclusive nature of this interview. He explains the omission in terms of modesty. But the one-on-one character of the interview surely affected what Enrile said and how he said it. Should Fineman have described the circumstances of this important interview?

3) On page 82, Fineman introduces a new section by listing its themes: "And Enrile is also very much a product of his past—six decades of learning about war, religion, and survival." Readers need reorientation as they read along, not just at the beginning of stories.

4) Fineman has several sources for this story, although it turns on his interview with Enrile. See if you can find at least five other voices besides Enrile's. Even a single-source story does not have to read like a monologue.

5) This interview explains Enrile's role in the coup, his motivations, and his ways of analyzing people around him. But notice also how much it tells us about Marcos.

6) On page 85, Enrile speaks a sentence that makes very little sense as prose, but perfect sense as conversation: "If I wanted to hit the president—you know, some of the men under me asked permission to hit the palace and I said, 'No,

don't hit the palace.' " Normal journalistic
practice would suggest either paraphrasing or
cleaning up that quotation. But think about it
as emblematic of a man thinking, and you might
just leave it alone, as Fineman did.

7) Early in this story, we hear that "Enrile
threw...three books on war, revolution, and law
into a bag" on his way to the rebellion. And
almost at the end, we learn their titles and why
Enrile chose them. Speculate on why Fineman
splits these two passages. Don't settle for easy
answers.

8) Enrile's son Jackie speaks in the beginning,
middle, and end of this story about his father.
Consider the unifying effect of this spacing.

9) In the introduction to last year's *Best
Newspaper Writing,* I spoke of "the most basic
principle of newswriting: reveal the character of
human beings by telling stories about them."
Mark Fineman proves the point.

A conversation with
Mark Fineman

DON FRY: Tell me about your writing methods. Let's say that you've just finished the reporting for a piece. How do you organize it?

MARK FINEMAN: Usually frantically, with a lot of desperation and cups of coffee and cigarettes. [Laughter] The one thing that is absolutely crucial, especially when you're covering a breaking story, is that you must constantly be thinking about the writing of the story as the events are occurring in front of you.

Number one, it helps you organize the events while you're watching them, and number two, it forces you to think about what you must ask of a principal in that story, while you have access to that principal. When you come back with your notebook all stuffed full of great quotes and wonderful descriptions, you've got a pretty good idea of what your lead is going to be, and your main point, and what we used to call at *The Philadelphia Inquirer* the "nut graph."

Do you mark up the notebook?

I try to. I'll whip through there and say, "Well, this is a great quote. This is marvelous description." When I was in Philadelphia, I'd sometimes sit down with a blank sheet of paper, and not really outline the story, but put dashes after the main points, and sometimes under that, put "quote so and so," "description such and such," "event on February 12," or whatever.

Did you use a tape recorder or a notebook?

There was nothing on tape. Everything was in notebooks or on scraps of paper. I came back to the office so infrequently that I ran out of space in notebooks, so I was writing on the back of press releases, or on top secret documents that I'd picked up lying around, or whatever.

You say you don't use a tape recorder, but I've noticed a lot of long quotations in these pieces. How do you get long quotations down?

Well, sometimes I use tape recorders in press conferences. Because number one, everyone else does, and it's not going to upset your subject. And number two, you want to make sure it's exactly right, down to the last preposition, because you know that the guy who's running the press conference is also recording it, and you want every major nuance to be there. I write quotes down fast with ellipses in my notebook.

What next? Do you write an outline?

No. I probably have one or two images in my mind that I think are going to make the most powerful lead. I write that lead, and then move into what I think are the most important paragraphs, and go on through the key elements of the story. Then I'll go through the notebook and say, "All right, I really need to get this in here."

Do you spend a lot of time writing the lead?

Yes, I do. But again, you shouldn't be thinking about the lead for the first time when you sit down to write it. The image probably jumped out at you at the time you heard about it. On the story I'm working on now, I've been playing around with the lead in my head for the last two or three days. Maybe I'll be on a plane flying back to Manila, or in a taxi going to work, or daydreaming at a boring press conference, something like that, but I'll be thinking about that lead. So when I actually sit down to write it, I've pretty well thought it through. So it doesn't take that long. And then I find the bridge between that image and those two or three very important paragraphs.

Do you revise as you go along?

I revise as I go along, and then go back and insert stuff or move a graph around. I should spend more time going back over my stories, but in daily journalism, you just don't have time to agonize. You write it the best you possibly can when you first write it.

Do you always write in the office, or sometimes in the field?

I wrote one of the better stories I've ever written on the hood of a jeep in the middle of nowhere during the Bhopal disaster in 1984. [Laughter] I've written on the back of airline magazines when I was so turned on by a story that I couldn't wait until I got to the machine. Sometimes I find that I write much better when I'm just scribbling things out on the way from something to something. When you're in an office or a news-room, the distractions are so enormous that they tend to take your mind away from the story.

How long had you been in Manila when the Marcos story broke?

Six weeks. I landed here on January 10, and the story started immediately, and I didn't even have time to open a bureau. I was writing out of a hotel room, so I was at the mercy of the hotel tele-phones. We didn't even have a direct line to L.A.

Let's take a look at your first-day story: "Two leaders renounce Marcos, seize bases." Here's your lead: "In an act of open mutiny,

the Philippines' defense minister and the deputy armed forces chief seized control of the nation's military headquarters Saturday night, demanded that President Ferdinand E. Marcos resign because his Feb. 7 election victory was fraudulent, and pledged their support to opposition leader Corazon Aquino.

"Backed by hundreds of heavily armed soldiers, Defense Minister Juan Ponce Enrile and Lt. Gen. Fidel V. Ramos, deputy chief of staff, sealed off the Defense Ministry building inside Camp Aguinaldo, one of the capital's three large military bases, and called on the remainder of the president's Cabinet and the nation's 200,000-man armed forces to support them. The rebels also seized nearby Camp Crame."

That's a fairly dense lead, but it's got a lot of information in it.

OK, it's too long, by all rules. When I sat down at the machine that night, I thought to myself, "OK, this is it. History is being made here. And there are three incredibly important points to be made." Putting all the elements in has a hammering effect: "This is important. This is important. This is important."

Now, the readers have watched television for the last 12 hours, and they know what's happening over here in images. But they don't necessarily know what's happening here in context. That's what this lead tries to do.

There are a lot of people in this piece, and yet we're able to tell them apart.

This country has a tendency toward the dramatic, and some of us viewed what was happening here almost as a script, where you had key characters and minor supporting actors, whose roles were crucial. Our readers did not know most of their names before February. We ran the risk of bombarding them with a lot of foreign names with no faces, with no ideas, with no perspective. So I made a conscious effort to spread them out, because I saw it as a script.

You keep telling us what people *didn't* know. The generals didn't know how many forces they had, much less how many the other side had. And I suspect there were lots of things you didn't know. So you come clean with the reader, right?

Absolutely. The most important thing we had to convey to our readers that night was that nobody really knew which way this thing was going to go. Marcos clearly was concerned and worried. You could hear that in his words; you could see that in the timing of his press conferences. Enrile was distraught. Ramos was unsure of himself in many ways. Cardinal Sin was hopeful, but nobody really knew what was going to happen.

You needed a lot of explanation very high in this story, so you couldn't put these nice details that high.

You're right, and this is the bane of my existence as a journalist: I always want the description too high. I think the reader likes that, but editors know best. [Laughter] I often kick myself after I finish a story, because I look at it and say, "That's just so straight." You want the reader to see the story, as well as seeing the importance of the story. And it's not always possible; this is one of those stories where it wasn't. And in those cases, I often write a sidebar.

Did you feel any sense of personal danger?

Not at first, but later that first night we did. Very early in the morning, we were told by Enrile himself that Marcos would probably attack that building at dawn with helicopters. We stayed.

Dawn came and went. And then about three hours later, after this helicopter attack did not materialize, there were two armored columns of infantry on their way toward Aguinaldo, and they had every intention to launch some sort of limited attack on that building.

Now, here we get into the ethical question. We were told by some of these guys, "If you don't want to risk your life here, get out now, because once this thing starts, you never know where it's going to go. However, we'd appreciate it if you would stay. Your presence here would act as a deterrent to an attack by Marcos," because he's not going to want to blow away 50 foreign journalists.

Yipe! That put you in a box.

Well, that ultimately was not the question for us. For us, the question was, "If you leave now, you're not going to cover one of the most important stories in the history of this country." You gotta see what's going to happen. If they do mortar the place, if they do bomb the place, that's the story. So most of us stayed, and in fact the story itself was so fascinating that you didn't have much time to be scared.

Let's go to the second story, "Fall reveals a private world in palace." Tell me how this strange piece came about.

This one means a lot to me. We got to the palace just in time to see Marcos's helicopters leaving. A huge mass of humanity crushed down the giant iron gates outside the palace, and we got into the palace compound. Having been in Malacanang so many times, I knew where the family lived, but I had never seen the private rooms. For my own curiosity, I wanted to see how these people really lived, to see if those stories were true.

Were you alone?

No, I wasn't. I was with a reporter for NBC radio and another reporter from the San Francisco *Examiner.* The press corps was going through piles of paper and trying to put out fires on the lawn, pulling out documents, trying to see what they were burning, more of an investigative approach.

Soon after we found our way into the private rooms, the military had secured them from the outside, and wouldn't let anyone else in. But they eventually did find us about an hour and a half later, and after two very kind diplomatic requests to leave, finally lowered their M-16s and said, "You get out of here, or you're dead." [Laughter]

The next day, they said the palace had been booby-trapped, and they had to sanitize the palace. We woke up thinking, "Well, that was a great story, but what if we had blown ourselves to Kingdom Come!"

You went through and inventoried, just wrote down everything?

I was writing down each intricate detail, whatever I could find in about two hours, and about half of it didn't make it into the story. But that was part of the power of the story, that it was so short, it was so terse, and it was so graphic and visual. For the first time, we really did get to see behind the scenes of a dictator.

Why didn't you indicate in the story that you were almost alone in there? Listen to this: "*Touring* the most intimate corners of a palace that many Filipinos had come to view as a symbol of their oppression, a *Times* correspondent found...." I got the impression from reading this account that you were given a tour. You're showing the reporting, but you're leaving out the wonderful fact that just the three of you were there.

But it wasn't important that we were on our own and wandering around. Whenever we translate that notion into print, it looks like you're pulling out the old cornet and letting blow, "Boy, I did this great thing, and now I'm going to tell you all about it." And I've always had a real problem with that. I've worked for papers that wanted us to trumpet our horn like that, and I always did so begrudgingly. But maybe you're right; in retrospect, I could have cast it as a little bit more of an exclusive.

Not an exclusive, but an adventure.

An adventure, hmmm.

Beyond the graphic details, this story is really a list. You're taking the things you see as signs of the character of the Marcoses.

That's right. I let the objects tell the story. I knew these people, so I felt it was fair to make the link between those objects and those attributes. I was using those items as illustrations from the lives of this couple to show what had gone wrong in their administration.

Is there anything you saw in there that you wanted to get in the story, but didn't have the nerve?

Yes, Imelda's underwear.

Aha. Tell me about that.

Well, the floor of her closet was piled high with dirty underwear, and in the corner of the bathroom, dirty underwear all thrown in the corner. It indicated that she was a slob, and in a lot of ways, in her private world, she was kind of a slob, I'm told. But I wasn't willing to make that leap of faith. I wasn't willing to take onto myself the authority of saying just exactly what piled-up dirty underwear said about the personality of the presidential palace, number one.

Number two, why throw in a graph that, though it's true, would make our readers' noses crinkle up in the morning over their coffee? But I guess in retrospect it would have been fun to throw it in. [Laughter]

Let's go on to the retrospective story, "The 3-day revolution: How Marcos was toppled." When did you write this one?

Yes, the monster. [Laughter] I sat down at the typewriter about 18 to 20 hours after Marcos left. I'd been awake for four straight days and nights without any sleep whatsoever. About 6:30 in the morning, I had finished that palace story and the news story on Marcos's departure, and I was just dead.

Before I went to sleep, the foreign editor, Al Shuster, and Linda Matthews, the deputy foreign editor, who had been handling most of this copy since the beginning, had said, "We need a reconstruction."

I knew I only needed one or two more things to make the story work; I wasn't exactly sure what. But I said on the phone, "OK, great. No question. I can do it, it's in my notebook. When are you guys thinking about, Sunday?"

And this is Wednesday morning, Manila time. And Linda said, "No, I think in a case like this, we need it absolutely as soon as possible. Can you do it tomorrow?" [Laughter] And I said, "No."

But I thought about it, and about the importance of the story, and about time, which always works against us in daily journalism. By Sunday, it would be old, overtaken by events in the formation of the new government. And I said, "You're absolutely right. I'll try everything in my power to do it for the Thursday paper," which would have been the following day. And then I collapsed and slept for about six hours.

When I woke up, I still wasn't sure exactly where I had to go with the lead and the final pieces that didn't entirely make sense. There was a telex shoved under my door that said, "The Philippine pundits back here think it would be real interesting to see what Cardinal Sin has to say about all this and what was his role in it." We knew it had been an important role, but we didn't know how important. So I called a friend of mine, an aide to the Cardinal, and he said the Cardinal wasn't giving any interviews. And I said, "Well, my editor assigned me to write history tonight, and the Cardinal knows things that nobody knows, and I want to make sure that it's a correct representation of history."

Great line.

And the Cardinal said, "OK, come on over." And the whole interview was done in background because for political reasons within the church, he didn't want to be on the record that soon after Marcos had left. But then he came out with that quote about "the force of the Filipino people stormed heaven with prayer." At the end of the interview, I said, "I know, Your Eminence, that this whole thing was in background, but gosh, that quote is so good, do you mind if I use it and attribute it to you in the story tomorrow?" And he said, "No problem; you're welcome to use that."

That's *the* great quotation in here.

Right. But I hadn't known about these phone calls. Nobody knew at that point that Ramos had talked to Enrile, that both of them had called Sin in the ultimate leadership role.

You found out about the two phone calls from him in that interview?

Yes, in fact, that was the first thing he said. I said, "Cardinal, tell me what happened from the very beginning." And he said, "Well, you know, it all started at 3 p.m. when Johnny Enrile called me with his voice trembling." After that interview, I called one of my sources very close to Johnny Enrile, and he confirmed it. And I did the same with General Ramos. So it was originally sourced to the Cardinal, but confirmed by key people close to both of the other principals involved. So I felt confident in using it in a narrative without attribution.

How much time did it take you to write this piece?

[Laughs] This story took me longer than any story I've written in my life, but not because I spent so much time organizing it. I spent just a few minutes blocking out the important points. It was the physical process of writing that many words that took so long. I sat down to write it about 8 o'clock at night, and despite many interruptions, I finished writing it at roughly 2 o'clock in the morning.

Six hours! That's amazing.

By the way, I was so much on deadline that I never reread it after I wrote it.

No revision at all?

Not a one. No, I wrote it straight through, filled every memory bank in my Radio Shack lap computer, and I didn't go back. I have never written anything more carefully. I just made sure that every date and time and name was correct, and never went back to look at it, and felt confident in not doing so.

The communications facilities were all being disrupted during these three days, and I was not able to file electronically. After writing this

4,000-plus-word story on deadline, in the middle of the night, 3:00 in the morning, I couldn't get a telephone line that was good enough.

So what did you do?

I sat there and dictated the 4,000-word story into the phone. It struck me, here we are almost in the 21st century, and we're going from high tech down to the lowest tech. But I dictated the whole thing. It took me almost as long to read it as it did to write it, because I wrote it so fast.

You had a real epic story on your hands, and you had the chance to turn everybody into a larger-than-life hero, but you keep showing them as ordinary people.

That sums up so much of what this country is about. It is a country that puts people on pedestals as leaders, and at the same time insists on their constant fallibility and humanity. Cory Aquino has been compared to the Virgin Mary.

Oh, God.

Really. In the eyes of the mob, she's the Virgin Mother. But at the same time, the press doesn't treat her as a sacred cow, and when she does something stupid, the columnists blast her for it. Because their heroes are fallible, that makes them palatable. And this is one of the things that Marcos violated. He refused to admit he ever made a mistake. He refused to be human in those later years, and his people turned against him because he was not willing to bend.

You said you didn't want to organize this story chronologically. Why not?

It *is* organized chronologically, but not *just* chronologically. I wanted to put each day in a context, and each part of each day in a context, and flag it: "Here's the turning point," not just "Here's what happened Tuesday."

So chronology takes a subordinate role to the thematic points, and each day's events support a thematic conclusion.

That's right. Chronology makes wonderful journalism, and the more detailed, the more enjoyable. But that's not the way we see the world as people. We see the events of our lives on any given day in a context of what's happening to us as human beings at that point in our lives.

Now look at the very end of the story. Why did you choose to end with this young farmer beaten to death?

It was a thematic decision, number one; number two, it was closure; and a lot of other reasons. First of all, the story opened with larger-than-life heroes. But in the end, it wasn't the political powers who really mattered in this story; it was the people, the Filipino people. I tried to make that point as often as I could during the story.

I wanted to get back to the grass roots of the farmers, number one. Number two, everybody was talking about this "bloodless revolution." But I didn't want our readers to forget that this was a conclusion to one of the bleakest periods in this country's history, when thousands of people were killed for their political beliefs. I was there when this farmer was beaten to death, and I saw the absurdity in it. He still believed that Marcos was there, and he was sacrificing his life for Marcos, after all this Marcos rhetoric: "I will not leave Malacanang. I will die here with the last drop of my blood." And this was the last thing that I saw before going into the palace, and going through Imelda's dirty underwear.

Let's look at the last story, headlined "Enrile's revolt sparked by his children."

Now that I shot my wad on this big reconstruction piece for the Thursday paper, what could I do for Sunday? I could have done a big thing on Cory, but we'd already done a big thing on Cory the day that Marcos fell. Linda sent me a telex saying, "[Managing Editor] Cotliar thinks we should touch base with Johnny Enrile." But Enrile was not giving interviews because he wanted to let Aquino take the limelight, and he was just going back to being the lowly defense minister, ha, ha.

But at 10 o'clock Friday morning, I got to the ministry and sat down with my friends, who are his PR people and aides, and said, "Well, I have to talk to the Minister, and I'm not leaving here until I do." And they said, "Well, he's real busy, but let's see how the day goes." At 9 o'clock that night, he called me into his office, so I sat there 11 hours waiting to see him.

However, during that period, I talked for two hours with Enrile's son Jackie, who apparently had been there through this whole three-day thing. And I spent the rest of the time talking to aides, and moving around and developing the whole story except for what Enrile had to say for himself. During those 11 hours, I found key areas to ask him about to make the interview intimate.

So when I finally went in there, I could tell him, "Hey, you know, your son just showed me this letter he wrote to you. What did this have to do with the whole thing?" It all really came together, and all of a sudden Enrile said, "You know, I could have gotten out, but I couldn't because I really was thinking about my children's generation. I was thinking about where this country was headed. And mostly, I was thinking about my interest in history and how history will view what I do." I usually use research to get anecdotes, but in this case, it was just blind sheer luck. By doorstopping him for 11 hours, I saw everybody who was important to him.

Luck? Not luck, but persistence. How long did you talk to him?

Well, it got out of hand. It went on and on and on. I'd interviewed him before, but we had just been through something together. He viewed this core group of foreign press as his friends in a very Filipino way, as a force that protected him from the howitzers of Marcos. And when I started prying him open with these little anecdotes his son and his top aides had told me, he felt an opportunity to get off on a tangent about himself. And they were the right questions at the right moment in his life, and he wanted to talk about them. It went on for three and a half hours, alone with him.

There's a lot of profound insight in here. You expect an explanation of the event, and you get an explanation of the man. I'm also struck by how much we learn about Marcos in this interview about Enrile. Is that what you were up to?

I thought about that, sure. I look at daily journalism in terms of what Ed Miller in Allentown used to call "daily nonfiction." I use some of the tried and true techniques of literary writing as opposed to journalistic writing. This is one example of what you can do, of the finer, subtle forms.

If I had pulled off the coup of getting this interview, and it went as well as it obviously did, the minute I got out of that room, I'd have jumped in the air for joy. What did you do when you came out?

The only thing that was in my mind was that I was one hour's drive from my office, that I had to sit down and write a megamonster story for the Sunday paper, and I was so tired from those four days I just wanted to die.

You and I have a mutual friend, Wilbur Landrey, foreign correspondent of the *St. Petersburg Times*, and....

He is a real hard worker. I have never seen anybody work that hard in my life. He won't stop. He'll start at 7 o'clock in the morning. He'll keep going until midnight. He's terrific.

I sent him a note saying, "I'm getting ready to interview Mark Fineman; tell me about him." And this is what he wrote back: "Mark is known as one of the hardest working correspondents in the Philippines. He never stops reporting, and he never stops writing when a lot of others have quit for the night." And you just said the same thing about Bill.

Wow. Thanks, Bill. Oh, boy. That's really...oh, boy. That's about as high a compliment as you can get.

It's true, isn't it? There's more than good reporting and good vision in here. There's also a lot of energy.

No question. I believe that this business is a total commitment, and you've just got to be willing to subjugate the private side of your life, having a good time. I think that if the people in this business don't have that kind of commitment, don't take this more to heart than the other media, we're just going to lose, and newspapers are going to fall by the wayside. The one thing that keeps newspapers way ahead of television is the context and the nuance and the personality and the behind-the-scenes. And we only get that if we work hard. You just have to work harder than the other guys.

What a great exit line.

Iditarod '86

Craig Medred
Deadline Writing

CRAIG MEDRED, 35, was born and reared in Staples, Minnesota. He was graduated from the University of Alaska at Fairbanks with a degree in journalism, and worked briefly at KTVF-TV in Fairbanks, at the Bureau of Land Management, and as assistant press secretary for Senator Mike Gravel, before joining the *Southeast Alaska Empire* in Juneau in 1976 as an environmental reporter. He worked his way up to city editor before leaving in 1982. Between March and August 1982, he worked for the Associated Press, *Alaska Fisherman, National Fisherman Magazine, Seafood Business Report*, and eventually the *Anchorage Daily News*, where he has stayed put as the outdoors editor.

Anchorage Daily News

Happy River is an angry trail

MARCH 4, 1986

HAPPY RIVER GORGE—Coming down into this cleft through the Alaska Range, the Iditarod Trail is an angry serpent.

It snakes through deep snow across a steep hillside covered with birch. The trail zigzags all the way. Gravity wants the sleds to slip off the edge and tumble.

That's what happened to Roger Roberts of Ophir in the early morning hours. And that's why Alan Cheshire of Great Britain found Roberts in tears amid a tangle of dogs and sled at the bottom of the hill.

A tall, hardy man from the Bush, Roberts is not a man given to crying. But he had been knocked from his sled by a branch at the top of the hill, and by the time he got to the dogs at the bottom he was beginning to fear they might have been hurt.

"The only thing I'm worried about now is Dalzell Canyon, because if I lose them there, they'll drown.

"I've fallen off a couple of times. They surprised me when they ran (so fast). I'm not used to a dog team that runs."

Iditarod dogs normally move along at a fast trot—10 or 12 mph. But the hills above Happy River always seem to encourage them to break into a lope.

The team pulling Frank Torres of McGrath was screaming down the hill when disaster struck Monday morning.

"The team went on one side of a tree and the sled went on the other," he said. The towline popped and Torres's dogs were off and running on their own.

Other mushers resting at the bottom of the hill after their terrifying ride down helped catch Torres's team. He muscled his sled back onto the trail and rode it down.

"It's easy coming down without a dog team," he said.

The story "that Frank cut 'em loose to get down the hill" would spread fast among the mushers, Steve Bush of Aniak predicted.

"A little damaged pride is all," Torres countered. "I'm lucky. It could have tore the whole front of my sled off."

"Ya," said Bush, "somebody said it's the kind of hill where when you go over the edge you start to scream, but before you can get it out, you're too busy."

Mushers are forewarned of this—more so than ever this year.

Trail breakers for the Iditarod Trail Committee have posted obvious red signs with black letters at the beginning of the run down into the gorge.

"Happy River just ahead," says the first sign.

"Get a grip on your sled," says the second, 100 feet farther down the trail.

"When you start over the lip," says the third.

"You may scream, Oh ----," says the fourth.

"Burma Shave," says the last.

Torres is glad he waited for daylight before making his attempt.

"That would have been something last night. I can't imagine what it would be like if it was icy. If it was bad, it would be real bad."

Observations and questions

1) I could argue that the lead in this story ends at "slip off the edge and tumble," and I could make an equal argument that this story has no lead at all. What do you think? Ask the same question about Medred's other pieces. If the story has no discernible lead, does it risk a feeling of shapelessness?

2) Medred does not clean up quotations because he wants the characters to shine through in the richness of their own lingo. An anecdote in the interview about quoting the native Indians shows the hazards of cleaning up the speech of minorities, but we might also ask how those Indians would feel about being quoted in non-standard English.

3) Medred believes that common sense and high-speed storytelling will overcome any trouble the reader might have with the jargon of mushers. What tests can we apply to determine how much definition and explanation to use in describing technical subjects? How do we know what our readers know?

4) Study Medred's sentence structures in terms of the placement of the subject and verb near the beginning and near each other. Notice how such positioning promotes an effect of vigorous action.

5) Would you be tempted to end this story two paragraphs from the bottom with "Burma Shave"? How would such an ending affect the rest of the story?

Musher uses extra stove to save his life

MARCH 6, 1986

RAINY PASS—A ground blizzard raged across the barren tundra high in the Alaska Range Tuesday night when Bobby Lee of Trapper Creek drove his dogs out from Puntilla Lake.

Ahead of him waited the 45 miles of trail over the pass and down through the Dalzell Gorge to Rohn.

Once before in an Iditarod Trail Sled Dog Race, Lee had been over this trail behind a dog team. He figured if he left in the wind he could gain a small advantage on the other mushers bunched with him at Rainy Pass Lodge.

It was not to be. Instead, Lee almost lost everything.

"I got out there, and I had to stop; I was shivering so bad," Lee said. "I thought I was going into hypothermia."

Lee knows about such things. In last year's race he nearly died of hypothermia on the ice of the Bering Sea outside of Shaktoolik.

That time, Lee was out in another ground blizzard. He had left his team with several others and hiked ahead through the blowing snow to find the next trail marker.

When he came back, the team was gone. The other mushers gave him a sleeping bag and went to get help. Lee was badly hypothermic when help arrived.

Out in Rainy Pass in another storm, he thought about last year, and he knew it best to heed his body's warning signs.

"Remembering my experience last year on the ice at Shaktoolik, I thought, 'Whoa boy,'" Lee said.

He started looking for someplace to hide from the storm, but there is little shelter in Rainy Pass.

Down in a shallow valley where the Happy River starts eight or nine miles below the summit of the pass there are some willows and a few scraggly spruce trees. Lee spotted a tiny spruce tree.

"I finally found about a 6-foot snow drift," said Lee. "I just trotted them off the trail there."

The dogs dug in and took care of themselves. Lee knew he had a bigger problem. He had to find some way to warm up, and warm up fast, if he was going to avoid a serious, mind-blurring loss of body heat that could prove deadly in a storm.

"I could tell I wasn't thinking quite right," Lee said. "It was blowing kind of slightly over there (behind the drift), but more than that it was the temperature drop."

In the wee hours of the morning, the temperature in the pass had plunged down to minus 20 degrees, maybe colder.

Lee dug a two-burner Coleman stove out of his dog sled to heat water, but he couldn't get the stove going.

"I put Fire Ribbon all over it (to preheat the stove)," said Lee, "and it just wouldn't start."

Worried now, knowing he was in trouble, Lee began rummaging through his sled bag for a single-burner stove he had brought just in case the other failed.

"That little...stove saved me," Lee said. "I had uncontrollable shivers by the time I got that going."

Lee boiled a half-gallon of water and drank it all. The hot water helped warm him; at the same time, the fluid helped battle the hypothermia.

After that, he emptied his sled bag of gear, rolled his sleeping bag out inside that protective nylon shield, and crawled inside.

"I got a wonderful three hours sleep in the sled," Lee said. "I think the dogs appreciated the stop, too."

In the morning, the winds subsided, and Lee took to the trail again. He hit Rohn at midday, feeling fine and happy to be alive. "Everybody made fun of me for bringing two stoves, too," he said. "It saved my butt."

Observations and questions

1) This simple story has three local terms in it: "ground blizzard," "hypothermia," and "Fire Ribbon." Medred says most readers will understand them from context, storytelling, and general familiarity. But notice the handling of the quotation from Lee: "I put Fire Ribbon all over it (to preheat the stove),...and it just wouldn't start." The parenthetical phrase explains the use of Fire Ribbon without stopping to explicate the reference. We serve our reader, even the sophisticated or local reader, by not taking too much for granted.

2) The time scheme in the first 10 paragraphs seems confusing. How could Medred handle the flashbacks and memories to help the reader keep them straight?

3) This story about a man nearly freezing to death has only three references to emotions: "worried now," "the dogs appreciated," and "feeling fine and happy to be alive." Would more information about feelings help or hurt the story? Would you be tempted to delete the phrase "worried now"?

4) Medred's kicker ends with the word "butt." Nothing gives the reader a sense of closure like a word with a solid thud.

The Farewell Burn tests mushers' grit

MARCH 8, 1986

McGRATH—For two days now, battered and jerry-rigged dog sleds have come trickling one by one into this community of 500 on the Kuskokwim River.

The sleds are pulled by teams of dogs fit and ready to run, but they are ridden by tired and bloodied mushers—men and women who have known the horrors of the snowless Farewell Burn.

These are people who will not soon forget what they have seen there.

Across the Farewell Burn is 93 miles of the worst trail the Iditarod Sled Dog Race has ever witnessed.

"I've never seen anything like that trail," said Joe Redington Sr. of Knik, the man who helped invent this 1,100-mile marathon from Anchorage to Nome in 1973.

"I didn't think I was going to make it. Worse as anything I've ever seen."

On the Burn, the trail snakes through land laid bare by the largest wildfire ever recorded in Alaska. Today, dog sled parts are littered among the sedge tussocks, testament to the 61 mushers who have picked their way across the Burn.

Most mushers have taken 24 hours or more to make the trip—24 hours of hell, 24 hours of slamming and pounding from frozen sedge tussocks to fire-scarred trees to clumps of willows.

"It's nice to think you can drive a dog sled through that, but there's no way you can. It's a controlled fall," said a gaunt and rasping Ray Dronenburg Thursday night. "I ended up pushing a couple trees with my nose and that kind of stuff."

"It's a good thing that there's no checkpoints out there people could quit at," the Willow dog driver said. "I think if they'd had a checkpoint out there, a lot of people would have quit."

Few dog sleds have come through the Burn unscathed.

Dewey Halverson of Trapper Creek broke the runners off his sled and he had to ride the basket or walk. Terry Adkins of Sand Coulee, Mont.— already ailing with a bad back—broke off one runner and had to ride much of the way balanced on the other.

Gordon Brinker of Shell Lake lost his sled brake. Ray Lang of Nome broke his sled in eight places. Redington smashed support posts. Ted English of Chuguik ripped his sled bag.

The list goes on and on.

"It was so bad, it was horrible," said Dronenburg. "It was incomprehensible."

Before this race began, the mushers knew this wind-scoured section of trail would be bad. They knew there would be no snow.

"We'll just have to go out there and be gladiators," Jerry Austin of St. Michael said, and the words became prophetic.

No musher was without a personal horror story.

Each now has memories that will live forever in infamy.

Perhaps the saddest tale belongs to Bill Cowart of Anchorage. He is a rookie musher who was expected to do well running the dogs of Herbie Nayokpuk, the fabled Shishmaref Cannonball who is not racing this year.

Cowart fared well in the early going. He had a strong team, and he held with the leaders in the race going into the checkpoint at Rohn on the north side of the Alaska Range.

Then, disaster struck.

"I got behind a moose after I left Rohn River. The moose trotted in the trees, and the dogs went after him," said Cowart.

He hung on as long as he could, but as the sled caromed from tree to tree and tipped side to side, he was finally knocked off.

On Friday in this city, Cowart still sported the marks of that adventure: a big bruise split by a nasty red scar under his left eye, a puffed and swollen hand that may be broken, and a bruised leg.

"You look like you've been through a war," someone told Cowart.

"I've been through that," he said. "And I can tell you this was worse."

It had taken Cowart eight hours to get his dog team back after the incident with the moose. Martin Buser of Eagle River eventually caught the dogs as Cowart hitchhiked rides with other mushers down the trail.

"Everybody was giving him rides," said Dronenburg. "And Herbie Nayokpuk's dogs were gone."

Dronenburg said he could empathize.

"I jumped a cow and a calf moose," he said. "When the dogs give chase you're all over the trail, just praying you won't go down."

Cowart said his main concern after the accident was for the safety of the dogs. They were OK.

All in all, added Jim Leach, the chief veterinarian for the Iditarod, dogs did a lot better than mushers coming through the Burn.

"Overall, the teams were good," he said. "They were a little tired coming across the Burn, but not as tired as I expected them to be.

"I flew over the trail, and I said at the time, 'Oh boy, trouble city.' We thought we'd have a lot of foot problems because of the rough ground, but a lot of their feet actually improved coming out of the Burn.

"That probably makes us as happy as anything."

In fact, the vets at Nikolai and McGrath were almost as busy offering first-aid advice to mushers as they were tending to dogs.

Observations and questions

1) Study each of the first six paragraphs as a potential beginning of the lead. Any of the six would work, but they would produce very different effects. Speculate on those effects.

2) We often improve the clarity of quotations by inserting bracketed phrases, as in the previous discussion of "Fire Ribbon." Try that technique with this statement from Joe Redington: "I didn't think I was going to make it. *Worse as anything I've ever seen.*" No addition can improve that quotation without killing it.

3) A musher describes the impossible Farewell Burn: " 'It's nice to think you can drive a dog sled through that, but there's no way you can. It's a controlled fall,' said a gaunt and rasping Ray Dronenburg Thursday night. 'I ended up pushing a couple trees with my nose and that kind of stuff.' " This racer, who has just crossed the Burn, says there's no way it can be crossed. Medred captures the paradoxical humor of men under stress.

4) We would normally trim off the end of a quotation like the one above, deleting "and that kind of stuff." What does Medred gain and lose with his typically sprawling quotations?

5) Medred frequently presents a series of similar actions simply by listing them, as in this passage on page 113: "Few dog sleds have come... incomprehensible." How can we use lists for economy without seeming mechanical? Should we hide the form of the list from the readers, or should we let them see it to keep them oriented within the form?

6) Even with people who are famous, Medred indicates that they are famous. He tells when they've won, lost, etc. I think readers like reminders of the accomplishments even of famous and familiar people, as long as we don't go too far (e.g., "Joe DiMaggio, a famous baseball player").

7) Medred says his average reader always worries about the Iditarod's effect on the dogs. Dogs are one of the three favorite subjects of readers (money, cute children, and animals), and we need to anticipate the sympathies of certain segments of our readership, especially in sports stories. Remember to tell what happened to the animals, or readers will fret about them.

There's no time to dream on the trail

MARCH 9, 1986

RUBY—For three hours Saturday, as clothes dryers whirred and washing machines throbbed, musher Rick Swenson of Manley slept like a dead man on a hard bench in the village Laundromat.

The room was warm, and the 1,100-mile Iditarod Trail Sled Dog Race was, temporarily, a million miles away.

Swenson, the four-time winner of this 1,100-mile marathon, was oblivious to the world. He stirred no more than the plank on which he slept.

He lay fully clothed with his hat pulled down and his mukluks under his head for a pillow. Pile booties for his dogs tumbled in a dryer nearby.

Swenson had arrived in this village on the Yukon River at shortly after 8 a.m. He was three hours behind race leader Susan Butcher of Manley. She had already tended to her dogs and bunked out in the home of a friendly villager.

Swenson was quick to feed and water his dogs. Then he went looking for a place to hole up.

As the dogs slept curled in tight little balls for warmth in the yard of a villager, Swenson found the comfort of the community laundry. Outside, it was minus 10 degrees.

"A little cold for the mushers," Swenson said when he woke blinking the sleep out of his eyes just before noon.

He pulled a bottle of eye drops from a breast pocket and dribbled saline solution onto sleep-dried contact lenses. Some of the water ran down his nose and cheek.

"This was a good place to sleep," Swenson said. "Nobody could find me."

Seven days into the Iditarod, sleep has become a precious commodity, maybe the most precious, for the top 10 mushers rushing for Nome.

They are running at a record pace toward the city of the golden beaches, and they know they have become the weakest link in their teams.

Well-cared-for dogs can get by on several hours of rest each day. But performance suffers if the dogs are left short of food, water, or foot treatments.

Tired mushers have a tougher time with those chores than mushers who are rested, and some mushers are renowned for their ability to operate with little rest.

Swenson is acknowledged as one of the best, able to function in the sleep-starved state of a zombie for days on end.

"There's nobody we're running with who's like Swenson," said Lavon Barve of Wasilla. "Swenson is smart, and I feel as far as a man who thinks it out, he's one. He doesn't make mistakes. I feel my percentage of mistakes are a lot higher than somebody like Swenson."

But Swenson is human, and at this point in the fast-paced Iditarod 1986, sleep has become as great a fixation for him as for anyone.

"I got a good nap yesterday," Swenson said. He found a windless spot in the sun among some spruce trees in the rolling hills near Ruby. His dog sled was his mattress.

Swenson rejoiced in that small comfort. They have been few and far between on this trail.

Nighttime temperatures in the Alaska Interior have plummeted as low as minus 30 degrees.

When Butcher arrived before dawn to the ringing of Ruby's church bells and the barking of village dogs, she was coated with a layer of frost that grew thick where her breath moved across her face.

She was quick to grab her food and make for the home of an accommodating villager. The welcoming residents of this community of 250 immediately retreated to their log cabin homes or the log cabin community center, where a warm wood fire raged in the stove made from two 55-gallon drums.

They watched Roy Rogers and Gabby Hayes on a small portable television as they waited for the next musher to arrive so the scene could repeat itself, which it did with a steady regularity from early morning through midday.

Dog team after frosted dog team came into town to be met by well-wishers. The dogs looked good. The mushers were grimy and tired.

Terry Adkins of Sand Coulee, Mont., had fallen in some overflow on the ice of a creek. He came in looking like an ice man.

Joe Runyon of Nenana came in with his eyelashes nearly frozen shut, but his team was full of energy. His dogs wanted to start a fight with a big, black Newfoundland sitting on a dog house near the checkpoint, and Runyon had a tough time holding them back.

Dewey Halverson of Trapper Creek came in behind fresh-looking dogs, but with a half-frozen face. He was still riding a sled he borrowed from Swenson in McGrath that was now lashed together with a willow branch. The new version replaced the one Halverson pulverized two days earlier in the Farewell Burn.

"I can hardly wait to get on the Yukon (River)," he said sarcastically.

Then Jerry Austin of St. Michael came roaring through town, his cheeks the hue of the pink sunrise starting to color the river outside of town.

Joe Garnie of Teller came in looking weary, but his dogs whined and tugged at their harnesses as he tried to sign the check-in sheet.

Nobody had much to say. All of the front-running mushers were playing it close to the vest. All said they planned to rest five to six hours before leaving.

That is what most of them did, with the exception of Butcher. She rested nearly eight hours.

"Susan had to push a little coming over because she didn't have enough dog food in Cripple, I guess," Swenson said.

The front-runners started pulling out of town just after noon on the 146 miles of river to Kaltag.

Butcher was the first to arrive in Galena. Adkins, the Montana Ice Man, pulled in 28 minutes behind her at 8 p.m.

Just behind the front-runners was Barve, still confident he could catch up.

"I'm sure they ain't pushin' that hard yet," Barve said. "Once you catch up with them, then you can see what you can do."

Observations and questions

1) This piece discusses the strategies for rationing sleep, not by analysis, but by telling little stories about the tired mushers. It begins with Swenson zonked out on a bench, not moving at all. But notice the action verbs in the description of the dryers.

2) On page 117-118 ("Seven days...as for anyone."), Medred shifts into the present tense for seven paragraphs. Study this technique in terms of immediacy for the reader. Also think about its potential for distracting the reader as the first verb ("has become") changes from the expected tense.

3) In this quotation on page 118, the last sentence has a subject-verb error: " 'There's nobody we're running with who's like Swenson,' said Lavon Barve of Wasilla. 'Swenson is smart, and I feel as far as a man who thinks it out, he's one. He doesn't make mistakes. I feel my *percentage of mistakes are* a lot higher than somebody like Swenson.' " Medred recognized the fault, but left the verb alone to show the speaker's personality. If we leave such lapses in without flagging them in the attribution, will our readers wonder about our knowledge of English grammar?

4) The last half of this piece, beginning at "When Butcher arrived...," pictures character after character covered with ice. Notice the unifying effect of this image, and the wordplay as Adkins, the Montana "Ice Man," pulls in at the end.

5) Medred liked the detail of Alaskan villagers watching "Roy Rogers and Gabby Hayes on a small portable television as they waited for the next musher to arrive...." Think about how the idiosyncrasies of the immediate audience can enrich the telling of a sports event.

6) Medred weaves in themes from earlier stories, such as, "The dogs looked good. The mushers were grimy and tired." Unity and concern for the reader transcend individual stories in a series.

7) This story has no news peg, but the jump headline (not included in this reprinting) reads: "Butcher grabs the lead, but others not far behind." Study how Medred weaves this piece of news through a story essentially about sleep.

Garnie, Butcher race through bitter wind

MARCH 12, 1986

KOYUK—All through the day, Joe Garnie and Susan Butcher rode behind their dog teams across the wind-scoured ice of Norton Bay.

A 20-mph wind blew the 5-degree cold down across the bay from the northeast. It clawed at their faces like an angry cat.

Out on this same ice a year ago, in a ground blizzard that made conditions even worse, Libby Riddles of Teller won the 1,100-mile Iditarod Trail Sled Dog Race from Anchorage to Nome.

Now two other mushers were vying for the title, and they were an ironically matched pair.

Garnie, the soft-spoken Eskimo mayor of Teller, the boyfriend and racing partner of Riddles.

Butcher, the woman from Manley who had wanted so badly to be the first of her sex to win this sled-dog marathon, the woman who has twice finished second and wants desperately to win at last.

They left the checkpoint at Shaktoolik 10 minutes apart as dawn came to the Bering Sea coast Tuesday. Fifty-eight miles down the trail, Garnie had squeezed out a 28-minute lead.

He and his dogs worked for every second of it. The dogs fought the bitter wind, and Garnie helped them all he could.

For much of the day, he could be seen working behind the sled—pedaling first with his right leg and then with his left, sometimes running beside the sled with one hand on the handlebar.

In this way they moved across the bay, following a line of scraggly spruce trees planted in the ice to form a well-marked trail.

"The dogs are doing all right," Garnie said as he came into a rousing welcome in the village.

"Tired is all. This run tired them out. I'm tired, too."

It had been a rough trail across the bay, he said. There were patches of snow mixed with glare ice. The dogs needed booties to keep from injuring their feet in the snow, but they needed bare feet for traction on the ice.

"That's what was frustrating out there," he said to veterinarian Bob Beiermann. "You didn't know whether to boot or not to boot. It was a real toss-up between pulling muscles or getting cuts.

"If we'd had any decent trail, it wouldn't have been so bad." But bad trail has been the story of this Iditarod. Though the front-running teams are moving along at a pace almost certain to break the old record time of 12 days, 8 hours from Anchorage to Nome, it has been bad trail of one kind or another most of the way.

It has taken a toll that is beginning to show on the mushers even more than on their teams.

After 10 days of racing with only a few hours of sleep each day, Garnie's eyes are thin slits in his wind-burned face. Bags hang beneath them. His hands are bruised and scraped from the chores of the trail. He chews gum constantly, nervously. He moves stiffly, jerkily.

Ahead of him on Tuesday waited another 175 miles of trail, more than a day's run to Nome. Another day would pass without sleep.

"I've just got to hitch them up a couple more times," Garnie said. It was a tired but determined statement.

To win, Garnie knows he must best Butcher, who appeared more confident and better rested on Tuesday. She had been seen trying to catch some sleep while riding hunched over on her sled early in the day, and she was smiling when she reached the village checkpoint.

She expected to set a new record for the race to Nome, she said. She expected to beat Garnie. She worried most about her old nemesis, Rick Swenson of Manley.

Somewhere back on the trail, the four-time winner of this race continued his run north. At noon he had been camped near the high bluff of Island Point on the far edge of the Norton Bay ice.

Butcher was unsure of what he was up to this time.

She cared for her team near the checkpoint, warmed herself an aluminum-wrapped dinner of ribs and potatoes with cheese on a pile of charcoal, and waited for Swenson.

All the time, her dogs slept curled up on straw, catching up on vital rest. Swenson was expected for hours before he showed.

Just after Butcher ducked into the checkpoint for a quick nap, his team came in off the ice. Butcher woke and watched from the shadows of the arctic entry on the checkpoint cabin.

For 24 hours, Swenson had been dogging her trail north from Unalakleet to Shaktoolik across frozen tundra hills and meager forests of spruce and alder, then across the sea ice of Norton Bay.

His arrival here was her signal to leave. She began hitching up her team as he pulled in. Garnie, too, took the cue.

Swenson was three hours behind the leaders. He said he had stopped to rest on the ice. "It got pretty warm out there," he said. "In the middle of the day, the dogs don't do so good."

He said he was out of the race, that he had no chance to win.

That is what he said. "I ain't got the dog team" were the words.

Reporters refused to believe him. They kept asking if he could catch Butcher.

"What about Garnie?" Swenson answered at last. "You guys seem to have forgotten him. You've got a shoo-in (victor) already."

Garnie was harnessing his team. He crammed equipment into his sled bag and tied it shut. Swenson went over to offer advice and encouragement.

"Don't let her beat you," Swenson said.
"There's nothing I can do about it."

Garnie nodded his head. Swenson returned
to his sled and his dog team. He said nothing to
Butcher, though they were parked only feet
apart, though they are good friends in Manley
when they are not racing.

Butcher, likewise, spared no words on
Swenson as he walked by her to the checkpoint
to get water.

Garnie was the first to get a team hitched up.
He eased the dogs past the decaying log cabins
and the drying caribou skins in the middle of the
village. They stepped into a steady trot as they
passed the newer frame homes on the way out
to the trail.

"At least the wind will be with you this
time," a villager yelled from behind.

Butcher watched them go before finishing
with her team. As the sun set, she followed
Garnie out on the trail.

"He should have let her go first," said
Swenson. "He's playing his cards wrong, for me,
but it's his game. I guess he thinks he can wear
her down.

"If I know Joe Garnie, those dogs of his aren't
going to wear down. I think he's got pretty tough
dogs."

It would be Garnie vs. Butcher now, racing
for the $50,000 and the glory in Nome, Swenson
said. But before their trail could grow cold, he
was readying to follow.

"A lot of things can happen between here and
Nome," he said. Sleds break, mushers get lost,
and teams quit.

"I don't think I can win, but they get to
racing, one of them might not make it," Swenson
said. "They had to take something out of their
dogs coming across (the sea ice)."

Observations and questions

1) Medred's lead tells us that the wind "clawed at their faces like an angry cat." In a story about a dog sled race, we get hostile nature personified as the traditional enemy of the dog. Medred will develop this image later with his emphasis on the contestants' faces.

2) Medred presents his principals, Garnie and Butcher, as "an ironically matched pair." Reread the piece and consider other adverbs to replace "ironically."

3) This piece has the feel of a televised sports event, with many angles of viewing, "close-up and personal" interviews, crowd reactions, etc. What tricks can we borrow from our sister medium to make our storytelling more vivid?

4) Medred describes a musher: "...Garnie's eyes are thin slits in his wind-burned face. Bags hang beneath them. His hands are bruised and scraped from the chores of the trail. He chews gum constantly, nervously. He moves stiffly, jerkily." Notice how the staccato rhythms in the last two sentences imitate Garnie's gestures.

5) In a story about Garnie and Butcher, Medred waits 21 paragraphs to introduce Swenson, the dark shadow in third place. Would you be tempted to hint at Swenson earlier, maybe in the lead?

6) Review the five stories, keeping in mind that we have not reprinted all the stories Medred wrote. Which scenes and images stick most powerfully in your mind? Now go back and find out how Medred makes those parts graphic and therefore memorable.

A conversation with
Craig Medred

DON FRY: Who reads your stuff?

CRAIG MEDRED: I write a lot of stuff that appeals to people who live adventures vicariously. Anchorage is a place that's particularly full of those people. They kind of like to live in the bush, but are not quite crazy enough to do that. They're attached to jobs and homes and the standard middle-class things we all get attached to, and they're somewhat removed from these other things that they'd really like to try.

It's like wearing L. L. Bean clothes so you can think of yourself as an outdoorsman. Had you covered the Iditarod race before 1986?

I covered my first Iditarod in March '83. There was a little village called Koyuk, and there were some real characters there. Three of them were leading the race at the time: a guy by the name of Herbie Nayokpuk, whom they called the "Shishmaref Cannonball," a real round-faced, good-humored Eskimo from Shishmaref; and a guy by the name of "Cowboy" Smith from the Yukon Territory, who had these incredible Siberian husky eyes (I mean, they were blue!); and a guy by the name of Rick Mackey, whose dad had won the race back in '78. And they sat in the National Guard Hall there in Koyuk and plotted how to beat a guy by the name of Rick Swenson, who's the only four-time winner of the Iditarod.

And the quotes were so good that they were almost like fiction. I mean, when I went back and read it a year later, if I hadn't known I wrote it down, I would have thought I made it up. I mean, Cowboy Smith was saying things like, "Well, Rick, daylight has to see you there."

In '85, I did a magazine story about how Libby Riddles won the race. She took a very bold gamble and went on into a huge storm and won the race. She had left home at 17 to come to Alaska with a guy by the name of Dewey Halverson, who happened to finish second to her that year. She'd left him and gotten involved with a guy by the name of Joe Garnie, who is the Eskimo mayor of a little place called Teller, and who's been a key player in several Iditarods, and who had once gone out on the same ice and almost died. He had barely managed to get his dog team back to the village of Shaktoolik, and had dropped from the race.

Were you writing sidebars or the main coverage in 1986?

I was doing the main coverage, and some days I would write sidebars, too. I had made the decision that I didn't want any advice on how to do it that year. I mean, it's a lot like covering a war: it moves every day. And I didn't want people 500 miles away telling me where they thought I should be, or what they thought I should hit. And we had several interesting times when I just hung up on editors who started to offer advice. I had worked it out that I was going to go out there and do what I thought I should do, and the rest of them should stay the hell out of it, and that's how it worked.

Did you follow the route of the race? And how did you travel?

Well, we did something we'd never done before. Our photographer Jim Lavrakas and I flew to Skwentna and took snow machines from there on up into the Alaska Range, up into Rainy Pass. The trail down the other side goes through a long gorge, and it's a very difficult trail. So we left the snow machines in Rainy Pass and had them taken back, and we skied again over Rainy Pass and down through the Dalzell Gorge and into Rohn. And we were met by the plane there and pogo-sticked by light plane from Rohn to McGrath and on up to Ruby.

And how did you file?

I usually wrote one or two stories a day. The first part of the race is the worst, because between Skwentna and McGrath, there are no telephones. So in places like Rohn and Puntilla Lake, you write it out longhand, and then you find some pilot who's going somewhere, and you hand him the story and the film, and you pray it gets back to the newspaper.

Did you ever lose a story?

No. I had more trouble with the portable computer, which you can use from McGrath on, because all the checkpoints and villages after that usually have at least one phone. For some reason, there were a lot of satellite problems that year, and we were having garble problems, and we'd lose it in mid-send. Several stories were sent over and over to get them to Anchorage.

Which computer were you using?

I was using the Radio Shack 100. At times it was a great asset, and at other times a great liability, because when it gets real cold, the batteries fail. [Laughter]

And you didn't have a printer with you, so you either had to write it in longhand or send it back electronically, right?

Yeah. Fortunately, my printing is real good and rather fast, because I usually take notes that way, and they all got back here readable. I wrote a lot of them while very tired, near brain-dead. Two of the stories were written out longhand with a pencil, because it was too cold to write with a pen. These stories were squirted out any way we could get them out. In rereading them, I was surprised at the amount of detail.

Wonderful details. These stories don't seem to have any contexts, and they don't seem to have traditional leads. They're very freeform...

No, no, no. Part of that is me. I tend to tell stories, rather than just report news. On these stories, I think there is enough oddity and enough inherent drama, that if you use the right verbs and build the sense of place, then you can get away with it.

Let's discuss the Happy River story. This wasn't a first-day story, was it?

This is probably a two-and-a-half-day story, when we were on snow machines.

Here's the beginning: "Coming down into this cleft through the Alaska Range, the Iditarod Trail is an angry serpent.

"It snakes through deep snow across a steep hillside covered with birch. The trail zigzags all the way. Gravity wants the sleds to slip off the edge and tumble."

The way you've written that passage, nature is not just hostile, but actively hostile. [Laughter]

Very hostile. And some of this is a payoff from past experience, from having been over that part of the trail in a snow machine, and remembering from '83 all the mushers talking about all the problems they had with the trail.

That hill is a horrendous drop. The dog sleds would come over, and the sleds wanted to slide faster than the dogs could trot. So mushers were running over their dogs, and it was just a nightmare. And having ridden a few sleds and getting a feel for how a dog team runs, you get an understanding of how bad this thing was. You could understand that they had to zigzag it down the hill, but even when you zigzag it, it doesn't become easy because the sled wants to tip over on the turns and tumble down the hill.

Indeed. Look at this passage about six paragraphs down: "The team pulling Frank Torres of McGrath was screaming down the hill when disaster struck Monday morning.

" 'The team went on one side of a tree and the sled went on the other,' he said. The towline popped and Torres's dogs were off and running on their own.

"Other mushers resting at the bottom of the hill after their terrifying ride down helped catch Torres's team. He muscled his sled back onto the trail and rode it down."

I'm impressed with the simplicity of the language and its vigor. Very powerful, simple writing.

Well, writing in a notebook, when you don't have a lot of time, tends to keep it real simple. In looking through my notebook, I find that I didn't put a lot of it in there. My notes were very sparse that year, and it was done intentionally to make the writing easier. I had a good sense of what I wanted, and when I got what I wanted, I'd write it down. And a lot of stuff I didn't want went in one ear and out the other. I find a lot of reporters getting buried in their notes.

How about quotations? Do you write out the whole quotation, or just a skeleton?

I save my scribbling for the good quotes; I devote more time to getting those down than to getting every word that's said. I write the good quotes all out. But I'm pretty selective in what I take, which gives me a little more time.

When you're ready to write, how do you organize your material?

In my head. [Laughs] The best training I ever got was working in radio in Fairbanks, because the pace was so hectic that I learned to write things in my head in the car driving back from a story. I would have the story half-written by the time I got to the typewriter, and I still tend to work like that. In fact, when I'm having writer's block, I get in the car and drive around. It can be a little dangerous, because when it gets going real good, then I'll start driving around and writing it down at the same time.

So you don't write from an outline; you just write off the top of your head?

Outlines have never worked very well for me. I'm better off to just sit down, rip through it, reorganize it where I need to, and be done with it.

So you write quickly when it's going well?

Yeah. I can often tell if I'm doing it well just by how fast it's coming out. If it isn't coming out fast, if I'm struggling with it, then I should probably go take a break and think about something else and get my head cleared out. I've got to get that sense of the story down and then come back and play with it.

Craig, how long did it take you to write the Happy River piece?

Jeez, I don't have any idea, probably 45 minutes to an hour. Just looking at it, I wouldn't think it took very long.

Come down three more paragraphs: " 'A little damaged pride is all,' Torres countered. 'I'm lucky. It _could have tore_ the whole front of my sled off.' " A lot of your quotations are

full of dialect and bad grammar. You don't clean up your quotations?

I don't like to clean my quotes up. In fact, we've got several big arguments around this newspaper about cleaning up quotes. There are several people that think you should clean up every quote. I don't think you should clean up any of them. I think it adds real texture to a story to let people talk like they talk. I don't, I don't want them to talk like I talk. I want them to talk like they talk. I mean, I get plenty of space in the story to talk the way I want to talk. And I would just as soon leave them to talk as they want to talk, and it, it's interesting.

We had a very good writer here by the name of Tom Kizzia who did this thing we called "North Country Journal," in which he went around to villages just looking for stories out in the bush. Tom's a very good writer and a very conscientious one. And there were several letters to the editor complaining about how he never wrote about natives, Alaskan natives, who are Indians. And Tom looked back through his stories, and something like 80 percent of them were about native people. I concluded (and I think Tom agrees, because his stories changed after the discussion) that he *had* written about a lot of native people, but he made them sound like white people. He'd cleaned up a lot of the quotes to make them sound better, and they'd all come out sounding like white people. The stories didn't sound like people out there sounded, and readers were left with the impression that we weren't writing about people out there.

Let's talk about the next quotation: " 'Ya,' said Bush, 'somebody said it's the kind of hill where when you go over the edge you start to scream, but before you can get it out, you're too busy.' " When I try to analyze what that wonderful quotation says, I can almost puzzle it out. [Laughter] But you don't seem tempted to straighten it out at all.

I don't think there's any need to. I mean, by the time I got there, I understood what he said; and if I told this thing well, by the time the readers got there, they would too.

Were you the only team from your paper covering the race?

Yeah. And this was one of those things we discussed before we started. Essentially, this race does not become a real man-against-man race until about halfway through. There's a lot of sorting out early in the race, almost like qualifying at Indianapolis. And we decided that we were going to poke around and look for people who got in trouble, people who had interesting experiences, people who were involved in their own kind of little adventure or drama. And we found one here.

Does your paper normally use that kind of features approach, or was it just for this race?

Early in this race, we mostly used that kind of approach. Having covered it in '83, I pretty much had decided that the good people-battling-each-other stories weren't going to come until we hit the coast at Unalakleet. And if we could find some good people-battling-nature stories before we got there, then we would have something.

Well, you got them, I must say. Let's take a look at "The Farewell Burn tests mushers' grit." Here's the beginning: "For two days now, battered and jerry-rigged dog sleds have come trickling one by one into this community of 500 on the Kuskokwim River.

"The sleds are pulled by teams of dogs fit and ready to run, but they are ridden by tired and bloodied mushers—men and women who have known the horrors of the snowless Farewell Burn.

"These are people who will not soon forget what they have seen there.

"Across the Farewell Burn is 93 miles of the worst trail the Iditarod Sled Dog Race has ever witnessed."

How did *you* get across the perilous Burn?

We flew across it, wisely, and got a good visual sense of it. It was bad, I mean, essentially a dirt trail instead of a snow trail, and the mushers slow down from about 10 miles an hour to 4 miles an hour. The dogs drag the sleds, and the mushers get out and walk.

The theme of this piece seems to be that the dogs did better than the mushers.

Oh, the dogs did much better than the mushers. The dogs probably enjoyed it. Some of the mushers are fairly fit, but some of them are not in the best physical condition, and it was a long and murderous walk. The dogs do the whole race, although you're allowed to drop dogs that are tired, and they're flown back to Anchorage. But essentially they get to Nome with all the same dogs they started with.

I like the way you handle this list of disasters: "Few dog sleds have come through the Burn unscathed.

"Dewey Halverson of Trapper Creek broke the runners off his sled and he had to ride the basket or walk. Terry Adkins of Sand Coulee, Mont.—already ailing with a bad back—broke off one runner and had to ride much of the way balanced on the other.

"Gordon Brinker of Shell Lake lost his sled brake. Ray Lang of Nome broke his sled in eight places. Redington smashed support posts. Ted English of Chuguik ripped his sled bag.

"The list goes on and on.

" 'It was so bad it was horrible,' said Dronenburg. 'It was incomprehensible.' "

That's full of technical terms, and I've never seen a sled in my life, but it's easy to follow.

Well, the sentences are quick enough there, that even if you don't understand them, you get this bang-bang-bang feel of something that's supposed to be bad.

I gather these are pretty famous people.

A good number of them are. Redington's real famous; Halverson's pretty well known; Adkins has been running this thing for 13 years; but Dronenburg's essentially a local.

Even with famous people, you remind the reader they're famous. You tell when they've won and that kind of thing, but there's not very much physical description of the characters.

There is at times, and there isn't at times. I usually throw it in if there's something worth describing, if the guy's nose is bloody or something like that. I often find that stuff gets in the way. I mean, some of that stuff seems somewhat gratuitous.

This piece is circular. It starts off in paragraph two, "The sleds are pulled by teams of dogs fit and ready to run, but they are ridden by tired and bloodied mushers," and it ends, "In fact, the vets at Nikolai and McGrath were almost as busy offering first-aid advice to mushers as they were tending to dogs."

Well, it seemed like a nice way to wrap it up. For our average reader, there are always questions about what the Iditarod does to dogs. So it seemed appropriate to come back and say that this was bad, but it wasn't bad for the dogs.

Take a look at the next piece: "There's no time to dream on the trail." Here we have a story about a race, and it starts off with a racer sound asleep. At one point, you say, "He stirred no more than the plank on which he slept." [Laughter]

Well, by this point, it's getting to be a race, and one of the key elements of this race is that these guys don't get much time to sleep. And the fact that this guy can sleep in a Laundromat just because it's warm gives a real good perspective on how tired they're getting.

After the last story here, "Garnie, Butcher race through bitter wind," Butcher went on to win, right?

Yeah, Butcher went on to win. This is about 200 miles from the end of the race, and we'd flown up to Stanton and landed on the ice. We'd spent about an hour and a half out on the ice at Norton Bay flying over them and landing ahead of them, so we could get photos and watch them as they made their way across.

And it was real cold. I mean, you'd get out of the plane and put on your wind gear and keep your back to the wind. Garnie and Butcher didn't have that choice. They had to cut right into it. The wind chill is vicious. There is nothing to slow it down. It's barren and flat and wind-scoured, and if there's exposed flesh, you feel it.

Lavrakas would try to get some photos, and we'd sit there and watch them, see how they were doing, see who was moving, see who was riding, who was doing what they call "pedaling," which is where they keep kicking with one leg. And you spend a lot of time watching and a lot of time getting cold.

Here's Garnie pedaling: "For much of the day, he could be seen working behind the sled—pedaling first with his right leg and then with his left, sometimes running beside the sled with one hand on the handlebar." That's so simply written and yet so vivid. I figured you must have seen it to write it that simply.

The best thing you can do is get out there. I mean, as a general rule, reporters don't use their eyes enough. They just don't get the richness of things without watching. And here it was real easy. It was a clear day, and we could fly all day, and we could land ahead of them and watch them go through. Ideal circumstances.

As Yogi Berra once said, "You can see a lot just by observing." [Laughter] In the rest of the piece, your attention passes back and forth from character to character. You're writing in blocks, right?

Very much so. It's getting to be a race now, and we're down to two players, and I play them off against each other. Swenson's stuff was especially useful in making that contrast because he and Butcher shared this great animosity when they're racing.

Let's back off and talk about these stories as a whole. When I first read them, I thought to myself, "Maybe this guy's coming from sportswriting," and the stories seemed very odd to me from that point of view. Now, of course, I know you're not from sports. But is there a tradition of writing about this race in this way?

Yeah, sort of a tradition. I mean, I do a lot of stories about people who have adventures and get into trouble, about people who freeze to death and get attacked by bears. And a lot of those stories are more interesting as stories than as just news. And that's shaped a lot of my style. It's more storytelling than straight reporting.

I often get into trouble with some of our editors for backing into stories. But, for a lot of stories I do, I have a feeling that the context is as important as what's happening. And if you don't put them in context high up, they're not much as stories.

What happens to your stories when they get back to the paper? Are you edited much?

[Laughs, long pause]

I'm not prescient. [Laughter]

[Laughs, long pause] Oh, suffice to say I'm not edited much. Suffice to say I threw fits around here. I mean, I stay at this paper because people have learned not to screw with me, and it's worked out well.

I had a reputation of being a prima donna for a while, but I just don't want people messing with my copy unless they can tell me why they're doing it. If somebody can tell me a better way to do it, I really am open to that kind of criticism. But with this "I don't like this" or "This doesn't feel good" stuff, I go ballistic.

You put that remark about being a prima donna in the past tense, but it sounds like you still are.

Well, I don't want to be called that. I mean, I'm not one. I'm more than open to discussion. Mike Campbell is my editor, and I'm the only guy he actively edits, because I was the problem child around here for a while. I mean, I had these reviews: "You don't listen to direction. You don't do this. You don't do that." And I would sit there and say, "Pay me more money, or I leave." But I've started working with Mike, and he's real good about saying, if he doesn't like something, "Why don't you go back and try and come at it from this way or that way?" But I just don't like this attitude of "It doesn't feel good to me" or "I don't think you know what you're doing."

Editors in general tend to treat reporters like they don't know what they're doing. And I generally tend to give reporters credit that they *do* know what they're doing. If they don't, fire them. I mean, it's very difficult to find editors who are secure enough so that they don't want to mess with things just for the sake of messing with things.

Well, what's in your future? What do you see for yourself next?

I really don't know what I want to do from this point on. I'm a little bit renewed now in being more of my old self and being more aggressive in pushing management around when I think things are not quite right. And I think I'll probably be doing more of that.

I mean, I'm in a job that I really like, but I would like to have a more active role in working with other writers.

Got any heroes, Craig?

Oh, yeah. I like to read a guy by the name of Pete Dexter, who works for the *Sacramento Bee* now, and I regularly read him up here and say, "Why can't we put this stuff in our paper?"

What does Dexter do that you'd like to do?

Oh, Dexter goes after a lot of those common stories about people who've been abused by the system. I mean, that's the kind of thing that I think newspapers should do, stand up for some of the little people out there. I mean, we lack people who get out of the office and do those stories. We tend to be a middle-class paper, and we're all living middle-class lives. I think that good journalism's got to go beyond that. We've got to open our eyes to the things that are going on out there that are the opposite of what we know. I wish that every newspaper in the country had a Pete Dexter, that there was somebody out there being a conscience, and writing about it with that kind of skill. I mean, it's wonderful to see people like that finding jobs in newspapers.

I think we've just heard the birth of a crusading journalist. Good luck, Craig.

Thanks, Don.

Dave Barry
Commentary

DAVE BARRY, 39, was born in Armonk, New York. After graduating from Haverford College, he started at the *Daily Local News* in West Chester, Pennsylvania, as a real reporter. He worked for the AP in Philadelphia until he got so sick of the inverted pyramid that he took a job as a Consultant Teaching Effective Writing to Business People with Burger Associates while his journalist wife sneaked his free-lance humor columns into her paper and some very generous people at *The Miami Herald* noticed him and hired him in 1983, and those very generous *Miami Herald* people now distribute him to 120 newspapers, or more. He sees like an angel and writes like a brat. Everybody loves his stuff.

SNEWS

Readers are sometimes critical of me because just about everything I write is an irresponsible lie. So today I'm going to write a column in which everything is true. See how you like it.

Our first true item comes from a news release from the J. I. Case company. For the benefit of those of you who have real jobs and are therefore not involved in the news business, I should first explain that a "news release" is an article that has been typed up by a public-relations professional hired by a client who wants to get certain information published, which is then mailed out to several thousand newspapers, almost all of which throw it away without reading it. If you ever commit a really horrible crime and you want to keep it out of the papers, you should have a public-relations professional issue a news release about it.

You ask: "Wouldn't it be more efficient if the public-relations professionals simply threw the releases away themselves?" Frankly, that is the kind of ignorant question that makes us journalists want to forget about trying to inform the public and instead just sit around awarding journalism prizes to each other. But I'll tell you the answer: because this is America. Because 200 years ago, a band of brave men got extremely cold at Valley Forge so that the press would have the freedom to throw away its own releases without prior censorship, that's why.

Anyway, this release from the J. I. Case company opens with this statement: "J. I. Case and Burlington, Iowa, the loader/backhoe capital of the world, today jointly celebrated the production of the 175,000th Case loader/backhoe." The release said they had a nice ceremony attended

by the mayor of Burlington, a person named
Wayne W. Hogberg, so I called him up to confirm
the story. He works at the post office.

"Does Burlington really call itself the
loader/backhoe capital of the world?" I asked.
Newsmen are paid to ask the hard questions. "Oh
yes," replied Mayor Hogberg. "We definitely lay
claim to that. We use it whenever we have the
opportunity. As a mayor, I sort of rub it in with
any other mayors I have occasion to meet with."
I bet that really steams the other mayors, don't
you? I bet they are consumed with jealousy, when
mayors get together.

Our second completely true news item was
sent to me by Mr. H. Boyce Connell Jr. of
Atlanta, Ga., where he is involved in a law firm.
One thing I like about the South is, folks there
care about tradition. If somebody gets handed a
name like "H. Boyce," he hangs on to it, puts it
on his legal stationery, even passes it to his son,
rather than do what a lesser person would do,
such as get it changed or kill himself.

What H. Boyce sent was a copy of a decision
handed down by the Georgia Court of Appeals
in the case of *Apostol-Athanasiou vs. White*. It
seems the former had hired the latter to mow her
lawn. What happened next, in the words of the
court, is that "...White allegedly slipped on some
dog feces concealed in the tall grass, and his left
foot was severely cut as it slid under the lawn
mower." I am not going to tell you how this case
came out, because you'll want to find out for
yourself in the event that it is released as a major
motion picture, but I will say, by way of a hint,
that in the court's opinion "...neither party had
actual knowledge of the specific deposit of dog
feces on which White apparently slipped."

Our next item comes from a release sent out
by the Vodka Information Bureau in New York
City. The Vodka Information Bureau has learned
that a whopping 42 percent of the women
surveyed consider themselves "primary decision
makers" in deciding what brand of vodka to buy.

This raises in my mind, as I'm sure it does in yours, a number of questions, primarily: What, exactly, do we mean by the verb "to whop"? So I looked it up in the *Oxford English Dictionary*, and there I found—remember, this is the column where we are not making things up—these helpful examples:

- "In less time than you can think, whop comes a big black thing down, as big as the stone of a cheese-press."
- "Mother would whop me if I came home without the basket."

So I called my mother, who said, and I quote, "I always make my vodka-buying decision as follows: the largest bottle for the smallest amount of money." So I called the Vodka Information Bureau and told them what my mother said, and they said, sure, you can buy the cheapest vodka if you don't mind getting a lot of impurities, but if you want a nice clean vodka, you want a brand such as is manufactured by the company that sponsors the Vodka Information Bureau.

Finally, and sadly, we have received word of the death, at age 85, of Sir Seewoosagur Ramgoolam, who of course was governor general of the island nation of Mauritius from 1968 to 1982. Mauritius has an area of 720 square miles and was once the home of the dodo bird, which is now extinct. It is hard, at a time of such tragedy—I refer here to the demise of Sir Seewoosagur Ramgoolam—to find words to express our feelings, but I think I speak for all of us when I say that a cheese-press is "an apparatus for pressing the curds in cheese-making."

Observations and questions

1) In the second and third paragraphs, Barry imitates at least three voices: a broadcast announcer, the public-relations professional, and an exasperated patriot. Watch the transitions from one to the other. Why doesn't the reader get confused?

2) Barry asks questions the reader would never think of, as if they had just occurred to every reader. Think about this device in terms of irony and surprise. Could we use it in hard news stories?

3) This piece parodies the un-selfconscious jargon of companies, courts, mayors, etc. Notice how Barry seems to accept them all without criticism. He ends each one with what comedians call a "blank-out."

4) *The Oxford English Dictionary*, Volume W, page 97, under "Whop," between "Whoo-whoop" and "Whopper," lists the following helpful examples:
"1870 E. Peacock *Ralf Skirl.* xviii, In less time than you can think, whop comes a big black thing down...as big as the stone of a cheese-press.
"1890 Henty *With Lee in Virg.* xviii, Mother would whop me if I came back without the basket."
Think twice before you doubt Dave Barry or the *OED*.

5) Count all the speakers in this piece, including Barry. In a hard news piece of this length, we would have trouble introducing this many voices. Study how smoothly Barry handles the attributions.

6) Notice Barry's rather shrewd characterizations of the press in this ironic piece about
truth. Do his observations ring true with your
experience as a journalist?

Campaign 86: And now for some comic relief...

APRIL 13, 1986

Big-time national politics has all but lost its Weirdness Quotient. More and more, high-level political races tend to be between identical slim men in identical slim suits. Rational men, cool men, men who know the voting market, men who never say the wrong thing, men who are *good on TV*. Candidates who don't fit this mold—the blatant hacks, the geeks, the loons, the people with bad teeth—tend to get filtered out at the state-legislature level. At the Senate level, you wind up with Ted Koppel vs. Ted Koppel, both speaking in perfect sound bites.

These people are boring. I ask you: What is the point of watching a politician talk if he doesn't make an ass of himself? Where are the weird candidates? Who, on the national level, will pick up the torch dropped, with a typical lack of manual dexterity, by Richard M. Nixon? Where are the fat candidates? Where are the ugly candidates? Where are the *stupid* candidates? Where are the candidates who go to formal dinners and pass out in the shrimp? Who set fire to themselves with cigars? I believe that if we are to keep the tradition of participatory democracy going in this country, if we are to revive voter interest, *we need more weird people running for high office*, and we need them *right now.*

And so I say: Thank God for Florida, whose very license plates should read, "FLORIDA: NOT A NORMAL PLACE." Because in a state like this, a state whose naturally humid climate has permitted a tremendous diversity of human and reptile life to flourish and mutate, we should not be surprised to find that this year, we are being treated to a Senate race between two politicians who are clearly not Standard Issue. I've spent some time watching both of them, and I can honestly state that regardless of which one is elected, we will all, as Floridians, have reason to be vastly amused. Here's a full report on the campaign to date.

* * *

We are in Gov. Bob Graham's rental campaign plane, which is stout and bouncy, not unlike the governor himself, and we are going to someplace called "Bartow." Rumor has it that there is agriculture in Bartow. Graham is going there to show his concern for it.

On the plane with the governor is the press corps, including a couple of political reporters from Big-Time out-of-state papers that are very interested in this race because (a) it is considered crucial to the Republicans' hopes of retaining control in the Senate and (b) it is nice and warm in Florida. The press corps is not crazy about landing in Bartow. The press corps frankly does not care about agriculture except insofar as it results in lunch. The press corps would rather hear Graham talk about his opponent, incumbent Sen. Paula Hawkins, and her hot new campaign issue, The Pipeline That Will Leak And Explode.

This is an issue that materialized out of the air, literally, in the form of two Hawkins campaign commercials suggesting that Graham is willing to let this pipeline spew oil and flame all over the state. Graham, who has long portrayed himself as a friend of nature, the Everglades, bunny rabbits, etc., fought back with a counter-commercial—featuring a photograph of Hawkins that makes her look like she lost the Miss Room Freshener Pageant because the judges thought she was too vacuous—in which prominent ecology nuts say that they favor the pipeline and like Bob Graham and think Hawkins' commercial is basically alligator poop.

But in a way, Graham has lost the round, because he had to spend money to make a commercial responding to an issue Hawkins raised in HER commercials.

The whole thing sort of reminds you of Coke vs. Pepsi, only with less substance.

Anyway, Graham would prefer not to talk about the pipeline because it's Hawkins' issue. What he often does, in situations where he doesn't want to talk about what the press wants to talk about, is launch into lengthy anecdotes with powerful sedative properties. This time, up in his rental plane, he decides to talk about the manufacturing of phosphate, which has something to do with agriculture and which they apparently make bales of in the Bartow area. Graham knows all about how to make phosphate. The trick, he shouts to the Big-Time reporters over the roar of the engines, is to get rid of the slime. The Big-Time reporters try very hard to appear interested in slime disposal—this man is, after all, a *governor*—but it is clear they would prefer to read the instructions on their airsickness bags.

Finally I get a chance to ask Graham: "Will Faye Dunaway be having your baby?"

"I have too much respect for Miss Dunaway and what she stands for in America to answer that question," he says. "If there's going to be any statement made, I think she should do it."

* * *

We land in Bartow, which apparently consists of a hangar. Inside the hangar is a smallish agricultural crowd, which Graham, using his oratorical skills, immediately whips into a stupor. He is not a gifted speaker. He is the kind of speaker who, if he were not the governor, people would shoot rubber bands at after a while. The high point of his Bartow speech comes when he holds up a can of Florida concentrated orange juice, which the crowd applauds, because frankly, and I am not trying to be cruel here, it exudes more charisma than the governor.

"Would you say," I ask, "that spending a lot of time around cows as a child could make a person kind of dull?" Graham grew up on a dairy.

"It could have that potential," he answers,
"but on the other hand, some might say—but I
am too modest to personally say this—that it
brings out a quickness of wit, a sense of ironic
humor, an ability to, with a—not a destructive,
but a positive uplifting way—with words to bring
humor into the world. That's what some people
would say. I am too personally modest."

During the Bartow speech, I locate, just
outside the hangar, an enormous insect of the
type that you would never find in a state such
as Ohio. I pick it up, using my notebook, which
it spits brown glop on, to test a theory I have
about Graham, which is that he will comment
on anything. I show it to him, and ask:
"Governor, would you comment on this insect?"

"This," he says, picking his words very
carefully, as he always does, "is an (*here he says
a name that sounds like 'Execretius Bolemius,'
which he is clearly making up*). It is a Friend to
Man. It is a member of the family of Almost-
Flying Insects, and one of the many things that
it does is that it titillates the toad."

He's very smart and he wants to be senator,
and he'll do whatever it takes. He knows he can't
get you with his voice or his looks. He has
trimmed himself down, but his face still contains
two-thirds of the known world supply of pudge.
So he compensates. He meets you personally.
Two or three times. If you're in the state more
than 12 hours, he'll track you down. Shake your
hand. Be Just Folks with you, cracker mouth
talking, Harvard eyes watching. He'll write down
your name in his little notebook. Send you a
personal letter. Carry your luggage. Make you
a sandwich. Take out your garbage. If you're a
cattle rancher, he'll pet your heifers. If you're a
humor writer, he'll give you funny quotes.
Whatever it takes.

* * *

Back up on the campaign plane, the press is
bitching to Graham that they have spent a whole
day flying around with him, and he has not committed any news. Graham argues that he has,

indeed, been newsworthy, and the press has missed it. Graham thinks the press should write about the Broad Sweeping Theme of his campaign, namely that Florida is a fast-growing state that must meet the challenges of the 21st century and needs to be represented by a person of competence, breadth, and vision, as opposed to some bimbo with hair like Harpo Marx. (The last part of the Theme is never actually spoken aloud.) This is the message Graham feels the reporters should focus on. So they ask him more questions about the pipeline.

***

Now we are somewhere around Orlando, and Graham is demonstrating his commitment to law enforcement by making a speech on the construction site for a new jail. He tells a small but extremely quiet crowd that he once did a workday as a SWAT-team member here, and—I'm pretty sure this is what he said—on that particular day, Central Florida was totally free of terrorists. Graham loves to refer to his workdays. They are a great idea, really: Here's a wealthy, highly educated man with all the power and prestige that go with being governor, taking off his suit and tie to go out amongst the common people and toil with them and sweat with them and get on their evening local TV news broadcasts.

By the way, if you ever need to get in touch with the governor and for some unusual reason he doesn't have a workday scheduled in your area that day, your best bet is to send a note to his wife, Adele, and ask her to tape it to the bathroom mirror. I got this tip from a story in *The Miami Herald* about this person named Alberto San Pedro, who is described in the story as a "crime figure," meaning we just *know* he must be guilty of something, and who is trying to get a pardon in connection with his 1971 murder conspiracy conviction.

So it seems this friend of San Pedro's who is also a friend of the Grahams sent Mrs. Graham a letter about what a nice guy San Pedro is now, with two children, aged 2 and 4, and stating that he is "active in the community" (the police agree with this), and Mrs. Graham taped it to the bathroom mirror so Graham would see it. Apparently this is a standard method of communication in the governor's mansion. According to a Graham spokesperson, "It's known by acquaintances of the Grahams that, from time to time, when Mrs. Graham wants the governor to be aware of something, she tapes it on the bathroom mirror." I imagine if the note is really urgent, aides unscrew the mirror from the wall and rush it down to the state capitol so Graham can read it.

But anyway, my point is, if you need clemency or anything, this is the correct gubernatorial channel to go through, although you should be aware that, according to the spokesperson, Mrs. Graham "obviously doesn't tape all (the mail) to the mirror." Of course not! How would he shave?

***

Now we're at the state fair, in Tampa. Graham lulls the crowd at a luncheon featuring an opening prayer in which the Lord is asked to "have mercy on people not only in this state, but in other states, and people throughout the universe." Then Graham wanders among these truly wonderful exhibits extolling the glories of the various Florida counties, exhibits that show what you can do with a little money and practically no imagination. He admires them all with sincerely feigned interest. There is a giant papier-mâché bird sitting on a humongous papier-mâché hand. This is of course illustrating the concept: "A bird in the hand," but it is not immediately clear, to the outside observer, *why*.

Next he goes to where they keep the cows. He knows cows. Knows their names. Seems to sincerely *like* cows. I think—this is pure speculation—that he likes cows better than people. But cows don't vote. If they did, Graham would have sent every one in the state a personal letter. But now he has to woo cow owners. Walks right up to them and talks cow. His press secretary, Ken Klein, scouts ahead for additional campaign livestock. "Governor," he says—I swear this is a true quote—"we have a *Palm Beach cow* over here." The press corps roars at this. "We have a Key West cow over here," we shout. We issue limp-wristed, lisping moos. Graham's Harvard eyes flash a laugh to let us know he heard us, then off he goes, bouncing away toward the Palm Beach cow.

Whatever it takes.

***

It's a beautiful morning in Fort Lauderdale, and the press has gathered outside the Broward County Commission building. Sen. Hawkins is scheduled to hold a hearing on The Pipeline That Will Leak And Explode, and the press is hoping for a Sighting.

Hawkins has been hard to see. Her chronic neck and back problems recently forced her into a hospital for tests. The press relations for this event were handled with all the smooth, suave, low-key professionalism of clowns hitting each other with dead fish. First, when Hawkins missed a couple of engagements and then disappeared, her office told inquiring reporters that she had taken an early vacation; then, when reporters found out that she was in fact in the hospital, her office announced that the previous announcement was—these are the exact words—*no longer operative.* This is of course the famous Watergate phrase that causes reporters to sprout facial hair and fangs and want to rip the flesh off everything that moves. Soon there was much speculation in the press about what was wrong with Hawkins, whether she was addicted to painkillers, whether she would drop out of the race, etc.

And so we are all standing on the corner in Fort Lauderdale, waiting to see if Hawkins will get out of the car and keel right over, or what. She does not. She gets out looking perky. She has huge perky eyes and a huge perky smile. She has perky hair. She wears lots of perky makeup and some big perky diamonds, which bring her weight up to maybe 18 pounds. One glance, and you understand why they whisper *That Name* behind her back. *Betty Boop.*

Well, forget Betty Boop. Hawkins is no nuclear physicist, and she does wear a *lot* of makeup (she looks like a person attempting to sneak valuable possessions through customs by hiding them under her mascara), and she does not have a dress-for-success hairstyle, but she is a very shrewd and tough woman who has managed to get herself elected to the U.S. By God Senate. She often refers to herself as "this senator," in case anybody forgets. But the point is, she IS a senator, which is more than you can say for the people who whisper Betty Boop. They are small jungle birds, chattering from the safety of the trees; she's prowling down in the tall jungle grass, where you either kill or get killed. Where Graham's every move and statement seem carefully planned, Hawkins seems to rely more on instinct and reflex. But her reflexes are pretty good. And for now, she's the one in the Senate.

The Big Pipeline Hearing is a wonderful example of how, for all of its faults, the American system of free, open, and representative government is still capable of being one of the silliest on earth. Your Objective Observers generally agree that Hawkins' concerns about the pipeline's environmental threats are short on logic, but of course logic has nothing to do with this. What we are talking about here is *street smarts.* This issue lets Hawkins hit Graham right where he is supposed to be strong. Right in his bunny rabbits.

And so she is in Fort Lauderdale to hold a hearing. With her, to help, is her friend and Senate mentor, Sen. Orrin Hatch of Utah, a thin man with thin lips. He looks like a funeral director, only not as much fun. This is supposed to be a hearing of the Senate Labor and Human Resources Committee's Subcommittee on

Children, Family, Drugs, and Alcoholism. But
Hawkins and Hatch, both Republicans, are the
only subcommittee members to show up. The
Democratic senators, back in Washington, say
the hearing is a sham. They say it's *political.*

Hatch announces that he is *shocked* by this
charge. "This isn't a political thing," he says,
looking for all the world as though he believes
there is nothing remotely unusual about a
senator from Utah coming to Florida under the
auspices of the Subcommittee on Children,
Family, Drugs, and Alcoholism to hold hearings
about a pipeline.

The highlight of the hearing comes early, at
the end of Hawkins' opening statement, in which
she voices grave concern that leaking fuel might
contaminate the groundwater. Suddenly she
brandishes a bottle of Perrier at Hatch, startling
him, and declares: "Not everyone, Mr. Chairman,
can drink Perrier. And Perrier *doesn't mix too
well with infant formula.*"

A wonderful move. Some of us in the press
are tempted to applaud. From deep left field, way
out near the warning track, Hawkins has
managed to drag in children, *little* children,
babies, as victims of the Pipeline That Will Leak
And Explode. It is a horrifying image: Mothers,
forced to feed babies formula made with *Perrier*!
Think of it! Think of the *burping*!

Hawkins brings up kids every chance she
gets. Kids are HER issue. Kids and drugs. She
is for kids, against drugs. She never misses an
opportunity to remind everybody of this. Why
not? Her concern is genuine, she conveys it well,
and who on earth is going to argue with her? Who
is going to come out *against* kids and *for* drugs?
Hitler?

Her critics say her near-obsession with these
two issues means she is *limited,* as a senator. A
lightweight. They chatter this, from the trees.

After the hearing, Hawkins and Hatch hold
a press conference, and of course the *last* thing
the press wants to talk about is the pipeline. (You

may have noticed a pattern here: the press and the newsmakers never want to talk about the same thing. This is why the vast majority of the news consists of vague and insincere quotations.)

What the press wants to talk about is Hawkins' health. She opens with a bombshell: "The good news," she says brightly, "is that I don't have cancer." This is a remarkable statement, since, as far as anybody knows, it was never reported that she *did* have cancer. Hawkins will sometimes emit offhand statements of the type that make press aides turn to hard liquor. She loves the quick quip, in sharp contrast to Graham, who usually speaks with all the spontaneity of highway construction. "Are you in discomfort?" a reporter asks Hawkins. "As long as I'm in politics, I'm in discomfort," she shoots back. She can be very funny, very sharp, when she quips. She is far less effective in her other major speaking mode, the Soaring Ramble, where she swoops and swerves sharply from topic to topic, at some length and seemingly without mental punctuation, until you, her listener, start getting nervous for her, wondering if she'll find a safe place to land before she runs out of fuel.

Driving back from the hearing, I listen to a radio news broadcast about the great pipeline hearing. "Hawkins says she doesn't have cancer," it says.

***

Now we are in Naples, where Hawkins is speaking at a Republican dinner at a very posh hotel, which is called "The Ritz-Carlton" only because it would be a little too obvious to call it "The Wealthy Protestant."

After she speaks, I corner her and tell her I'm a humor columnist for *The Miami Herald.* "*That* must be hard," she says. She is not nuts about *The Herald.*

I ask her if she sees any humor in the pipeline issue. This elicits a Soaring Ramble, which I will quote from here, verbatim, transcribed from my tape recorder, so you'll get a feel for what they're like:

"...So it's up to the people of Florida to decide
if they want to make a safe pipeline, and that's
why I'm trying to point the way towards that
pipeline. I drink lots of water, and I just must
tell you that we can live without a lot of luxuries
we have in Florida—we brag a lot about a lot of
more roads, and a lot more other of the luxuries
I call them, and yet we want to keep it rural like
it was 50 years ago, and we can't *do* that—people
are here—but the least we can do is provide water
for people who are here and for the future
generations—*my* children certainly don't want to
leave Winter Park; they love it there, and my
eight grandchildren, they intend to have water,
I have eight grandchildren under 8, and I want
to tell you they all expect great quality water to
come out of their tap. They think I should do that.
I think there's a little humor that I started in
politics, regulating 800 water and sewer companies. We used to regulate Florida Gas—I don't
know what they call themselves this year; they
keep changing their name..."

I interrupt. "What about Bob Graham?" I
ask. "You see any humor in Bob Graham?"

She stops toying with her pearls. Her eyes
cool; her smile hardens.

"*None at all*," she says.

About 15 reporters, mostly from Florida
papers, have gathered at the National Press Club
in Washington, D.C., to have breakfast with
Hawkins. This has come about because the
reporters have been complaining that they never
get to talk to her, and often can't even find out
where she is. The press does not like this. The
press is used to political figures like Graham,
who are at least willing to pretend they think
reporters are important. The Hawkins' camp, on
the other hand, gives the impression it wouldn't
have minded if the journalist-in-space program
had gotten an earlier start.

At the breakfast is Hawkins' chief campaign
strategist, Charlie Black. Black is 38, my age,
but he is far more poised, articulate, and mature

than I will be at death. He's a media-savvy
political consultant. His job is to take polls to find
out what the voters think, then make television
commercials showing that the candidate thinks
so, too. It's similar to what McDonald's does. A
while back, McDonald's must have done a survey
that showed that the public wanted lettuce and
tomato on its hamburgers, so they created a
massive advertising campaign for this *radical*
new product, the "McD.L.T.," which is a
hamburger with lettuce and tomato, but which
sounds like a wondrous innovation, along the
lines of time travel.

The pipeline issue came up pretty much the
same way. Charlie's polls showed that voters
were concerned about their water supply, so he
created: The McPipeline. If the voters had said
they were concerned about giant UFO beetles
from space, Hawkins and Hatch would have held
hearings on *that*.

The reporters ask Black if he hasn't made a
mistake with this pipeline issue, because the
newspapers have dumped all over it. It is all
Black can do to keep from laughing out loud. "In
Florida, especially, television is the king
medium," he tells us, amiably. "Advertising,"
he says, "has a much more dramatic impact than
daily newspapers."

We all write this down, to put in our
newspapers.

Hawkins arrives, and we have a tense little
breakfast. She picks at her muffin and smiles in
a bright and cheerful and obviously forced
manner, so as to make it clear that she would
frankly prefer to be undergoing eye surgery. Of
course she doesn't want to talk about her
health—she is sick unto DEATH of reporters
asking her about her health—so we mainly ask
her questions about her health.

Hawkins, always smiling, answers the questions patiently and sometimes condescendingly,
as if lecturing small children. She gets in her digs
where she can. Responding to a reporter's ques-

tion, she begins: "I read in one of your columns—
which I don't read very often (huge smile here);
I'm sorry, but they're *so* inaccurate that I have
to get a better source..."; then she goes on to
answer the question in her sweetest, most
cheerful voice. All in all, it's a fun half-hour for
everybody, and Hawkins' press secretary prom-
ises we'll do it again sometime.

So there they are, your Senate candidates,
both surrounded by little pieces of the molds that
were broken when they were made, both
desperate for the opportunity to Serve You. For
the record, Graham is favored to win. Not that
he's taking it for granted. He's probably mowing
your lawn right now. Because he knows, as
Hawkins knows, that it will be a long time before
this particular storm oozes off the radar map of
Florida politics. I think it's going to be a fun race.
I urge you, the voters, to follow it closely, maybe
even find out, by reading stories written by
responsible journalists, what the issues are.
Assuming there are any.

Observations and questions

1) Dave Barry assures us that he does not write to be read aloud. Pay no attention to him. Read the first paragraph aloud, noting the conversational rhythms and tone. What devices does he use to create that effect?

2) Barry wrote the whole Graham section and then the Hawkins part, and then tied them together with the ending and the beginning. But notice how he weaves Hawkins into the Graham portion and vice versa.

3) Except for flashbacks, this whole piece is written in the present tense, non-traditional for news writing and difficult to sustain. Study how Barry manages this feat, and speculate on its effects on readers, section by section.

4) Barry says that the governor "admires them all with sincerely feigned interest." Other than quoting someone else saying it, how could a hard news reporter convey such an observation?

5) Barry keeps assuring the reader of the veracity of his quotations: "I swear this is a true quote;" "verbatim, transcribed from my tape recorder;" etc. Do such asides convince readers or make them wonder even more?

6) Barry usually sets us up with something straight and then knocks it down with a zinger. But after getting Hawkins on the stage with four paragraphs of zingers, he delivers a serious appreciation of her as a politician, ending, "And for now, she's the one in the Senate." Of course, he promptly knocks her down again.

7) This piece starts off calling for more weird candidates. Are Graham and Hawkins really weird, or has Barry just made them sound weird? What would he do with Fritz Mondale or Gary Hart?

8) How can we get Dave Barry to run for the Senate?

The domino theory blues

I believe that from time to time every taxpayer should go to Washington, which is where we have our government and our government-related restaurants, just for the sheer fun of finding out what kind of comical high jinx grown people will engage in if you give them enough money to raise armies and hold hearings.

When I was there recently, they were holding hearings on the crucial question of how we can further screw up the situation in Nicaragua. Nicaragua has become a very hot foreign-policy issue lately, as is evidenced by the fact that President Reagan recently sent Philip Habib down there. Phil had just returned from the Philippines, where his job was to make sure that the Air Force courtesy getaway jet supplied to Mr. and Mrs. Ferdinand Marcos by grateful taxpayers such as yourself was nice and clean and had enough overhead storage space for the national treasury.

But Phil faces tough sledding in Nicaragua. For one thing, they never get any snow. (Ha ha! Who says foreign policy issues are dull? Many people.) Seriously, you have a very difficult and complex situation in Nicaragua, which I will attempt to explain in simplified terms that even a taxpayer who uses the short 1040 form can grasp. A few years back, there was this leader down there, a Mr. Somoza, who graduated near the top of his class at the Stereotypical Latin American Tinhorn Dictator Wearing Aviator Sunglasses Academy and who was—let us choose our words carefully here—a big fat tub of scum. But he was *anti-Communist* scum, so of course concerned taxpayers such as yourself gave him bales of money because we didn't want the

Communists taking over Nicaragua. And so of course the Communists took over Nicaragua, and of course they have also turned out to be scum. You wonder, sometimes, when you study foreign policy, why there can't be more nice countries out there, like Canada.

Anyway, this is a serious problem, Communists in Nicaragua, because of the Domino Theory, named in 1954 for Antoine "Fats" Domino, who was very big at the time. Not that he is what you would call petite today. The Domino Theory states that if the Communists take over one nation in a region, and they put down a tile with a certain number of spots, the United States has to put down a tile with a matching number of spots, or the Communists get to take over another nation, and so on until they take over Texas.

Actually, I don't think anybody of refinement would seriously object if the Communists got Texas, especially if they passed some sensible laws, such as: No More Big Stupid Hats. But the problem is, once they get Texas, what's to keep them from taking Oklahoma? OK, I guess that's not really a problem either. But eventually they're going to come to a really important state, such as Tennessee. Elvis is buried in Tennessee. When I think about Communists getting hold of a precious national resource such as Elvis, perhaps even selling him off in segments—think what a single toe bone would fetch, at auction—to raise money for their evil worldwide empire, well, you can call me a courageous patriot if you want, but my reaction is: yuck.

So we have to stop the Communists. The question is, where? President Reagan would like us to stop them right there in Nicaragua because that way (a) they won't be able to spread their vile poison throughout the region and (b) he won't have to learn the names of any additional countries. So he's always pushing Congress to send more money, provided by freedom-loving taxpayers such as yourself, down to an outfit called the "Contras," which is trying to overthrow the Nicaraguan government. There are pros and cons to the president's policy, as follows:

PRO—The Contras are brave, Valley-Forge-style patriots fighting for liberty and justice.

CON—The Contras are vicious baby-killing rapists.

I assume it goes without saying that both the pros and cons are provided by well-informed government leaders receiving salaries and limousines and subsidized haircuts courtesy of satisfied taxpayers such as yourself.

The way our leaders have dealt with this situation so far is, they came up with a compromise. Here's how it works: We send aid to the Contras, just in case it turns out they are good, but just in case it turns out they are bad, the KIND of aid we send them is "humanitarian," which means they can't use it to kill people. (Don't laugh! This is your foreign policy!) Like, if we send them some humanitarian shovels, they can use them to dig holes, but not so deep that if a Communist fell in, he would suffer a fatal injury. Also under the heading of "humanitarian" aid is cigarettes, which I assume the Contras are not allowed to share with Communists, because of course the surgeon general states right on the pack that they are hazardous. He works for you, too.

Observations and questions

1) Study Barry's lead paragraph, which is all one sentence. How does he keep such a long and intricate sentence running smoothly and clearly? Does it sound more like prose or conversation?

2) On the surface, Barry simply hops from thought to thought as he plays word games and tosses off gags. Outline the sequence of ideas underlying this piece to see its devastating logic.

3) The Domino Theory, as Barry describes it here, makes as much sense as it does when serious politicians wield it without thinking, or worse, wield it *with* thinking. Why do we need a humor columnist to make us see?

4) Barry uses the same phrases over and over again, such as "so of course" or "taxpayers such as yourself." Besides exasperating copy editors, what purposes can you imagine for such repetition? How can you tell when it works, and when it begins to get overdone?

5) The last paragraph reads more like real conversational speech than prose. Try rewriting it into traditional news prose, noticing what you delete. Why does Barry use such a conversational ending, especially in view of the prosy lead?

6) Count the number of references to "our," "you," "your," and "taxpayers" in this column. Who is the target of this editorial?

Commencement

SEPTEMBER 28, 1986

We're taking our son, Robby, to his first day of kindergarten. He is being Very Brave. So are we.

We're saying: "This is great!" And: "You're going to have a *wonderful time!*"

Robby's thinking: This is it. The fun part of life is over now.

We're thinking: Please, please, PLEASE let him not hate this and let the other kids be nice to him and let his teachers see, among all those little bobbing heads and skinny arms and Band-Aided legs, what a wonderful little boy this is.

I know this is just as rough for everybody else. I know *all* the kids are special. I know that the teachers are very, very nice, and that, over the years, they've had hundreds of kids like Robby.

But not *Robby*.

I think: If only they could put him to bed just one time, hear him talk to his stuffed dolphin, hear the dolphin answer back in a squeaky version of Robby's little voice. If only they could have seen him burst into tears in the part of the Saturday TV movie when it looked liked Godzilla had been killed by the Japanese army. He slept with his Godzilla doll that night, comforting it.

We're getting near the school, and Robby is trying so hard to be brave that I am about ready to turn around and drive back home and sit down on the living room floor and play with him and hug him forever and the hell with developing Motor Skills and Language Skills and Math Skills and Socialization and growing up in general.

"This is going to be *great*," I say. I give him his lunch money. I wish I could give him my muscles, to keep in the pocket of his little blue shorts in case a big kid tries to bully him. I wish I could give him my mind, so he'd understand why he has to go to school. I wish *I* understood it.

"I remember when I started kindergarten!" I say, sounding to myself like Mister Rogers. "It was scary at first, but I made a lot of friends!"

What I'm really remembering is the way kids got teased in kindergarten. Because they were fat. Because they were short. For no reason at all. We teased them and teased them and teased them, and it must have been hell for them. I still remember the kids we teased. I'm sure they still remember.

Please forgive me, Craig and Susan. Please God, don't let the kids tease Robby.

We're at his classroom. We're supposed to leave right away. They told us that in Parents' Orientation. They said hanging around only makes it worse. It couldn't be any worse. Robby is fighting panic, asking questions, stalling to keep us there, tears running quietly down his cheeks.

"How many hours will it be?" he asks.

Thousands, I think. Thousands and thousands, in classrooms, away from us, until you've learned to accept it, and you don't cry when we leave you, and your dolphin never talks anymore.

Observations and questions

1) This piece appeared in *Tropic* magazine's "Just a Moment..." series, which traditionally prints serious, rather weepy pieces. But it had Dave Barry's byline on it, and an editor's note identifying him as "*Tropic*'s humor writer." How can the usually comic writer signal serious intent and subject matter to avoid confusing the readers' expectations?

2) Barry tells this story in the present tense. Why? What would happen if we revised it into the past tense?

3) A list of Barry's standard comic devices would include the following: run-on sentences, emphatic capital letters and italics, imagined conversations and thoughts, highlighted jargon, sentence fragments, exclamation points, etc. He wields all the same tricks in this serious piece. The devices themselves do not create comedy; comedy results from how he plays them.

4) Barry normally writes in simple language. Notice how even that language gets simplified in this piece. What effects can you see?

5) This piece skates a fine line between capturing an exquisite moment and descending into sentimentality. Can you identify places where it seems to get out of control? Can you identify places where it seems too controlled? The answers to those two questions may depend more on your personality than on your analytical skills.

A conversation with
Dave Barry

DAVE BARRY: Is that it, Don? [Laughs]

DON FRY: That's it, Dave. Thanks for a great interview. It'll look terrific in the book. [Laughter]

Let's try this again. Let's talk about your writing techniques. When you first get an idea for a column, how do you develop it?

Well, I just sit down and start. I very rarely think it through. In fact, I virtually never have a real good solid idea of the whole structure of anything when I start to write it.

I'll write a line, and I'll really want that line to be funny. If it's not, I'll just keep diddling around with it until it is, and then I'll go to the next one, and I'll diddle with both of them, and then I'll go on to the third, and I'll diddle with all three. Then based on whether it's working or not, I keep going, and I let that determine whether I'll stick with one structure all the way through, or just take a radical left turn and try for something else. That will determine what shape the piece will ultimately have, rather than some preordained or preconceived idea of what would work well.

How can you tell when it works?

That's the hard part, isn't it? I've always been able to tell what was going to be funny when you read it, which is a lot different from what's going to be funny when you say it. And I'm willing to argue hard with other people about it if they try to change it.

Do you read it aloud?

No. And I really don't write my columns to be read aloud. I write very, very long, complicated sentences, enormous run-on sentences, lots of punctuation, ludicrous over-punctuation, and I do all those things because I think they work in writing.

How long does it take you to write a typical column?

Oh, six hours, spread out over two or three days. Unlike a real reporter, I spend a lot of time standing out in the yard, and I really ought to count that time. I'm usually just standing out there throwing sticks for my dog, waiting for something to happen in my brain that will strike me as funny. I can't make it happen, so I just wait.

Let's take a look at your long piece about the Florida senatorial campaign. How did you get all this wonderful stuff?

I traveled with Graham for a couple of days, and I traveled a lot to be with Hawkins for brief minutes. She was very, very inaccessible to the press, so that made the story tough. It was very easy to be funny about Graham and maybe too easy to make him look likable, because he goes along with all the jokes. Hawkins was the opposite. She's very distrustful of the press, and the *Herald* in particular. And I didn't want to look like I was painting her as the Dragon Lady. I had to be with her enough so that I could write funny about her. And I thought she was very funny, but not quite in the same self-aware way that Graham was.

   I went to one hearing of hers, and it was so surreal that I didn't know how the other reporters could possibly present it to the public as real. In fact, I often have that reaction when I go to big-time news events like the conventions. How do the real reporters get it to seem real? Are they really telling the truth when they do that?

Yes. Maybe they think they have to make it seem serious so somebody will believe them.

Yeah. They'll take what was obviously rampant buffoonery, and they'll make it look like actual political statesmanship or something.

   The most fun I've ever had in journalism was in '84, when the *Herald* sent me to New Hampshire to cover the primary. In some union hall somewhere, nobody would know who Fritz Mondale was, and people were there for free hot dogs and stuff, and then Gary Hart would come in with Stephen King, of all people, and it would just be hilarious from beginning to end. I'd write it up pretty much straight, and everybody would tell me how funny it was. Then I'd read what David Broder wrote, something like, "Contrasting calls regarding industrialization policies were heard yesterday...." [Laughter]

Do you write leads on your pieces, or do you even think in such traditional terms?

Well, in this column I did. I wrote the whole Graham section first. Then I did the whole Hawkins section next. And originally it had no beginning at all; I just plunged in with Graham, and then I wrote this lead.

Here's your lead: "Big-time national politics has all but lost its Weirdness Quotient. More and more, high-level political races tend to be between identical slim men in identical slim suits. Rational men, cool men, men who know the voting market, men who never say the wrong thing, men who are *good on TV*. Candidates who don't fit this mold—the blatant hacks, the geeks, the loons, the people with bad teeth—tend to get filtered out at the state-legislature level. At the Senate level, you wind up with Ted Koppel vs. Ted Koppel, both speaking in perfect sound bites."
You could take "the blatant hacks, the geeks, the loons, the people with bad teeth" out of that lead, and it would sound like fairly straight news commentary.

You're right. In fact, this was one of the straighter stories that I had ever written for *Tropic*. It's a fairly straight lead for a column, like a David Broder kind of column.

**David Broder wouldn't have said "Weird-
ness Quotient." He'd have been a little more
highfalutin' than that. Come down four
paragraphs: "On the plane with the governor is the press corps, including a couple of
political reporters from Big-Time out-of-state
papers that are very interested in this race,"
etc. Talk about your use of capitalization, as
in "Big-Time out-of-state papers." You're
always playing games with capitalization.**

I play a whole lot with punctuation. One of the
things I love about writing, as opposed to speaking, is finding ways to do what people do all the
time in speech with inflection. Most writers limit
themselves badly because of newspaper style. But
I love to capitalize phrases as an ironic way of
saying, "This is allegedly a big deal, although
you and I know it's not." I do that a lot. The same
with exclamation marks and italics.

**I like the way you capture the soporific
qualities of Graham as a speaker; listen to
this exchange you made up: " 'Would you
say,' I ask, 'that spending a lot of time
around cows as a child could make a person
kind of dull?' Graham grew up on a dairy.
     " 'It could have that potential,' he
answers, 'but on the other hand, some might
say—but I am too modest to personally say
this—that it brings out a quickness of wit, a
sense of ironic humor, an ability to, with a—
not a destructive, but a positive uplifting
way—with words to bring humor into the
world. That's what some people would say.
I am too personally modest.' "**

That's a real quote.

You're kidding. Verbatim?

Yeah. I've got that on tape. That's the only way
I would have been able to preserve it. Graham

would always do that when anybody asked him a question. He stops, he thinks, and then he launches into a very elaborately crafted sentence, or something that's like a sentence.

Lately I've been arguing that almost all quotations have to be cleaned up a little, because otherwise they wouldn't make sense, or would embarrass the speaker, or would offend public taste. Real speech quoted verbatim in a newspaper shocks the reader.

Yeah, I guess that's one of the things that you learn when you're a reporter, and we all have the problem of how we deal with it. No matter what your official newspaper policy is, everybody changes quotes, and the question is, "How much do you change them and for what reason?" But this quote was just too wonderful not to quote verbatim. Also, I did the same thing to Hawkins.

You're a very astute political observer. Listen to this description of Graham: "If you're in the state more than 12 hours, he'll track you down. Shake your hand. Be Just Folks with you, cracker mouth talking, Harvard eyes watching." You've really caught those shrewd, addressing eyes.

I was prouder of that sentence, that characterization, than anything else in this whole piece. Graham is a very difficult man to know, and everybody's very good at describing what he does, but not what he's like.

One paragraph later, you say: "Graham thinks the press should write about the Broad Sweeping Theme of his campaign, namely that Florida is a fast-growing state that must meet the challenges of the 21st century and needs to be represented by a person of competence, breadth, and vision,

as opposed to some bimbo with hair like
Harpo Marx. (The last part of the theme is
never actually spoken aloud.)"
    How do you get away with things like
that last bit?

This is where it's wonderful to be a humor
columnist, because you can tell the truth.
[Laughs] And the truth is that the Graham
campaign people had utter disdain for Hawkins,
as did many people. They never ever would say
any of that, but would never ever do anything
to discourage that assumption on your part. I was
just stating it. But that's where a real reporter
gets in trouble, because unless somebody says a
quote like that, he can't say it, whereas I can just
assume it, knowing that it's true.

**You're free to speculate on what people are
thinking.**

Yeah. And I can lie, because I'm a humor
columnist.

**In the Hawkins section, you say, "She often
refers to herself as 'this Senator,' in case
anybody forgets." You're a very close
observer, sir, but I'm not sure that's why she
does that. Do humor columnists have an
open license on ascribing motives?**

No. It's quite an assumption I'm making, and I'm
out on a limb, but I'm sure I'm right. I'm always
suspicious of people who refer to themselves in
the third person. Dave Barry would never do a
thing like that.

**Indeed. In the Hawkins section, I love this
wonderful scene with the Perrier bottle:
"The highlight of the hearing comes early,
at the end of Hawkins' opening statement,
in which she voices grave concern that
leaking fuel might contaminate the ground-**

water. Suddenly she brandishes a bottle of Perrier at Hatch, startling him, and declares: 'Not everyone, Mr. Chairman, can drink Perrier. And Perrier *doesn't mix too well with infant formula.'* A wonderful move. Some of us in the press are tempted to applaud. From deep left field, way out near the warning track, Hawkins has managed to drag in children, *little* children, *babies,* as victims of the Pipeline That Will Leak And Explode. It is a horrifying image: Mothers, forced to feed babies formula made with *Perrier!* Think of it! Think of the *burping!"*
She really said that?

Everything there is true. This is what I was saying about how I really felt sorry for the real reporters, because the whole hearing was so bizarre, and the moment of the Perrier bottle coming up was just wonderful.

You're also an astute commentator on the press. Listen to this: "After the hearing, Hawkins and Hatch hold a press conference, and of course, the *last* thing the press wants to talk about is the pipeline. (You may have noticed a pattern here: the press and the newsmakers never want to talk about the same thing. This is why the vast majority of the news consists of vague and insincere quotations.)" That's absolutely right.

It's not even humor; it's just the truth. But it's one of those things that you really can't say if you're covering the news, only if you're sort of detached from it somehow.

A little later you say, "I ask her if she sees any humor in the pipeline issue. This elicits a Soaring Ramble, which I will quote from here, verbatim, transcribed from my tape recorder, so you'll get a feel for what they're like."

Is the quotation that follows also true?

Yeah. That's why I put in "transcribed from my tape recorder." I was afraid nobody would believe me.

When you put that phrase in, ironically that's when we don't believe you. Truth gets so tricky here that the reader doesn't know what to believe.

This one's mostly true.

Actually, aren't most of these *mostly* true?

Yeah.

Let's look at your kicker. By the way, do you think in terms of stories having kickers, as having endings?

On this one, before I wrote the lead, I wrote the ending. I knew it had to have some kind of unity of structure. Having all that Graham and then all that Hawkins, I needed to bring them both back together again.

Whoa! You told me a while ago that you write sentence by sentence, but now you say you wrote the ending before the beginning?

Yeah, on this one I did. I really viewed this piece as three separate things: Graham, Hawkins, and the whatever I would need to tie them together. I never thought about either the beginning or the end until I'd written both of the middle parts.

Here you're telling the truth about these perfectly vapid candidates.

True. This was probably one of the more accurate pieces written about this campaign, in the sense of telling people what was really the issue, namely, there wasn't one. I got a lot of very nice comments on this piece from journalists who had covered them, who were really thrilled that somebody among them was allowed to tell what they considered to be the truth. In fact, most of the feedback was from journalists, and that's the best kind for me. That's what I like to hear most.

I was afraid that this column was unbalanced, which is a strange thing for somebody to say who freely admits to being biased and dishonest. I worried that it would cause people to like Graham a lot more than they liked Hawkins. And in some ways, I felt there wasn't a whole lot I could do. I tell you what they're like, but the truth is, if you met them both, you probably would like Graham more than Hawkins, if you were a reporter. And I was afraid that would come through.

I thought you were equally mean to both of them. Tell me how the piece headlined "SNEWS" came about.

One of the business editors dumped a bunch of press releases on my desk, and some of them struck me as so funny that I decided to write a column about it. I picked up the first one from this backhoe company and called them. And I went down through the list and called these people, and ended up calling my mother for no apparent reason, and one thing seemed to lead to another in a surrealistic fashion, and I put it all down. It's one of the weirder columns I've written.

It gets us into these weird problems of truth again. Here's your lead. "Readers are sometimes critical of me because just about everything I write is an irresponsible lie. So today I'm going to write a column in which everything is true. See how you like it." When I read that, I assumed that these were probably real news items and real press

releases. But it didn't occur to me that what you said *you did* was true.

Everything I said was true.

Of course, none of us believes that.

I know. I have this problem.

Tell me about "The domino theory blues."

I was really happy with this one. I went to Washington to watch Paula Hawkins. While I was there, I went to a hearing on Nicaragua, and I decided I had to write something about Nicaragua. At first I was trying to write about the hearing, but it came out too much like a news account. So I just chucked that story and wrote this impressionistic view of our policy in Central America. I was looking for laughs all the way through, but trying to link the laughs to the amazing illogic of our foreign policy.

Look at your third paragraph: "But Phil [Habib] faces tough sledding in Nicaragua. For one thing, they never get any snow. (Ha ha! Who says foreign policy issues are dull? Many people.) Seriously, you have a very difficult and complex situation in Nicaragua, which I will attempt to explain in simplified terms that even a taxpayer who uses the short 1040 form can grasp. A few years back, there was this leader down there, a Mr. Somoza, who graduated near the top of his class at the Stereotypical Latin American Tinhorn Dictator Wearing Aviator Sunglasses Academy and who was—let us choose our words carefully here—a big fat tub of scum." [Laughter]
That's the Dave Barry I'm used to.

It's just wonderful when you have an editor who'll let you bring out your absolutely most childish impulse [Laughs], and call somebody a really bad, stupid name right in the column. And I just enjoy that freedom so much that I abuse it immensely.

You take a common expression, "tough sledding," and go leaping off into "they never get any snow." And then that long sentence gets completely out of control, plus dashes, and suddenly inserted parentheses, like "(Ha ha...)." [Laughter]

It's sort of become my trademark. I have to fight, because I want to get it in all the time.

Do the editors try to take it out?

My wife Beth is always aware of how many times I do things. I think she has a running count somewhere in her mind. I could wake up in the middle of the night and say, "How many times have I used the word 'actually'?" She'd say, "3,754." So she'll keep me from (Ha-ha)ing too much.

This Nicaragua piece is vintage Barry. Let's look at "Commencement."

Hardly vintage Barry, this last one.

I think it is and isn't. Tell me about this one.

I've only ever written a couple of serious columns. The first one I wrote was when my father died a few years ago, and I didn't know how people were going to react to it. It was totally serious, totally sad, and it got an overwhelmingly positive reaction, which made me think, "Gee, it's kind of nice to write serious stuff, and I'm not going to get laughed at if I do it." But I just didn't have anything else serious to say. [Laughs] I'm either an optimist, or a shallow person, or something. I don't mean "shallow" in the sense of "stupid," but I tend to be superficial in my thinking about a lot of things.

I doubt that.

I appreciate that. But I really do think I am superficial, and, in some ways, that's good, because of what I do for a living.

Part of your equipment.

Yeah. When we took Robby to school that morning, I was just overwhelmed with sadness, a much...much more powerful sense of...gee, I can't think of quite the word. It's not "sad," it's not "sorrow." I was feeling very emotional.

Lost.

Yeah, and I couldn't say why. So I was going to start to write a humor column, and instead I wrote this. And of all the things I've ever written, this took the least time. I would say from beginning to end, I wrote this in 20 minutes, and then maybe a little polishing, but that was about it. I was crying the whole time I wrote it, tears pouring down my face. And I finished it and just sent it in, so I wouldn't think about it anymore. Felt fine after that. Went and got Robby after school. He was fine. All was fine. It got an incredible response, I guess because everybody has felt that way, everybody who ever took a kid to school. Beth loved it; she broke down and cried. [Laughs]

I cried over it.

Gee, I'm touched to hear that. I kept hearing that, and I couldn't understand it. When I was writing it, I kept thinking, "This is so obvious, everything I'm saying here. Everybody's going to say, 'Well, of course, everybody's been through that.' I'm saying nothing original here and nothing really new. Why am I saying it?" And I guess, in the end, people loved it because it *wasn't* original, it *wasn't* new. It was just something everybody had felt, and they liked it.

It was universal.

I'm not into symbolic writing, or writing on a bunch of different levels, or anything like that. I usually just say it, whatever it is. I'm a very obvious writer. Maybe people like that: seeing something simple and clear, stated simply.

This piece isn't just expressed well, it's also very keenly observed. Here's the turning point: " 'This is going to be great,' I say. I give him his lunch money. I wish I could give him my muscles, to keep in the pocket of his little blue shorts in case a big kid tries to bully him. I wish I could give him my mind, so he'd understand why he has to go to school. I wish *I* understood it."

Here I was thinking, "Why do I have to lose my little boy?" I was thinking back to *my* school, and ahead to what's going to happen to him. He's going to get farther away from us. He has to. He's going to get friends. He's going to have a whole life outside of my life now. And so the days of having this wonderful little boy, whose life and my life were almost the same, are over. A new phase is starting, and there's no little boy to replace him. And I just had a lot of trouble that morning accepting it.

Talk about the ending, especially that last line: "...your dolphin never talks anymore."

I didn't want just to say, "And you're all grown up." You have to give readers concrete things whenever you can instead of abstract statements. So I was looking for a really concrete way of saying what happens to you when you become a big boy. And one of the things you don't do is play with stuffed animals anymore, which seemed terribly sad to me just then.

Did you struggle with that ending?

No. No. I didn't struggle with one word in this. This was probably the easiest single thing I ever wrote. It just poured out. I had to get it out of me so I could go on and do something else.

I think it's one of the best things you ever wrote.

I appreciate that. I was struck by the response it got. It was really nice.

Let me ask your advice for writers who want to break into humor. I know reporters who are very, very funny observers and very, very funny talkers, who would like to write humor. But they're afraid to let their guard down and stop being the serious reporter. Any advice for people like that?

Yeah. If you decide you're going to write humor, don't hold back. Too many people try too hard to be dry or ironic or reserved or British almost in their humor, instead of really letting go and saying what they really think is funny. And don't try to write humor like anyone else. People try to copy the humor styles of other people, but it just never works, any more than a standup comic doing somebody else's bits looks real. All the people who are funny are funny because they're funny.

That's true. Thanks, Dave.

You're welcome, Don.

Don Marsh
Commentary

DON MARSH, 59, was born in Logan County, West Virginia, and was graduated from his state university with a journalism degree in 1950. He joined *The Charleston Gazette* in 1952, and served as a reporter and city editor before being named editor in 1976. He had the great fortune of working for Ned Chilton, a crusading publisher who sued every baddy in sight and kept his office in the newsroom. Marsh won a Nieman Fellowship in 1956.

the Charleston Gazette

Why we are in the Third World

FEBRUARY 15, 1986

I continue to believe that West Virginia is a Third World state, stuck unfairly in a developed country, forced into economic competition with more technologically advanced neighbors.

Despite my failure to persuade others, I proceed, exposing myself to the most serious charges that can be placed against a native—failing to talk about what's *right* with West Virginia.

It is a price I am willing to pay. I argue that understanding the problem is essential to finding a solution. As a consequence, I believe it is important for us to know just how far behind we are.

Who can deny our Third World status? What better proof was there than Gov. Moore's plan to borrow money to pay interest on the unemployment compensation debt we owe the federal government?

Does the approach not ring of Argentina or Mexico—pledging their gross national product to pay interest to the Yankee bankers? And the penalty is the same for us as for them: economic sanctions from Washington if we fail to pay up.

Another symbol of our Third World status, in my mind, is the increasing arguments being made in favor of a right-to-work law.

"Right-to-work" is code for "non-union," which itself is code for "cheap labor." Lysander Dudley's strident calls for right-to-work legislation are confessions that West Virginia cannot compete, even up, with industrialized states like Massachusetts or Ohio.

Therefore, to make ourselves more attractive to captains of industry, we tell them that they won't have to pay the kind of wages that would be required in Kentucky or Ohio. Presumably, we also would be willing to fix them up with our sisters, if the need arose.

A further indication of our Third World mentality is our treatment of education. Advanced states, like California or Illinois, have an advanced educational system. States trying to move up, like Tennessee and Kentucky, stress education as the best method of reaching 20th century standards.

We, on the other hand, make clear that as a people we have no commitment and little interest in education. Consider the current developments in higher education. The governor is cutting the budget by at least $20 million and politicizing the system, a process that may go unnoticed by presidents of state colleges and universities, a group which could be expected to lend tape recorders to observers sent to their campuses by the Accuracy in Media crowd, particularly if they thought Arch Moore wanted them to.

Their desire to please the governor was evident in their knifing of the chancellor of the Board of Regents and their personal silence on their budget problems. (My program for improving higher education, by the way, is to retain the Board of Regents and to abolish the presidencies.)

Then there is secondary education, supervised by a state Department of Education which is unsure whether it should favor property reappraisal, the only hope of paying for adequate schools. (Understandable, perhaps, in an organization headed by a superintendent who, upon taking office, announced that in a funding conflict between education and economic development, he would favor economic development.)

On another level, critics grimly pointed out that the reappraisal program would cause a 440 percent increase in Wyoming County property taxes. Since nearly 80 percent of the land in Wyoming County is owned by corporations, it is clear that our concern about shielding corporations from fair taxation exceeds our concern about educating our children.

And, speaking of Wyoming County, I noted a story in the *Independent Herald* of Pineville that parents in an area of the county were protesting. They were upset because overloaded coal trucks have forced school buses and private cars off the road.

The parents had a meeting at Glen Rogers High School and laid their complaints before a delegate and a union leader. What was local leadership's response to the petitions of the people?

"Let's try to maintain these jobs while keeping our children safe."—Delegate Clayton Hale, D-Wyoming. "You have to remember, we're talking about a lot of jobs."—Bill Legg, vice president of a United Mine Workers local. I know how it is. I have no objection to Carbide making poison gas upwind from me as long as it means jobs.

And my final bit of evidence of our Third World status is the increasing tendency of our political leaders to isolate themselves from reality and to create a fantasy world free of problems or criticism.

The most alarming case is that of Arch Moore who is acting as if he is failing to take his lithium. Is Moore coming unglued or, in a phrase passed on to me, overdriving his headlights? The answer seems to be yes.

His statements on the budget and casino gambling remind me of nothing so much as Capt. Queeg's explanation of the significance of the stolen strawberries on the *Caine*. I'm not the only one who is shaken.

Richard Grimes of the *Daily Mail* said something unflattering in print about Moore, a news story in itself. Grimes usually fastens the kind of critical eye on Moore that Nancy fastens on Ronnie. And Tom Miller, a reporter from Huntington, stalked out of a news conference the governor was holding the other day. That is unprecedented. The form has always been that Moore stalked out on the reporters.

And finally, there's the guy in the other party, Bob Wise, the man I have predicted will become the dominant Democratic politician in the state.

What new vistas has Wise discovered? How does his vision differ from that of Arch Moore, Lysander Dudley, or Mr. Cartoon? What new leadership frontier is marching on?

Make your own judgment. In his most recent speech, Wise quoted from Norman Vincent Peale's *The Power of Positive Thinking*, urged West Virginians to develop a positive mindset— like salesmen or pole vaulters—and, in a smash ending, summed up by urging us to think of the glass being half-full rather than half-empty.

That's the kind of thinking that's got us to where we are today. Alas.

Observations and questions

1) Marsh opens with a comic figure of West Virginia as a Third World nation, and continues with a series of economic and political gags. But he is not a humor columnist. How does the reader know when to take him seriously and when not to?

2) Marsh begins with two charges against himself: failure to persuade others and "to talk about what's *right* with West Virginia." How will readers respond to such mock vulnerability?

3) In the eighth paragraph, Marsh uses the phrase "fix them up with our sisters." Try substituting different verbs for "fix up." Your choices will range from "introduce" to "pimp for." Project the effects of each word choice through the rest of the piece.

4) This piece consists essentially of a group of lists. Study how Marsh alternately reveals and conceals this structure. Why?

5) How does Marsh present himself as a character in this piece? What effects does he create by weaving himself through the arguments?

How to identify politicians

MARCH 21, 1986

It is outrageous that three members of the Nicholas County Board of Education are suing citizens who criticized the board. It is more outrageous that they are using school money to pay a private lawyer $100 an hour to pursue the suit. Were it possible to sputter in print, I would be sputtering.

I have long suspected that shame and common decency no longer influence many office-holders in West Virginia. The examples of board members Patricia Bright, Norma Bush, and Lewis Worlledge are among the reasons I feel as I do.

The money they are using was placed in their trust to educate children. Instead of using it for that purpose, they have hired what has to be the most expensive lawyer in Nicholas County to sue a group of citizens. The group went to court in an effort to undo the board's firing of a former superintendent and hiring of a new one.

It is impossible to find a charitable excuse for the three board members. They are either power mad or appallingly ignorant. My instinct is toward ignorance. Nobody in Nicholas County is as contemptuous of the democratic process as they appear to be. I have to conclude they are too dumb to know what they're doing.

They clearly don't know that part of the deal of being elected is that they accept the burdens as well as the benefits of office. Part of the burden is the criticism of citizens who don't agree with them.

Just as clearly, they don't know, or don't care, that the people have a right to complain and to go to court to change things they don't like. Those rights are contained in a document that the

Nicholas County board members don't know about or are indifferent to. It is called the Constitution.

They are civilians and boondock politicians. Abstractions like the Bill of Rights may be over their heads. But what about their lawyer? His name is Dan Callaghan.

Callaghan is a former president of the West Virginia State Bar. He once visited the newsroom in an effort to convince Ned Chilton, the publisher, that the Bar was a high-class organization and that its members were concerned with ethics and responsibility.

I cannot believe that Callaghan doesn't know that what the board is doing is wrong. He already is on notice. Gary Johnson, the county prosecutor, is the board's official lawyer. He refused to represent the three in the suit against the citizens. "I feel that they (the parents) are just exercising their political rights," Johnson said.

I assume, as do others in Nicholas County, that the purpose of the suit is to silence criticism. "Obviously, when you get hit with a $180,000 countersuit it chills your desire to get involved in anything the board of education does," Carl Harris, the lawyer representing the citizens, told the *Gazette*'s Eve Epstein.

Clemente Diaz, a doctor at Sacred Heart Hospital, had the same reaction as I had. "Here we are. Our taxes support them and they are going to sue us with our own money. It doesn't make sense."

Indeed it doesn't—or it wouldn't in a civilized state. In fact, I don't believe it makes sense in West Virginia. Chilton said that if the board members continue their march down the path of folly, he is leaning toward suing them himself.

He said they should be removed from office and they should have to personally repay any public money they have spent on their private lawyer. Chilton said he is thinking of filing an ethics complaint against Callaghan for his part in the suit.

But Chilton has limitations. He can't sue in every instance of the insolence of office. It would be cheaper to finance a Jay Rockefeller election campaign. If you doubt me, consider the additional examples of:

• Martha Wood, a member of the Kanawha County school board. She accused the school system's professional staff of using a "Gestapo Swat Team approach" to bully and harass teachers in the classroom. But she wouldn't say where, when, or who. Stuart Calwell, another board member, endorsed her refusal to allow the staff to confront its accusers, saying: "The fact is we want you to get to the bottom of it."

• Phyllis Rutledge, the circuit clerk, and members of her staff. They were discovered Sunday in the courthouse addressing envelopes amid boxes filled with her campaign posters.

What were they doing? Sending invitations to wine and cheese parties for lawyers, she said, adding that her employees "volunteered" to do the work. Rutledge is shameless, a two-bit politician who, if she were on the Nicholas County board, would drag down the level of service.

• Harry Price, city finance director. Price refused to tell a councilman the cost of a trip that Police Chief Kent Carper and three—count, them, three—other city employees made to Orlando, Fla., to "inspect" and return an ambulance to Charleston.

Price, keeper of the financial records, said that the councilman, Ernie Layne, talked mean to him. "In fact, his tone of voice was quite abusive. I don't feel that employees should be subjected to the type of tirade that I experienced. I feel that I am due an apology."

What self-serving sniveling. One has to wonder if the mean old councilman reduced him to tears. I don't feel Price is due an apology. I lean toward a kick in the backside.

I also think that Mayor Mike Roark has a perverted idea of public records. Roark apparently takes the Arch Moore, or imperial position, that the only person who can discuss public records in the city is him.

"If somebody needs to know something, they can call me and I'll say 'fine' and I'll make sure they'll get everything," Roark said. Wonderful. And when he's out of town, as he was when Layne asked, everyone should be happy to wait.

• The state Health Department. It issues special "certificates" to mothers of illegitimate children. The certificates omit the names of mother and father and are so peculiarly written that they clearly identify the holder as illegitimate.

The department says the purpose is to protect the child. If I had my way, I'd hand the certificates to a number of officeholders, regardless of their legitimacy. If they persist in acting like bastards, why not identify them?

Observations and questions

1) Marsh uses "outrageous" twice in his first two sentences. Normally we save such a potent adjective for the kicker. Why doesn't he? Would you be tempted to start somewhat cooler?

2) Find all the first-person references, and imagine this piece without them. What, if anything, does Marsh gain by including himself in the column?

3) In the middle, Marsh puts Dr. Diaz on the stage to explain why the Board's action "doesn't make sense." Why should Marsh bother with such a simple quotation? Why doesn't he just say it himself?

4) The last third of this column consists of a list of other public servants treating the public insolently. Does Marsh diffuse his point by this scatter-gun approach, or does he show how endemic the problem has become?

5) The last two paragraphs haul in the state Health Department to set up the concept of bastardy. Why does Marsh need all this apparatus to call the board a bunch of bastards, especially after he's already called them "power mad" and "appallingly ignorant?"

Solitary, poor, nasty, brutish, and short

JULY 18, 1986

I doubt if any justice of the West Virginia Supreme Court will follow Ken Faerber's advice. Faerber, who is commissioner of the Department of Energy, recommended that justices visit a thin-seam mine so that they could further their understanding of life underground.

"It is very easy to paint a picture—a vision of miners crawling around in a dark place with a huge mountain hanging over their heads with no control over the situation," Faerber said. "That simply isn't so."

Well, everybody gets to paint his own picture. The kind of mines that Faerber was talking about are tunnels that are 28 to 42 inches high (give or take a few inches), running miles underground. I measured the distance between my desk and the floor. It is 28 inches.

There are 44 thin-seam mining locations in West Virginia. They employ about 2,000 workers and produce about 3 million tons of coal a year.

A special kind of machine called an auger-type continuous miner makes them feasible. The machine, a Wilcox miner, is manufactured by Fairchild International, a company that bailed out of Beckley recently and moved to Glen Lyn, Va.

A crew of five is needed on an auger miner. I share the technical deficiencies of the Supreme Court. Faerber said justices had a vision of miners crawling in a dark place with a huge mountain hanging over them. My vision of a Wilcox machine in operation is more lurid.

It is based on a description I read in the paper. The story said the machine has two four-foot augers that swing back and forth, boring coal and dumping it on conveyor belts. As the machine sweeps back and forth, miners must continuously knock down roof-supporting timbers on one side of the machine while replacing timbers on the other side.

The top is so low that men work on their backs or from a crouch. They can't straighten up to eat a sandwich, drink water, or urinate. One can only imagine the noise, the dust, the darkness.

They have to go in advance of the machine to set the wooden timbers that keep the roof from falling. The work is very dangerous. Between 1974 and 1975, 17 workers on Wilcox miners were killed by roof falls.

The United Mine Workers union estimates that one in four members of a crew will be killed in a working lifetime. I have seen no estimates of injuries, but they must be high.

As a consequence, my vision of thin-seam mining is a scene from a darkened hell. Hobbes must have been thinking of a Wilcox crew when he described the life of man as "solitary, poor, nasty, brutish, and short."

Paul Nyden wrote a story about one man who was killed while working with a Wilcox miner. His name was Charlie Lanham. He was 29. His father had died in a mining accident. He left a wife and a 5-month-old son.

"He didn't talk much about that mine," his widow, Brenda, said. "But I never seen Charlie so scared as when he worked there. The night before he went back he laid awake, trying to figure out what to do. We couldn't make it on unemployment. That's why Charlie went back to work."

He died setting timbers in a 28-inch seam. He was paid $80 a day, about $30 less than a union miner earns. His company paid no workers' compensation, provided no medical insurance, pension, vacation time, or sick leave.

His widow was billed for the ambulance that took him to the hospital where he was pronounced dead. None of his employers called or sent a card.

Men work at such places because they are desperate. There are few decent mining jobs. "Charlie said they fired someone every day at the mine. They never had any reason. They just didn't get along with the boss," his widow said.

Mark March, an international representative of the United Mine Workers, said there is a large pool of laid-off miners. As a consequence, the little mines get all the manpower they need. "If you object to anything, they'll tell you, 'I've got 200 other people waiting for your job.' When I visit these mines, people are scared to death even to talk to me."

Not all thin-seam mines are that way, of course. Peter Sigler is among operators of a mine near Gauley Bridge. The mine has been using Wilcox machines for three years.

In that time, only one of his employees has been injured by a roof fall. Sigler said that his company started the mine that Lanham died in, but abandoned it because operators knew the roof was bad.

But Sigler doesn't contend all operators are as responsible as his group. "There is no doubt that there are some outlaws in the coal industry. Prices being down, people do what they can."

The Supreme Court became involved because the UMW sued to require Faerber to order thin-seam mines to use roof bolts. Roof bolts are steel rods that are driven through the ceiling of a mine to pin layers of rock together to keep them from falling. Nine thin-seam mines use roof bolts. None has had a miner killed by a falling roof.

The court, by a 3-2 vote, upheld the union's contention that all thin-seam mines must use roof bolts. Some can't. Faerber said that 400 workers will lose jobs.

I thought his reaction was consistent with those who lead us. Economics are worth the risk of death and injury. One of the lawyers for the coal companies argued that roof bolting would make the mines less safe.

"Death comes from a failure to comply with state and federal approved roof control plans, not from a failure of the plans themselves," he said. It is a familiar refrain: miners are guilty of killing themselves.

The court ruled on unemotional grounds. It held that the State Code requires that roofs be adequately supported or controlled to protect miners. There was one hint of passion. It was in a section quoting from an earlier Supreme Court mining case. That section said, in part:

"...We are not concerned with a mere point of law in routine civil litigation, but rather with the lives and limbs of countless thousands of living, breathing, human beings who, along with their families, have suffered needless loss since time out of mind in an industry which appears inevitably to suck the life's blood from the miner as he takes the coal from the earth...."

It is not Justices McHugh, McGraw, and Miller, the three who ordered roof bolting, who need to go into a mine. It is Justices Brotherton and Neely, the two who voted against roof bolts.

I hope they will go and that Kenneth Faerber will lead them. I recommend that they start at the mine which employed Charlie Lanham.

Observations and questions

1) Marsh compares the 28-inch-tall mining tunnel to the 28-inch space beneath his desk. Think of all the 28-inch things he could have selected. What makes his choice a good one?

2) In a frighteningly claustrophobic passage, Marsh describes in detail how a Wilcox miner works. At the beginning, he tells us that he based his vision "on a description I read in the paper." Does this vague attribution strengthen the authority of his telling, or does it distract the reader from his graphic account? In answering this question, try to think like a reader, not like a journalist.

3) Study the transition between the Wilcox miner and the death of Charlie Lanham, keeping in mind that we don't usually regard numbers and references to philosophers as likely materials for transitions.

4) Brenda Lanham's first quotation ("He didn't talk...") contains two grammatical errors. Why doesn't Marsh clean them up? Should he do so to avoid an accusation of condescension?

5) Marsh presents a sequence of actions the mine company did *not* take, even after Charlie Lanham's death. Why does Marsh end this list with the detail of not sending a card, which seems like such a minor omission?

6) Who is the target of this column, and what changes does the writer recommend? Don't settle for easy answers.

Arch Moore's make-believe world

NOVEMBER 28, 1986

I can understand why Arch Moore is upset over his $2,084 bill for a night at The Greenbrier. The economy is going very badly in the state.

If West Virginia were a private company, its leaders would be asking for protection from bankruptcy court. The image of the chief executive of a depressed state lolling in a $2,000-a-night suite is as distasteful as the pictures of Imelda Marcos's 2,000 pairs of shoes.

Last week, *Saturday Night Live* showed news clips of Ronald Reagan explaining his reasons for sending weapons to Iran. Each time the president's picture came up, the words "He's Lying" started flashing at the bottom of the screen.

I had the *Saturday Night Live* reaction to Moore's explanation of the bill. He said The Greenbrier overcharged him by $1,769. He attacked Paul Nyden, the *Gazette* reporter who broke the story, saying Nyden hurried into print without giving him a chance to respond adequately.

Moore stayed at the hotel in July as part of a coal symposium sponsored by the Department of Energy. The hotel bills were submitted in August. At the state's request, The Greenbrier revised them in September, omitting sales tax which government doesn't have to pay (indicating, by the way, that someone had checked the governor's charges).

Nyden had to use the Freedom of Information Act to get the bills (alerting Moore's people to a reporter's interest). Nyden picked up the bill on Friday, Oct. 31. He asked the governor's press secretary about the hotel charge that day, and was told on Saturday that one reason might have been the cost of rooms for the state policemen who accompany Moore. The story appeared on Sunday.

A week later, Moore went semi-berserk at a news conference, accusing Nyden of not asking him about the bill (and then saying "So what?" when told an inquiry had been made two days before the story appeared). Moore also said the symposium caused $100 million to be invested in the state. He produced a letter from the general manager of The Greenbrier saying the hotel had made a mistake.

The man at The Greenbrier called it a computing error. I called it a diplomatic one. *Saturday Night Live* would have called it something else.

On Nov. 20, Moore's office mailed out a five-page press release, repeating the governor's story. There was only one new note: According to the handout, Moore and his wife were at The Greenbrier for 12 hours, six of which, the governor said, in a phrase that I thought went out with Greta Garbo movies, he and Mrs. Moore were "in repose."

I thought the $2,000 hotel bill was a better-than-average story. It seemed to me that Moore magnified the impact by the fervor of his attack.

I may be wrong. I am not a big fan of Arch Moore. Where others see the doughnut, I see the hole. The last act of Moore's that I approved of happened in 1980. He lost the gubernatorial election to Jay Rockefeller.

My personal theory is that Moore was as much upset by events as he was by the story. Moore has been governor more than two and a half years. The state is falling to pieces around him.

The highway commissioner says that half of the 6,800 bridges in West Virginia are structurally deficient. His department is too poor to fix them. It doesn't have enough money to fill routine potholes.

The work force keeps shrinking. There were 11,700 fewer people in the work force in

September 1986 than there were at the same time a year ago. Federal statistics show that 37 of the state's 55 counties had double-digit unemployment in September, led by McDowell County with 32.3 percent. Since then, U.S. Steel has laid off a thousand miners in McDowell.

The state is so hard up that it can't afford to pay teachers on time. Officials other than Moore talk of the need for a spending freeze. Legislators want to transfer road maintenance to counties and to raise the amount of fees students pay at state colleges.

Moore ignores them, announcing instead that he will build a $25 million football field at Marshall, put gold leaf on the Capitol Dome at an undisclosed price (but one greater, I assure you, than whatever the estimates have been), and repair the South Side Bridge in Charleston at a cost of perhaps $6 million.

Meanwhile, Moore ignores a report by a management task force that could save a lot of money. As a consequence, the state spends $3 million a year to grow food worth $1.6 million and continues to pay the cost of keeping two planes at Yeager Airport, even though the planes haven't flown for six years.

And what of the faithful assistants he had named to run departments of government? One, the commerce commissioner, is extolling the desirability of a $30 million fish tank as a way of revitalizing Huntington.

Another, the energy commissioner, would be an embarrassment to another administration, holding secret meetings with polluters and warning inspectors not to enforce laws without his permission. Statements by the insurance commissioner cause me to wonder if he needs custodial care.

But I really don't hold Moore personally responsible. The state's difficulties are such that there's not a lot that he can do about them. Moore's announcements of economic miracles and progress are growing threadbare. Even the merriest whistle becomes shrill at last.

The state is in the grip of tough times. Moore is trying to ignore them. It is getting harder to do. Stress is getting to him, as witnessed by his reaction to the hotel bill story. Living in a make-believe world is not easy. Reality keeps trying to intrude.

Observations and questions

1) Marsh usually writes his column with the assumption that readers know the general outlines of news events. Yet here he retells the intricacies of the story, which revolve around reporting processes. How much telling do we need in columns?

2) Marsh plays games with the *Saturday Night Live* references, evidently to keep from saying that the governor lied. Why doesn't he just say so?

3) Marsh tells us that "Moore went semi-berserk at a news conference." Why "semi-"?

4) The second half of this column moves at a rapid clip, faster than the first half. Study the sentences and the spacing of information in each part to figure out how and why.

5) This column contains many detailed numbers. How does Marsh incorporate them without slowing up his blistering pace? How can we use his techniques in calmer government stories?

6) Five paragraphs from the end, Marsh lists the deficiencies of three government officials. Why doesn't he mention their names? Should he?

7) Three paragraphs from the end, Marsh seems to let the governor off the hook. Does he really?

Liberals, virtue, and golden domes

DECEMBER 19, 1986

I confess that I am ill at ease when I think of myself as a liberal. The word is in disrepute. Some words are like that. Liberal is one example. Secular humanism is another.

George Orwell had the same problem with socialism. He spoke of the disquieting prevalence of cranks when socialists got together.

"One sometimes gets the impression that the mere word 'socialism' draws toward it with magnetic force every fruit-juice drinker, nudist, sandal wearer, sex maniac, Quaker, nature-cure quack, pacifist, and feminist in England."

I recognize the symptoms but I personally deny having the illness. I believe it is possible to have liberal—i.e., humanistic—attitudes without being fuzzy-headed.

The other day I saw a story saying that the Kanawha County Commission had paid a woman $4,000 to settle a sexual harassment suit. Her case was that her boss kept nude pictures on his desk and she saw them.

I am offended by the payment. The $4,000 was yours and mine. We did not harass anybody. We did not display nude pictures. Why should we be punished? The male superior is the guy to deal with. If he is guilty, why is he untouched? If he is not guilty, why pay $4,000?

I felt satisfaction when I read the story about a judge overturning a civil service case. An employee of Pinecrest Sanitarium got a warrant for her boss for slapping her. Later, she admitted she had not been slapped. She had lied.

The boss fired her. Civil service said that was too tough. She could only be suspended. The judge said the decision was crazy. And it was.

I think that one can be a liberal and recognize that the poor and the oppressed are as ready to profit personally as the rich and powerful. The big difference is that they have fewer opportunities.

Those of us who are working can feel smug and superior. If the poor don't like welfare, let them get a job. Tell that to the thousand or more miners who were laid off this month in McDowell County when the mines closed.

Tell that to the 50-year-old in Mingo County who is banned from employment near his home because he went on strike against A.T. Massey. Tell that to the man who was living in a cave in Logan County. Tell that to the pregnant women who can't get a doctor to see them or a hospital to deliver their babies in most of southern West Virginia.

What I yearn for, I think, is fairness to those who need help and virtue from those who can give help. I don't even blame the bad guys. Ronald Reagan cuts child care, but I am sure that he would personally pay to have a sick child hospitalized if he chanced upon one.

His charity, like so many others, is personal. In the abstract, it is fine to say that churches or private charity will take care of the poor. In practice, it doesn't work. The Salvation Army in Logan has reduced the amount of food in its Christmas baskets, and cut the number it will deliver, because the demand is so great.

There is no virtue in our leaders. I define virtue as a willingness to set examples. The virtuous governor does not stay in $2,000-a-night hotel rooms or drink from coffee cups that cost $49 each. The virtuous governor does not insist on gold on the dome at a time Christmas baskets are going unfilled.

My opinion of Arch Moore is no secret. I think he is a petty, mean-spirited, overrated blusterer. I have repeated that view so often that even my colleagues tell me that further criticism is ineffective.

It may be ineffective, but it is nonetheless heartfelt. I give you two recent causes. This week, there was a story that the number of mine deaths was the greatest in three years.

A few days later, there was a story from the man who Moore picked to enforce mine safety. He said that the Supreme Court didn't know what it was talking about in ordering roof bolting as a safety measure and that mines would be closed as a result.

I have no doubt that the Moore administration would be willing to take a chance on a few more deaths in exchange for a few more mines. The position is silly. West Virginia's problem is not too few mines or too few miners. The problem is too few places to sell coal.

The Moore administration condones the exploitation of desperate men who are willing to forgo safety in exchange for a job. Similarly, it allows six convicts to be killed in this year at Moundsville without a sense of emergency, a sense of inadequacy, or a sense of regret.

Within the past week or two I've gotten a couple of letters from former legislators. They said that the *Gazette* is too negative toward the Legislature, and by being more positive, the newspaper could contribute to progress.

I don't question their sincerity. But I disagree with their conclusions. The state Senate is led by a man who, as a "public relations" specialist, regularly does business with private firms that lobby the Legislature. The majority leader, a man the *Gazette* commends, nominates the leader for another term, citing his integrity.

In the House, a new speaker is chosen, a "liberal" who won a battle for control from a "conservative." Who does the new speaker pick for his leadership team? Why, the very people who extol the merits of the conservative case.

I said earlier that it really made no difference whether Tweedledum, the liberal, defeated Tweedledee, the conservative, for speaker. I little realized how right I was.

It is profoundly depressing. I remember reading a poem a long time ago about a sweatshop being located near a golf course. The poem said the location was fortunate because it allowed the little children at work an opportunity to watch the men at play.

I see an analogy. The unemployed soon will be able to promise their kids that, while they won't have anything for Christmas, they may one day be able to go to the Capitol where they can look at the gold on the dome.

Observations and questions

1) Marsh starts off talking about liberalism, secular humanism, and socialism. Do those themes get lost, or do they get transformed?

2) This column dumps on courts, plaintiffs, the civil service, the poor and the rich both, doctors, Ronald Reagan, government leaders in general, Governor Moore, expensive hotels and coffee cups, Marsh himself, his colleagues, Energy Commissioner Faerber, mining companies, the coal economy, the entire Moore administration, a warden, former legislators, the state Senate leader and the majority leader, the new speaker of the House and his leadership team, and the Capitol dome, in that order. Should Marsh provide the reader with a scorecard to keep the players straight?

3) In the middle, Marsh gives us his opinion of Governor Moore as "a petty, mean-spirited, overrated blusterer." Nothing that follows this blast makes the slightest attempt to support the characterization. Why not?

4) Do you regard this column as fair? Must columns be fair, or complete, or balanced? If you give up the first three, how about accurate?

5) Marsh's sig always depicts him smiling. Why is this man smiling?

A conversation with
Don Marsh

DON FRY: How did you come to be editor in Charleston?

DON MARSH: Well, my old man was a coal miner, and I grew up in a coal camp in the '30s. That was a grim and barren and depressing kind of place, and those people got screwed by the world, and still do.

How did you escape?

The GI bill. I went into the service in World War II, and the GI bill was there available to me. My one career goal was *not* to be a coal miner, and I couldn't do math, so I got into journalism.

Who are your readers?

I really don't know. I aim toward what I hope is an informed audience, people up in the legislature, some in state government, and some in academia. But in the end, I write for myself.

How many columns do you write a week?

I did write two, but it got too busy, so I write about one-and-a-half. Once or twice a month, I try to write one about newspapers. But I find that subject kind of limiting, and I enjoy writing general interest columns. I really hadn't thought of writing a political column; it just turned into one.

Tell me about your late publisher, Ned Chilton.

Well, Chilton had to be the only publisher in the country who had to be inhibited by his editor. He

said, "Our editorial policy is to piss people off."
I admired a man who would say that in print.

Indeed, [Laughter]

Yes, and it's kind of nice, pissing people off. When
I started out, I was deferential and worried about
doing damage to people, and I always tried to find
the good thing to say, or I tried not to name the
department head who screwed up. But Chilton
said that was wrong. Since he was my employer,
he convinced me of a lot of things, but he was
right.

He hated things like printing "p--s off" when
you want to say "piss off," and he went into a
frenzy about that. He said, "Goddamn it, if you're
going to use 'piss,' write 'piss.' If you're not going
to use 'piss,' don't write 'piss.' " [Laughter] He
would say, "If so-and-so is a goddamn thief and
scoundrel ('goddamn' was one of his favorite
words), then use his name. Screw this business
of saying, 'some department head' or 'an
unnamed official.' "

**Tell me about your working methods, from
getting an idea to finishing the story.**

Well, if I have an idea, it's pretty easy. But I tend
to procrastinate, and I never write columns in
advance, which is probably a mistake.

You mean you don't keep one in the drawer?

Hell, no, I never have one in the drawer. Seven
o'clock in the evening is always my magic
number.

But sometimes I have ideas, or clippings, or
knowledge about what I'm going to write about,
and those are easy days. And other days I come
here thinking, "Oh, my God, what's it going to
be?" And I fumble and bumble around and get
very mixed results.

Do you write from an outline?

No, no. I just sit down and start writing, and I get up and write a paragraph, and pace around and answer the phone and pace around, drink a cup of coffee and pace around, and write two or three more paragraphs.

I tend to write too long. I keep thinking I should write 20 inches, but I always write 30. But once I get started, the beginning is difficult, and the end is semidifficult. But the middle comes out too long, and that's where I think I would profit by editing, if I were a quicker writer.

When you say "the beginning," you don't mean just the lead?

No, no. The beginning is when one has made one's statement, and then one gets into one's facts; and the end is where one comes to a conclusion of some kind or another. Usually the end is a paragraph or so.

Do you revise much?

No, no. I read through it two or three times on the screen, but I'm a terrible editor. I'm kind of a scanning reader, and I miss a lot of things. There's a guy in the next office, Jim Haught, who will often read my piece. He's a slow reader, and he catches a lot of the minor things.

Is West Virginia's government especially bizarre, or do you just see government more clearly than anybody else?

Well, I think West Virginia government is especially bizarre, and it baffles me why other people don't see it the same way that I see it. There is endemic corruption, with an almost gamelike quality that people admire. The more outrageous your behavior is, the more successful,...well, that's an exaggeration. Often though, people don't react as they do in moderate, middle-class America.

Let's look at "Why we are in the Third World." Tell me how this piece came about.

Well, the coal-mining areas of southern West Virginia, a desolate and devastated region, are now being touted for toxic waste disposal sites; they'd put it down the abandoned coal mines. Eighty percent of that area is owned by coal and timber corporations. The elected officials there do not represent the people; they represent the great conglomerates. As in India, the colonialists take the native talent into the fold and use them against the peasants.

I read a book called *Power and Powerlessness* written by John Gaventa, who runs something called the Highland Center in Tennessee, an extraordinarily bright man. He used the Third World imagery, and that reinforced my own instincts, so I adopted it.

Take a look at these two paragraphs: "The parents had a meeting at Glen Rogers High School and laid their complaints before a delegate and a union leader. What was local leadership's response to the petitions of the people?

" 'Let's try to maintain these jobs while keeping our children safe.'—Delegate Clayton Hale, D-Wyoming. 'You have to remember, we're talking about a lot of jobs.'—Bill Legg, vice president of United Mine Workers local. I know how it is. I have no objection to Carbide making poison gas upwind from me as long as it means jobs."

Talk about irony and sarcasm. They're hazardous, you know.

Yes, they're often misunderstood. Bhopal is another Third World reference. They made poison gas there and at Institute, the only two places in the world; Institute is only five or 10 miles from here. We had great hassles about whether we should do away with the poison-gas-

making plant at Institute. We had a survey about
this time that said that 70 percent of the people
thought we could have the same disaster as
Bhopal, but 80 percent said that it would be better to keep the plant and keep the jobs and take
the chance. So that was the background of that
remark.

**But don't you run the risk of readers mis-
understanding you?**

Oh, yes. Sarcasm and satire are often misunderstood, and that's why I say that I really don't
write for everybody. The people I hope are
reading it know what I'm talking about. I'm often
misunderstood, particularly about references to
religion. But on the other hand, I do try to goad
the religiously fervent around here. [Laughter]
But, what the hell, the ones who know better will
know better, and the ones who don't, what can
you say about them?

   In this column we're looking at, the people
that read me regularly, the ones I'm trying to
reach, know what I'm doing. So nobody really
thinks that we're going to give our sisters to the
out-of-town corporate giants. On the other hand,
a lot of people would say that they wouldn't take
our sisters. [Laughter] So it works out.

**Let's take a look at "How to identify politi-
cians." Tell me the background on this one.**

Well, let me collect my thoughts before I start
sputtering again. There is a tendency in West
Virginia (West Virginia is the only place I know,
so I keep acting as if it's the only place in the
world.)...there's a tendency to politicize
everything, and if a politician wants to pay
somebody off with public money, what the hell
is it to him?

   We had a great, long-running fight here with
the county clerk, who was indicted for vote fraud.
She was indicted on seven or eight charges, and

she won her case and promptly presented the county court with a bill for $260,000 in legal fees. Well, they were going to pay it, but we sued them and stopped the payment. We have gone to court a couple of times and have established the principle that there has to be some reasonable charge and some reasonable service, that the county commissioners and state government can't just get together and say, "What the hell, just pay him whatever he wants." And we've had two or three other cases of what I regard as excessive payoffs. So that is a recurring theme of mine and something that always angers me, and the idea of public officials using public money that cavalierly offends me, and then the idea of public officials taking public money and suing the public with it, that just.... See, I sputter.

This column made me angry as hell, and I don't even live there. [Laughter]

It makes me mad just thinking about it! It's endless! But at least the board is not using public money to sue those who disagree with them!

Try to calm down while I read your lead [laughter]: "It is outrageous that three members of the Nicholas County Board of Education are suing citizens who criticized the board. It is more outrageous that they are using school money to pay a private lawyer $100 an hour to pursue the suit. Were it possible to sputter in print, I would be sputtering."
I was interested in the ending of the first paragraph: "Were it possible to sputter in print, I'd be sputtering." In this piece, I think you are sputtering.

Well, I was trying to! In my theory of writing, in any kind of story all you need is two or three or four good figures of speech or good similes, and that makes a well-written story.

So when I can discover a line like that (if that is a good line, and I think it is), I like to insert it wherever I can. Because you only need three or four of those, as I said.

It's a wonderful attention getter.

Well, it does show that this is a goddamn outrage! Hey, that's Mayday, the flag is going up!

Yes, well, you did use the word "outrageous" twice in one paragraph. We're not going to miss the point of that.

Right. [Laughter]

In the fourth paragraph, you really get into high dudgeon: "It is impossible to find a charitable excuse for the three board members. They are either power mad or appallingly ignorant. My instinct is towards ignorance. Nobody in Nicholas County is as contemptuous of the democratic process as they appear to be. I have to conclude they're too dumb to know what they're doing."

It is kind of mean, isn't it?

It is, yes.

Well, goddamn it, that's what I meant! Why not? Why pussyfoot around, saying, "These people are probably sincere but really aren't informed on all the issues, and if they really gave some thought to it, they might change their opinion." [Laughter]

Talk about fairness in columns. You're not making any effort to balance this at all.

No, no. I'm writing an opinion, trying to reach a conclusion. What is balance? That's another Chilton theory. He said the editorials that appalled him most were the ones that say, "There's a lot to be said on the one side, but on the other hand, there's a lot to be said on this side. Therefore, it's up to every informed person to make his own conclusion." He said, "That's crazy! It's insane! What the hell are you writing editorials about?!"

A friend of mine said that when you talk to a post, you have to talk in a loud voice, otherwise you won't get its attention. So I was trying to embarrass those board members. I don't feel apologetic at all. There are so many bad things done out of ignorance and power and indifference to the welfare of people. So screw those board of education members!

What the hell, I get excited about this! Take Ronald Reagan. He doesn't pay any attention to the law. He does whatever he wants to do. They all do that, to some greater or lesser degree, and that throws me into an absolute frenzy, whether they're board of education members, governors, or, or, or presidents. [Laughter]

In the very middle of this piece, we read: "Clemente Diaz, a doctor at Sacred Heart Hospital, had the same reaction as I had. 'Here we are. Our taxes support them and they are going to sue us with our own money. It doesn't make sense.' " That's the pivotal quotation in the whole column, spoken by the common man, even though he's a doctor. Actually, unlike many columnists, you don't invoke the common man very much.

Well, in my heart, I think the common man shouldn't be invoked. He's a product of ignorance, of possum-headedness.

"Possum-headedness?" [Laughs]

"Possum-headed" means ignorant. We had a guy up here who called all West Virginians "One-Eyes," because, as he said, "Inbreeding is making their eyes grow closer and closer together, and eventually they'll all be Cyclopes." And so I think of the common man as a possum-headed one-eye.

A possum-headed Cyclops boggles my mind. [Laughter] In the next paragraph, your publisher, Ned Chilton, threatens to sue the board members himself. Chilton was famous for lawsuits, wasn't he?

Yes, he was hell on suing everybody. He insisted that I say that he was going to sue them. In my heart I thought that was an unneeded aside. But, there was the publisher reading what I'd written, saying, "That's great. Goddamn it, say that I'm going to sue them!" And I said, "Oh, yes, Mr. Chilton, I'll do it."

I notice you saved your old nemesis Arch Moore until four paragraphs from the end. You seem to hold him up as a standard to judge other people by, perhaps a standard of idiocy.

In my cool and calm moments, I think he is really the lowest common denominator, and what baffles me is why others don't recognize that. He's generally praised here. He got indicted for taking money and beat the rap, because the only guy they could get to testify was a known criminal, and the judge wouldn't let him talk about the two or three hundred thousand dollars that went into his office and never came out.

His Liquor Commissioner got indicted for shaking down the liquor companies, and went to the pen for it, and all the money went to Arch Moore. And he's announced he won't pay any attention to this law, he won't pay any attention to that law. We've had six guys killed in the penitentiary, and Moore won't replace the warden, who everybody says is a terrible administrator. He says, "The press won't tell me what to do." And he's insisting that West Virginia is on the comeback trail. He's making it new and great again. And we're all starving to death, except me.

Stepping back, this piece blasts all the local villains at once. Do you see risks in such a scatter-gun approach?

Yes, yes. I was just unloading all my spleen and venting all my anger. You do diffuse any kind of focus, on the one hand. On the other hand, you gain a wider audience. The ones who aren't interested in this sort of thing, or aren't interested in the Nicholas County School Board, may be interested in Phyllis Rutledge, and so forth. Anyhow, it makes me feel good. I just get to raise hell with whomever I feel like raising hell with.

Maybe that's the whole point of having your own column. [Laughter] Let's take a look at the next one, headlined "Solitary, poor, nasty, brutish, and short." This column made me so angry that I went around reading parts of it to my colleagues.

Well, Don, I'm certainly glad to hear that. One tends to think that people only get interested in the great events of the world, about war in the Sudan or somewhere, or starvation in Africa. And you forget how little things are common to us all, arguments over parking places, or the pettiness of bureaucrats, or the unfairness of coal mining. I think about coal miners as an exploited and isolated and unknown breed of people who get screwed by everybody. And I forget that people like you or anybody, just normal human beings, say, "My God. That's terrible what they're doing to them." But I don't think in those terms when I'm writing it. I do it for my own satisfaction and to vent my own spleen. [Laughter]

There's a lot of good reporting in this piece,

a lot of good details. Did they come from the clips?

That came from the clips and from my own eye for things. If you get good details, it makes it believable. What really stuck with me in one of those stories was a reporter who went into the mine, and he said you couldn't even stand up to eat, drink, or urinate. And that kind of detail and the imagery of that machine, whirling around with those goddamn arms going, where you had to lie on your back, desperately pulling poles out, in imminent danger of the whole top of the mountain falling on you, is some kind of inferno. It's Dante's inferno, and a short, brutish, and unnatural life for these people!

Absolutely frightening...

...and then to have Faerber in a business suit with a million bucks saying, "This is OK; this means jobs"...that's my position: close the damned mines down! Nobody should have to work in those surroundings. No American should.

Let me ask you about what I call "local context," the problem of explaining local terminology. You've really bent over backwards to tell what this Wilcox miner machine looks like. Would your readers know what a Wilcox miner is?

I don't think so. I'm from a coal mining background myself and cover coal hearings, and I didn't know what the hell it was. I really don't think that explanation is adequate. I got it from the clips and from talking to a reporter named Paul Nyden, who was up there. I have a strong suspicion that I could have done better, or would have been more satisfied with my own description, if I had seen it myself.

Halfway through, you tell the story about Charlie Lanham's death. Is Charlie Lanham typical, or is he just a particularly excruciating example?

The work is very dangerous, with 17 workers killed between 1974 and 1985. And they become kind of clichés, tragic stories of guys born at a place and a time, born to their bad luck. There is a kind of uniformity about how they died, often needlessly, almost always tragically, and almost always with a grieving but inarticulate family behind them. My own guess is that Charlie would have been typical.

Well, let's look at the next one, which is about your favorite subject, "Arch Moore's make-believe world."

My man. [Laughter] This was more of an explanatory column as opposed to an opinion column. I really prefer the opinion columns, right or wrong. I like to use reporting details, the concrete things that give body and substance to anything you write. But I don't want to report it. Why the hell should I write a news story? Get a reporter to write it; that's not what I'm doing.

You put a wonderful paragraph right in the middle: "I may be wrong. I am not a big fan of Arch Moore. Where others see the doughnut, I see the hole." [Laughing] I almost fell out of my chair when I read that, not just the understatement in "I'm not a big fan of Arch Moore," but the comparison to the hole.

Yes. The *Gazette* is always perceived as negative. We don't boost, we knock; and this is a great "Let's boost" state. So the images of "seeing the glass half-empty and half-full," and "I see the doughnut and you see the hole," are really common parlance here. It's common bullshit. We're constantly filled with stories about what's right with West Virginia.

Two paragraphs from the end, you say, "But I really don't hold Moore personally responsible. The state's difficulties are such that there's not a lot that he can do about them. Moore's announcements of economic miracles and progress are growing threadbare. Even the merriest whistle becomes shrill at last."
You're letting Moore off the hook; have you gone soft?

Well, Rockefeller was attacked viciously when he was governor, and supposedly Moore, the miracle man, would change all these things. I was saying in 1984 that Rockefeller is not responsible for the sad condition of the state, and that no one person could change it, and that Moore can do no more about improving the state than Rockefeller could do. So that paragraph is kind of a ha-ha-ha.

You keep on railing against this and that, but nothing changes. How do you keep from getting shrill and despairing?

I really think that it's the duty of everybody to try to make the world better, and one has got to keep plugging away, keep dripping water on the granite. Some writers do it by saying, "Let's do this, and let's do that." I keep trying to do it by hitting people over the head, or trying to humiliate them, or embarrassing them.
Arch Moore is the world's largest bullshitter. With him in command, we can't do anything. And I keep thinking maybe if I keep sneering at him enough, maybe I'm changing six or eight votes. Maybe he'll lose by four votes, and I can say, "Aha. I did that." [Laughter] That's the whole secret: make the world better, and keep trying.

Good for you. Finally, let's look at "Liberals, virtue, and golden domes." I look at this piece in terms of the attitudes of columnists. You've been at this awhile, and you're struggling uphill. Near the end of this column, you exclaim: "It is profoundly depressing." Maybe it's getting to you.

Well...take the example of Nicholas County, where our side won. Now we find out that our side is doing what the other side did, and the citizens are protesting that. It seems to me that the whole structure of government, of justice, of public opinion is directed against the people. And then you see the most exploited people in the state electing the most regressive legislators in the state. And so, yes, that does get depressing.

And you don't foresee any change in that?

No.

No. Well, I've only read five of your columns. If I had read a whole year's worth, would there have been some that were bright and cheerful?

No, those five were pretty representative. I'll have to think about that. I'll have to write a bright and cheerful column. I'll have to find somebody who did something good and just say, "This was a hell of a guy." [Laughter]

Thanks, Don, and good luck.

Jim Nicholson
Obituary Writing

JIM NICHOLSON, 45, grew up in his native Philadelphia and graduated in journalism from the University of Southern Mississippi in 1964. He worked as a reporter in New Orleans, Baltimore, and Wilmington, Delaware. In Philadelphia, he served as a reporter for the *Daily News* and *The Inquirer, Philadelphia Magazine, The Evening Bulletin,* and WCAU radio. He did brief stints as a political campaign manager and a private detective. He takes credit for putting over 150 baddies in jail during his career as an investigative reporter. At the *Daily News,* he created the obituary page and invented the feature obituary for ordinary mortals. His colleagues call him "Dr. Death."

Edward E. 'Ace' Clark, ice and coal dealer

MARCH 19, 1986

Edward E. "Ace" Clark, who hauled ice through Port Richmond by horse-drawn wagon and by truck for nearly 40 years, died Saturday. He was 85 and lived in Port Richmond.

Clark also had been active in church activities and local sports teams since the mid-1930s.

"Ace," who got his nickname as a kid from the gang that hung out at Tucker and Cedar streets, quit school in the sixth grade because life on his father's ice wagon seemed more interesting than books. He took over the business—Pastime Ice & Coal Co.—when he was 17.

His favorite among his horses, which he stabled at Seltzer Street below Somerset, was one named "Major." He could go into a house with ice, through the back door, across the alley, and out the front door of the house in the next street, and Major, who knew the route, would walk himself around the block and be there waiting on the next street.

"We used to say that if us kids had of been horses, we'd have been the best-raised kids in the neighborhood because Dad knew more about horses than he did kids," said his son Bob Clark, with a laugh.

Powerful arms and shoulders atop spindly legs, Ace Clark was a man of many friends who had a zest for life and would toss out the old icemen's line: "Every man has a wife, but an iceman has his pick."

Bob Clark said his father had keys to many of the homes; if someone wasn't home, he would bring in the ice, empty the refrigerator, and then repack the food around the ice.

"Can you imagine someone doing that today for a quarter?" said Clark, adding that the only day's work he ever knew his father to miss was when he got loaded the night of V-J Day and couldn't get up the next morning.

In the winter, when the ice business dropped off by as much as 75 percent, Ace delivered coal.

Though he loved horses, getting a Ford truck in 1937 meant he didn't have to feed the horses on Sundays. And Sundays for Ace Clark were for the church.

He was a past president of St. Anne's Holy Name Society and the St. Anne's Men's Club. He also was one of the organizers and first president of the Icemen's Union in Philadelphia in 1933.

"We had the first telephone in the neighborhood," said his son. "I think it was a fringe he got for being president, to do union business. But I don't think he did much business on it."

Ace Clark loved sports. He was manager of St. Anne's softball team in the 1930s and '40s and the basketball team in the 1940s and '50s.

Normally an easygoing sort, Ace Clark turned rogue elephant when his team was on the court or field.

"People used to go to the games just to watch him," said Bob Clark. "He'd throw his cigar down and get on the referee's case. He always thought his team was getting shortchanged."

By 1950, the ice delivery business itself was going the way of the iceman's horse a decade before, and Clark went to work for A&M Beer Distributors in Frankford. His son said he believes his father enjoyed that job even more than delivering ice because he could pause for a "boilermaker"—a shot of whiskey chased by a glass of beer—to get him on his way.

After six years delivering beer, he went to work for Highway Express and was still loading and unloading trucks when he retired at age 68.

After retiring, he became involved with senior citizens' organizations.

His late wife was the former Agnes M. Bannon.

In addition to his son, Robert J., he is survived by two other sons, Edward A. and Francis X.; two daughters, Anna M. McMenamin and Agnes M. Conahan; 29 grandchildren; and 27 great-grandchildren.

Mass of Christian burial will be celebrated at 10 a.m. tomorrow at St. Anne's Church, E. Lehigh Avenue and Memphis Street. Burial will be in Resurrection Cemetery, Hulmeville Road below Bristol Road, Cornwells Heights, Bucks County.

Friends may call from 7 to 9 tonight at the Hubert M. McBride Funeral Home, 2357 E. Cumberland St.

Observations and questions

1) How does Nicholson structure this piece? Is it simply one interesting bit after another, or do you see patterns?

2) Clubs and memberships often dominate ordinary obituaries. Notice how Nicholson integrates them into the narrative and the character development.

3) Nicholson attributes the first quotation: "...said his son Bob Clark, with a laugh." Do we need the last phrase or will the quotation carry the tone by itself?

4) I could read the sixth and seventh paragraphs ("Powerful arms...around the ice.") as hints at a covert sex life. How would we evaluate such a suspicion? Should Nicholson have removed the potential ambiguity?

5) The son Bob Clark never quite makes sense in what he says, but Nicholson does not clarify the quotations. See, for example, the statement about the boilermaker. How does the son's way of speaking affect the portrait of the father?

6) We learn in the survivors list that Ace Clark had 29 grandchildren and 27 great-grandchildren. Would you have included this feat in the body of the obituary?

7) Nicholson's obituaries all use the same opening and closing formulas. Study all five and describe the pattern and its variants. When does he vary his template, and with what effects? How do such formulas help the reader?

Tastykake retiree Marie Byrne

APRIL 2, 1986

Marie Byrne, a lovable Irish mother who took in neighborhood runaways but was tough enough to keep them and her own kids in line, died Sunday. She was 65 and lived in Havertown, Delaware County.

Raised in the Swampoodle section of Philadelphia, the former Marie Kelly was a 1938 graduate of John W. Hallahan High School. She worked at Tastykake's Hunting Park plant for more than 20 years.

Her house was a gathering place for all of her children's friends and occasionally would be a refuge for the youngster who had a rip at home. The runaway might stay a few hours or a few days. But any youngster soon found out that "she wouldn't be soft on anybody," recalled Brian Byrne, a son. "They would get whacked by Mrs. Byrne, too. You could come home for supper and never know who would be there, sitting at the kitchen table for supper."

Kids and adults liked being around her. It wasn't the lure of her kitchen, noted Brian. "Her idea of a meal was opening three different cans." Nor was it her ability to tell a good joke; she usually popped the punch line first, if she remembered it at all.

"She was the adopted American mother for kids who came here from Ireland," said Jean Marie O'Neill, a daughter. "They all loved her."

One who loved her was family friend Mary Byrne. Since there were already two Aunt Mary Byrnes in the family, the kids called her "Uncle Mary." After Marie died, "Uncle Mary" dropped off a letter to the kids which was written to Marie. In the letter she wrote:

It was 43 years ago we met. You were so full of life, so outgoing, so determined to make life easier for all around you. You were so smart at work, so quick to learn. You were the one chosen for all the special jobs. The rest of us were just part of the group....

Strict about education, she drove all four of her children toward college degrees, which they all obtained, and two of them earned master's degrees. And she helped find them jobs to pay for their educations. Their careers were a great source of pride to her in later years.

Brian said that if he or any of the other kids got into trouble at parochial school and got thrashed by the nuns, "mother would give me another beating for making the nuns upset."

For about 15 years, Marie Byrne played Santa Claus for the family, the neighborhood, and at Tastykake. She donned the red suit, and her kids, who had jobs at the plant at various times to earn college money, would get red faces.

"Mom would make everyone in the cafeteria sit on her lap and tell her what they wanted for Christmas," said Jean Marie, "even the president of the company. I think one year he told her he wanted a new Lincoln."

She retired from Tastykake in 1974.

A member of St. Bernadette's Church, the Legion of Mary, and the Cavan Society, she was a regular churchgoer who had a private prayer list with countless people on it. She was always volunteering her service. When her own efforts didn't seem to be enough, she volunteered her children.

"She was always the boss," said Jean Marie. "She had written instructions on how everything was to be done when she died. She wrote what Irish songs were to be played after the Mass and at the open-bar gathering later."

Despite two years of illness, she wouldn't give in.

"One day she would be in intensive care and the next day out shopping," said Jean Marie.

"She loved to shop and spend money. The Saturday before she died, we shopped and she joked that she would 'charge up everything and if I die, you don't have to pay for it.' "

Her husband, Eugene Byrne, died in 1971.

She also is survived by another daughter, Margaret Byrne Campbell; another son, Kevin; three grandchildren, Maura Jean O'Neill, John Henry O'Neill, and Sean Andrew Campbell; a sister, Katherine Lenahan; and a dear friend, Tom McDonagh.

Mass of Christian burial will be celebrated at 10 a.m. Friday at St. Bernadette's Church, Turner Avenue near Bond Avenue, Drexel Hill. Burial will be in Holy Sepulchre Cemetery, Cheltenham Avenue above Easton Road, Cheltenham Township, Montgomery County.

Friends may call from 7 to 9 tomorrow night at the Robert L. D'Anjollel Building, 8645 West Chester Pike, Upper Darby.

Observations and questions

1) Marie Byrne represents a real test for Nicholson's idea that everyone's life deserves a feature obituary if the reporter digs enough. We can see his obvious reporting skills here, but how does Nicholson keep the reader from asking, "So what?"

2) What qualities does Nicholson celebrate about Marie Byrne? How does he make her into a figure of some stature without straining?

3) The fourth paragraph tells us two of Marie's failings. Ironically they contribute to the overall positive picture. Explain how that effect works.

4) In the sixth paragraph, I find Nicholson's set-up of the letter confusing. How could we introduce this document without losing the reader in the two Maries and Marys?

5) Halfway through, Nicholson introduces the Santa Claus motif. Would you be tempted to move it higher, or at least to hint at it earlier?

6) Notice the lack of any obvious chronology in this obituary. In fact, Nicholson's structure seems aimed at defeating chronology.

7) Nicholson's obituaries teem with people, but he keeps proper names to a minimum. Why?

John Ciavardone, veteran blinded during WWII

SEPTEMBER 3, 1986

John "Skinny Lead" Ciavardone, a blinded war veteran who, with his wife and mother-in-law, lived a story of great courage and love, died Thursday. He was 60 and lived in South Philadelphia.

"They knew his habits; the neighborhood people looked out for him," Rose Surace, who grew up with him, said. "He was part of it. The whole neighborhood. When I look out, everybody looks so sad. It seems lonely already without him."

Ciavardone's story was unknown beyond the one-block world of 7th and Washington in which he grew up, lived, and died. It is within that block that the story begins and ends.

The pencil-thin corner kid was nicknamed "Skinny Lead" sometime in the early '40s. He was drafted into the Army in 1944, shortly after he finished vocational school. He didn't complain, he just kissed his childhood sweetheart Anna Domeratzski goodbye and went away.

On March 19, 1945, 19 days short of his 19th birthday and less than two months before the war in Europe was to end, Ciavardone was blinded when a shell exploded on a battlefield in Germany. He spent four years in Valley Forge General Hospital convalescing. And for the next decade he would have 76 operations to rebuild his nose.

Rose Surace remembers the first time family members and neighbors went to see Skinny Lead in the hospital.

"We were all sick and shocked," she said. "He was the only one in the room with a big smile on his face. He was so glad to hear our voices. Everyone was crying and looking at him. He took his injury better than we did."

Skinny Lead only cried once over his injuries.

"His family had just left," recalled Mickey DiSanto, a lifelong pal. "The doctors had just told him he wouldn't see again and he didn't want to break down in front of the family. He said, 'I can't cry over it. Life has to go on.' "

The neighbors said Ciavardone put off marrying Anna Domeratzski until he got out of the hospital. They had a big wedding in April 1949.

"He was terrific. You wouldn't know he was blind unless we broke it to you. He wouldn't make his burden your burden," said Mickey DiSanto. "He never used a cane or a seeing-eye dog because he didn't want to draw publicity to himself. Sometimes he would take my arm and affectionately refer to me as his canine."

In 1952, while pregnant with their second child, Anna developed a blood clot that caused her left arm and leg to be permanently paralyzed.

"He became his wife's arm and she was his eyes. Him and his missus worked in concert. They were very close and in love," said Mickey. Actually, living with his mother-in-law, Millie Guglielmo, the three formed a perfect and beautiful tripod.

"When I first went into the home, it struck me that they functioned like a team," said Carmel Ciavardone, Skinny Lead's daughter-in-law. "What one couldn't do, the other could. They cooked meals together that way, one cutting onions, one giving directions, one making hamburgers."

Living on a 100 percent disability pension, Ciavardone loved following sports and simply being part of the 7th and Washington neighborhood. The neighbors and a generation of children also loved Skinny Lead. He enjoyed babysitting his grandchildren and loved conversing with people. He also liked playing the slots in Atlantic City. And he would be the first to break into song at parties.

But most of the singing stopped and he became more subdued about two years ago when

Anna died. After that, the neighborhood ladies kept a closer watch on Skinny Lead.

"We looked out in the morning," said Rose, "and if he was out there, I asked him to come in for some coffee until the retired men came out to sit with him."

John Ciavardone, the oldest of Skinny Lead and Anna's three children, said, "Both my mother and my father certainly never let any handicaps they might have had dictate how they led their lives. He was the best father anyone could ever want to have."

Recalled Mickey DiSanto, "He was very happy-go-lucky but very thoughtful when it came to his family. They never were wanting for anything. Most of all love."

Ciavardone was a member of St. Mary Magdalen de Pazzi Church, the Blind Veterans Association, and the Disabled American Veterans.

He is also survived by two daughters, Marilyn Candeloro and Anna Marie Calhoun; two sisters, Anna Grande and Dillie DiSantis; four brothers, Joseph, Andrew, Frank, and Albert; and four grandchildren.

Mass of Christian burial was to be celebrated at 9:30 a.m. today at St. Mary Magdalen de Pazzi Church, 714 Montrose St. Burial will be in Ss. Peter and Paul Cemetery, Sproul and Crum Creek roads, Marple Township, Delaware County.

Observations and questions

1) In the third paragraph, Nicholson tells us that Skinny Lead's story is confined to one block. Study how Nicholson breaks out of that geographic restriction without calling attention to his variations.

2) This obituary seems more a portrait of a family than of an individual. We could even call it a portrait of one block and its web of connected people.

3) Nicholson spreads out the speakers. In a piece this short, any bunching of characters will probably confuse the reader. But notice how he frames each character who reappears, often by repeating whole names.

4) Notice all the visual imagery and references to sight in this obituary about a blind man. Would you guess that device is deliberate or inevitable?

5) Does the inherent interest of Ciavardone generate a feature obituary, or does the obituary itself create the interest? Here lies the secret of Nicholson's contention that anyone's life can sustain a feature obituary.

6) This obituary has the potential to become a real weeper. Study how Nicholson keeps it restrained. Do you think he succeeds?

7) If these pieces have a message, it probably lurks somewhere in this obituary. What themes or agendas do you see?

Vincent 'Cous' Pilla Sr., Italian chef extraordinaire

OCTOBER 10, 1986

Vincent "Cous" Pilla Sr., a Runyonesque character whose Italian cuisine and quick wit made his South Philadelphia restaurant a favorite stop for movie actors, mob bosses, and Mom and Dad, died Wednesday. He was 58 and lived in South Philadelphia.

A chef for more than 40 years, Cous worked at and operated a number of restaurants. His most famous eatery was Cous' Little Italy at 11th and Christian streets.

Philadelphia organized-crime boss Angelo Bruno had his last meal there before he was murdered the night of March 21, 1980.

Cous' Little Italy closed about three years ago, and until the day before he died, Pilla was working at Big Ralph's Saloon on East Passyunk Avenue. The day before he died of heart failure, he and his son Vincent Jr. had agreed that the father would go in on Vincent's restaurant on Main Street in Manayunk.

In fact they had ordered the new sign: Cous' Canal View.

The talented and gregarious Pilla was known throughout Philadelphia for his Italian specialties, which included chicken Neopolitan, sausage Genovese, shrimp scampi, and an array of delicate combinations with veal.

His pleasure didn't end with the cooking. He loved to watch his customers and friends eat and enjoy. Often he would pull up a chair and tell jokes.

"He was a beautiful man, a giving kind of man," said his other son, John Pilla. "He always had a big smile on his face and loved to greet people. When you saw Cous he just put a smile on your face. He dealt on life's level and made a joke of everything. He laughed at people, with people, and about people."

Cous taught his son Vince and his daughter Marcella to cook. John said he didn't want to know about cooking: "Dad makes me gravy and I take it home and freeze it."

"He was more than a father, he was a buddy," said John. "He taught me everything good— how to live. He had charisma. People loved him."

As a corner kid growing up around 6th and Montrose streets, Vincent Pilla Sr. never thought he would wind up a famous chef or any kind of cook. Downtown, a youngster can aspire to be a contractor, a priest, or merely a numbers runner for the guy who owns the candy store. But nobody in his right mind talks about growing up to be a cook.

In fact, it was in that environment that Pilla got his nickname. In a July 27, 1986, *Inquirer* magazine article by Mary Walton, Cous recalled: "I got the name 'Cous' from 7th and Washington Avenue where we hung out on the corner as little boys, the Sunshine Playground. And while I'm in there, my name was Pilla and the toughest kid in the gang was named Pilla, too. And he didn't know my first name, and I didn't know his, but he told them to leave me go, 'He's my cousin.'

"From then on in, it was 'Cous.' Eighty-five percent of the people you stop will not know that my name is Vincent. My mom, when she died, called me Cous."

Pilla dropped out of school in the ninth grade and joined the Merchant Marine at 16, the Army at 18, and married the former Anna Amato at 19.

After the Army, he went to work as a soda jerk in his aunt's restaurant. He remembered for reporter Walton the night behind the grill that changed his life:

"Once there was a black fellow by the name of Scotty. I was on night work, and he comes in, and he said, 'Can I have two eggs?' At night we didn't do anything like that, so I says, 'Yeah, sure Scotty.' I always felt a little sorry for him.

"So I scrambled him three eggs. To me, an omelet always called for three eggs. I put salt and a little grated cheese in there and I mixed them, and I scrambled them on the grill and made him a flopover omelet.

"He went to eat. He says, 'I ain't never tasted anything like this in my life.' This was the turning point in my life. This was satisfaction."

A lot of people loved the "Cous" touch and would trek to a restaurant to eat his cooking whether it was his place or another place where he was working.

Customers included actor Sylvester Stallone and ex-Eagles coach Dick Vermeil. City Councilwoman Joan Specter invited him to teach a class at her cooking school. The "boys" also came to eat.

Of course, this attracted the people who follow and keep tabs on the "boys." As *Daily News* columnist Larry Fields pointed out once, "Cous' only crime is making the best pasta in town."

One story goes that federal agents came in one day to question Pilla about some of his diners. Now it is in the mob manual somewhere that the first item a connected guy buys is the most expensive hand-tooled, imported shoes he can find.

As one agent started in on Cous, he was cut short by the exasperated chef who said, "Hey, look at these," pointing to a scuffed, obviously cheap pair of Buster Browns. "Do these shoes look like I'm a gangster?"

Even at home, Cous wore his "chef whites." Said John, "They were his dress whites."

His main diversions were sports and the track. He loved football, "but he was too hyper to sit in front of a television all afternoon," said John. "He would check the scores against the point spread."

In his last years, his world also revolved around his grandson, Vincent, taking him on rides and buying him pretzels and toys.

Cous loved to eat, especially cupcakes, peach pie, and ice cream, and constantly fought the battle of the bulge. He also was put on a salt-free diet five years ago by his doctor, said John, "but if he got a good report from the doctor, he would grab a bologna sandwich or put a little salt on spaghetti." He had suffered two heart attacks in recent years.

Pilla was a member of St. Mary Magdalen de Pazzi Roman Catholic Church.

He also is survived by a brother, John, and a granddaughter, Lauren Pilla.

Mass of Christian burial will be celebrated at 9:30 a.m. Monday at St. Mary Magdalen de Pazzi Church, 714 Montrose St. Entombment will be in Holy Cross Mausoleum, Baily Road and Wycombe Avenue, Yeadon, Delaware County.

Friends may call between 7 and 10 Sunday night at the Achille A. Ingenito Funeral Home, 705 Christian St.

Observations and questions

1) Study Nicholson's first sentence. Normally readers stumble over complex sentences with separated subjects and verbs. But here the formula tells the reader from the start that the verb will be "died."

2) Nicholson lets Pilla retell the story of Scotty as "the turning point in my life." But neither Nicholson nor Pilla explains why it was a turning point. Study how Nicholson tells us a lot without explaining a lot.

3) Notice how Nicholson spreads the various food descriptions throughout the obituary. Would you be tempted to bring them together, or to expand any of them? Remember, Nicholson's subject was a famous cook.

4) Nicholson normally does not list the cause of death, but here he makes a point of it. Why?

5) Pilla seems almost too famous for Nicholson's democratic agenda of presenting only plain people. Is Pilla notable for himself or just "connected"?

6) Study Nicholson's use of dialect in quotations: "he told them to leave me go," "so I says," "ain't." In this context, he can use it without fearing accusations of mockery or condescension.

7) This obituary has no obvious section divisions. Notice how Nicholson slides from paragraph to paragraph by connecting images and themes.

Richard 'Boss Hog' Hodges, school custodian, bon vivant

OCTOBER 28, 1986

Richard "Boss Hog" Hodges, a retired Philadelphia school custodian and veritable social lion, died Friday. He was 49 and lived in the Mantua section of the city.

Richard Hodges had been a custodian at the Ferguson School at 7th and Norris streets for more than 15 years and custodian at Drew School at 38th Street and Powelton Avenue for a number of years before that. He retired on disability in October 1985.

But beyond his outstanding record as a custodian, Hodges is remembered as the man who for some 20 years operated and hosted the greatest after-hours spot in neighborhood memory.

He liked to think of it as an "open house." It didn't have a name—other than being referred to as "Richard's Spot" or "Cafe Richard"—but the house on Brandywine Street was where the action was. It was a house that Hodges owned, located two blocks from his own home.

Friday and Saturday nights and all day Sunday people gathered there who had two things in common: they wanted a good time and they were personal friends of Hodges, the smiling man in the sharp slacks and sport shirt. The gathering cut across the socio-economic spectrum.

There was food and music, laughter, card games, and lots of good cheer.

"It was fabulous," said William L. Jackson, director of personnel testing for the School District of Philadelphia and a lifelong friend of Hodges. "There would be beautiful women with well-dressed guys and guys in work clothes, and all of Richard's high-roller buddies.

"There was camaraderie and Richard was the nucleus of it all. There was never violence or insulting behavior. Everybody knew who everybody was. They were all friends of Richard.

"He didn't have an A or B list. Everybody was on his A list. It was always a place to feel comfortable."

If things did get out of hand, Hodges would appear—waving the ever-present Camel cigarette—and defuse the situation with humor. He kept things smooth, said Jackson, "through his sheer force of personality."

"He could talk the birds out of the trees," said William H. Hodges, Richard's brother. "He was that type of guy. If he had $20, you could have 15 of it. If he could help you, he did it without question."

The 5-foot-8 Hodges tended toward being overweight, but that was understandable because he was a gourmet cook. If someone had a birthday, "Boss Hog" would dress up in his best suit and put out a big birthday cake and dinner at his "open house."

"Cook?" said an incredulous William Hodges. "His roast beef melted in your mouth. And fish and grits. His biscuits and cornbread talked."

Hodges was raised in Mantua, but then—before the neighborhood started getting dressed up—the area was known as "The Bottom." His father, Nathaniel, was a construction worker who, recalled William Hodges, "wore an iron glove and didn't spare the rod."

Richard went to work young and brought in his share of money to help the family. He also was a member of Mount Olive Baptist Church and sent in his offering with a family member when he couldn't make it to Sunday service.

Hodges also liked to visit race tracks and occasionally took trips to Atlantic City, Las Vegas, and Haiti. He enjoyed traveling.

"He was a black Damon Runyon," said his friend Jackson. "Without question he was one of Mantua's most colorful and beloved figures. He was known for his love of good times and a high-rolling lifestyle.

"Everyone who knew him loved and admired him for his ability to befriend, and be a friend to, people in all walks of life. He was a friend of senior citizens in the neighborhood, professional men and women citywide, the cop on the beat, neighborhood youth, businessmen, and fellow school district employees.

"His passing will be sorely felt in the community. The guys who knew him at (the fire house) will blow the whistle for him at 4 p.m. Friday when his viewing starts, in honor of Richard's memory."

Hodges is survived by his wife, Marva; three daughters, Debbie, Linda, and Nicey; two sons, Poogie and Ricky; and four brothers, William H., Tilman, Arthur, and Cleveland.

Services will be at 8 p.m. Friday at Mount Olive Baptist Church, 37th and Wallace streets, where friends may call after 4 p.m. Burial arrangements were incomplete.

Observations and questions

1) Nicholson grabs our attention in his first paragraph by pairing "retired Philadelphia school custodian and veritable social lion." Consider the gulf of social class between those two phrases, and the effect of the adjective "veritable." Track this theme through the piece.

2) Nicholson begins his third paragraph, "But beyond his outstanding record as a custodian...." Analyze the democratic and blue-collar values in this phrase, as well as its potential (perhaps in any other paper) for irony and condescension.

3) Nicholson knew the source of the nickname "Boss Hog," from a character on the television show *Dukes of Hazzard,* who also wore white suits. Why would he leave this source out?

4) Toward the end, William Jackson says, "He was a black Damon Runyon." Try moving this quotation around for various effects.

5) Study how Nicholson integrates his themes of memory and neighborhood fame.

6) This eulogy for a bon vivant describes the sociology of a whole neighborhood. In fact, many of Nicholson's individual portraits actually portray groups.

A conversation with
Jim Nicholson

DON FRY: What did the obit page look like when you took it over?

JIM NICHOLSON: The *Daily News* has never had an obit page. They would run obits if someone big died in Philadelphia, but there was no obit page. So I started writing the thing, and I'd like to say that I had the great inspiration that I would do this common-man page, but I really didn't.

Whose idea was it?

Nobody's. It evolved within a few days. It became apparent that if we were going to be a little different from *The Inquirer,* rather than just the stepchild, my page had to look like the rest of the paper, which was pointed at the row houses and the blue-collar and the river wards. I decided that I would do the average person, and it just fell into place within a few days.

No funeral directors would call in obits. I didn't even have paid notices in my paper. So I'd go down the notices in *The Inquirer* and see something like, "All snake charmers of America, Incorporated, invited to the funeral," and I would say, "Hey, this guy was probably a snake charmer."

So I'd call the funeral home and I'd say, "I'm so-and-so, I'd like to talk to the family. This guy looks kind of interesting." The funeral director would say, "Yeah, yeah. The guy had a whole basket of snakes, and he used to blow on his flute, and they'd come out of the basket." So I learned how to pick out the little tiny clues, like if he was a member of Lodge 5 F.O.P., he was a cop. I'd find these professions, especially in the service sector: police, fire, teachers. This way I knew for certain these people were deserving and worthy of something. But it was very slow going the first year or so.

Did you establish an obit page, or was it still treated as just news stories?

Oh, no. From day one, they gave me a logo, "Deaths," which was not my favorite one. Everyone else says, "Obituaries." We had to say the most negative possible word: "DEATHS." There were a lot of funeral directors who would not talk to me, and there were a lot of families who refused to be in the *Daily News*. Many years ago, this was almost a scandal sheet. We're talking about low-cut dresses and bloody dead gangsters. And I met a lot of resistance inside the paper, but not on the top management level; I had their support, or at least their acquiescence.

Where did the resistance come from?

Mid-level management copy readers thought they were working for *The New York Times,* and they would see an article about a plumber that ran 15 inches, and it blew all their fuses. They said, "My God. Fifteen inches for a guy that fixed toilets, in our newspaper? What is all this drivel?"

So I would be edited pretty heavily, and I'd fight the good fight. To give you an example, I would write about, let's say Guido "Crazy Ralph" Bongiovani, and I'd get a memo saying, "Why do we have to have nicknames like this?" Well, in South Philadelphia, you are born, raised, live, and die with a guy, and you never know his name is Guido Bongiovani. He's "Crazy Ralph." And if you went in the neighborhood saying, "Where is Guido Bongiovani?" they'd all stare at you.

I had to explain why I would use a nickname and how important it was, because these downtown people would read an obit and if it wasn't in there, they would just pass over it and never know that their friend had died.

So then they came out with another directive, saying to explain the nicknames. Well, you can in a lot of cases, but some are lost in antiquity and some I couldn't explain, like a guy whose nickname was "Joe Tickets." He worked at city hall, and he fixed everyone's tickets. [Laughter] How am I going to say in the guy's obit, "He was a fixer"?

Tell me what the page looks like. Do you have one lead obit, and the rest are little capsules, or what?

Yes. I'll have a lead obit that will run anywhere from eight to 20 inches. I'll then have three or four small obits. Sometimes the gates open, and you wind up with three lead obits; and the next day you've got no lead obit, and you just put five shorts on your page.

How do you pick your subjects?

Burr Van Atta of *The Inquirer* and I meet every single day for coffee, once or twice a day, and we talk about obits. Burr and I are the only two obit writers in Philadelphia, but we share. So if his deadline's coming up and mine is not until the next day, I say, "Burr, you'll want to know about so-and-so." Or he'll tell me, "They went past our 48-hour rule; maybe you ought to do something." See, if they're dead longer than 48 hours, *The Inquirer* won't write an obit. I'm the safety net.

He covers prominent people, Jewish, businessmen, government. I cover black, Irish, Polish, lower class. He'll do the president of United Fruit; I'll do the fruit vendor. Between us, we're able to give the kind of public service and coverage that's encompassing, and we can only do this by throwing away this *Daily News* versus *Inquirer* nonsense.

Having divvied up the dead, how do you pick the lead obituaries?

You can almost close your eyes and put your finger on the death notice page, and that could be the lead. Every person is a lead obit. There are no unimportant obits. There are only reporters who ask unimportant questions or bad questions.

You mean that everybody has this kind of interest. It's all in the reporting.

Yeah. I'll call the funeral home, and no one ever gets in the paper unless a funeral director says they're dead. [Laughter] I don't care if my brother calls and says my other brother is dead, I'm going to call the funeral director. Anyhow, I'll talk to the funeral director and get the basic information, including the family's phone number. I'll call and say, "Don," (and I always use a first name) "Don, I'm Jim Nicholson with the *Philadelphia Daily News.* Mr. McBride at the funeral home said you might be interested in an obit, and I'd like to do one on your uncle," and so on. And then I get all the basics. I don't ask any personal questions until I get them talking about things they really know and are sure of, and would have no problem telling anybody who came to their door. Then I'll say, "All right. Let's talk about your uncle for a little bit. He sounds like a pretty interesting guy. You say he was a fireman until he was 70 years old. That's kind of old for a fireman, isn't it?" And he starts telling me the guy was in great physical shape because he worked out with weights all his life and was a boxer. I say, "A boxer? Really? Amateur or pro?" And pretty soon, things start coming out of the guy's past.

So you get reactions wrapped around the facts.

Yeah. Sometimes, if the person on the phone keeps asking somebody else, I'll say, "Why don't you put Lucy on? Let me talk to her." [Laughter] Then we cut out the middle man, because Lucy really knows it all. But families will sometimes put on the family member by protocol, the oldest son or the daughter who ran everything, but they often don't know the story.

I tell the family, sometimes in these exact words, "I'm not working for the *Daily News*. I'm working for you. You're the boss. I'm writing this obituary for the family. If there's anything you don't want in here, you tell me. I'm not trying to sell newspapers, so you make the call."

In spite of that promise, do people tell you the negatives in people's lives, and let you use it?

Yes. Now, some of them are surprised when I use it, because they start forgetting that they're talking to a reporter.

Do you encourage that forgetting?

Not really, but we get talking and I can identify with a lot of people I'm writing about. If a guy was a stevedore, well, I loaded trucks. I worked in the oil fields. I was a salesman. And when you start showing the people that you understand who their loved one was, they start talking more and more.

I wear a headset, and I type the information on a word processor. I just use two fingers, but I can type as fast as the average person can talk, which is very important because I must capture the argot.

I notice you print it that way, too.

Yeah. We've got prepositions hanging at the end, and we've got all kinds of stilted dialogue, but it can't come out sounding like Jim Nicholson.

You do all of this on the phone, not in person?

Oh, yeah. All on the phone. It's better on the phone. The worst interviews I ever had were in person. There's just enough anonymity created on the phone so that they can relax.

Is your obligation to the families or to the dead?

Both. I believe that every person I can do an obit on is one that didn't get through without being noticed. And if it was possible, every person who ever died should have a good good-bye. I wish what I do would become commonplace, that everybody would do this.

Do you interview several people?

Oh, sure. Sometimes a wife or brother will be unable to articulate, so I'll say, "By the way, does he have a close pal that I could talk to?" The close pal will give me the whole story, and I'll just use a paragraph from the family member. But the close pal will always come through.

How do you deal with all this emotional baggage?

We're celebrating life, not death. Death is incidental to the story. If you took the phrase "died on Tuesday" out of the story, it would be a feature. It would not be an obituary. It would be a human- interest feature about a hell of a nice guy or girl. And the death is almost incidental in most of the obits.

How do you know when you've got enough?

I know an obit will be successful (and I think most are) when at a certain point in the interview, it clicks in my mind, "I know this guy," and from there on, it's all downhill.

Once you've done all the interviewing and looked at the clips, what is your writing process? Do you outline or just sit down and write it out?

No. I'll print out a hard copy of my notes, and read them over, and start making little stars and underlines here and there. And sometimes I know my lead during the interview. I don't do fancy leads or real feature leads. I always say that he died and when in the lead. In a complex sentence structure, I'll use phrases like "a Runyonesque character." But I try to make leads pretty uniform. It's kind of simple, but the obits write themselves.

So it just flows out when you've got it organized?

I don't rewrite, except to check my spelling. It's rare that I take a sentence out. I may insert here and there, but I never rearrange at all. I trust my gut feelings, and a little voice says, "Do what got you here." [Laughter] And sometimes it writes as fast as I can type, and I get excited about it, and I'll get so pumped up I'll call somebody over and say, "Look at this. Look at this quote." And I'm as pumped up as I was at 20 years old on my first newspaper.

I notice that you don't indicate the cause of death.

Here are the problems. Number one, in about 40 percent of the cases, you don't know the cause of death, and neither does the family. Unless you have an autopsy, it's going to be heart failure, or a stroke, or something of that sort. The paper has a rule: under 40, I will say "natural causes," only to eliminate the possibility of gunshot, auto accident, suicide, etc. If they're under 40, I have been including the detailed cause more, because of AIDS. If you've got a young, single musician who dies at 35 from a heart attack, and I don't list the cause of death, the public wrongly attaches a stigma. They think he died of AIDS.

If you know a person has died of AIDS, do you put that in?

I have known, 99 percent sure, in about three cases, and I did not use it. Again, going back to the original philosophy, if the death is incidental to my story, the cause of the death is even more incidental. Now, in a lot of my stories I mention cancer, because it's part of the drama. Maybe it's a five-year battle, and the courage and dignity are incredible.

Number two, there's also a social stigma against listing the cause. *The Inquirer* can list it more often, because with a more prominent person, they feel compelled to say he died of cancer or a heart attack. But for your average row-house person, cancer is still a taboo.

Many newspapers don't indicate the cause of death because they're trying to avoid trouble. For you, if the cause of death isn't part of the story, it doesn't go in the story.

Yeah. It's really not part of the story unless the events leading up to it are intertwined. If you look over these obits, you could take two words out and not know it's an obit. And people frequently refer to my obit page as my "column." I've never considered myself a columnist, but I'm viewed by other columnists as a columnist.

This stuff will outlive any kind of investigative work I ever did. It's hanging on walls. It's laminated. They'll copy maybe 200 of these at the viewing and have them next to the registry; as people come in, they'll pick one up, or they'll use them for the eulogy, and they put them in the caskets.

They put them in the casket?

Oh, yeah. A lot of people put the obits in the casket. With one old Irish guy I did, the family said, "Well, Uncle Tommy can read this later," and they put it in the casket right in his pocket.

How did you pick 'Cous' Pilla?

Well, I didn't pick him. I got several calls from our "Night Life" columnist and others that I should do this one, and I had heard of the guy. I don't generally do people who are well known; that's handled by the city desk.

I wasn't sure the family would talk. This guy had been maligned a lot because he was often mentioned in mob stories, like, "The mob gathered at Pilla's Restaurant." Well, hell, the mob's gotta eat somewhere, you know. [Laughter] And 'Cous' could care less about being in the mob. Obviously the guy wasn't, because he never had any resources; he was on his heels at the end. But the family did talk.

Look at the lead: "Vincent 'Cous' Pilla Sr., a Runyonesque character whose Italian cuisine and quick wit made his South Philadelphia restaurant a favorite stop for movie actors, mob bosses, and Mom and Dad, died Wednesday. He was 58 and lived in South Philadelphia." You use that formula for all your openings.

Every one of them. People don't have to read any further. I make it easy by giving his age and where he was from, and if they want to go further they can, but they have the basics there. I think it's unfair to the reader to bury the age in the eighth graph. I could probably do feature leads, but it would not be fair to the reader.

Yes. You put the feature stuff between the guy's name and the verb "died." Beautiful characterizations, by the way.

Well, the challenge is to tell who he was in about seven words or less. If you want to read further, this sketch is going to be supported.

You use a lot of long quotations with pretty rough edges.

That's how people talk. They don't punctuate, and they don't pause at the end of a sentence, or even complete a sentence. And if that's how it came out, that's generally how I try to get it in.

My favorite anecdote in this piece comes right in the middle, the account by Scotty.

I took that out of Mary Walton's story in *The Inquirer*. The same story was told to me in a very rough form by the son, but it was so much better in Walton's version that I decided to lift it.

All of the papers I ever worked for were very petty about one thing: they would not name another newspaper or the writer they were taking something from. I absolutely put my foot down here and said, "We will quote the writer and the newspaper if I use somebody's stuff," because I use some very good stuff from some very good reporters. They did the work, not me, and I want to credit it. So you'll find in all my obits that I credit reporters from *The Inquirer*, although there's fierce competition between us.

Good for you. I find the anecdote interesting because it doesn't exactly explain anything, and yet you understand it.

Well, see, what you're saying is the very heart of the obit. If you took out things that, by our rules of the business, were not germane or significant, you could wipe out every one of my obits. You could go through line-by-line and say, "Well, what's that got to do with anything?" And pretty soon, you'd have a blank hole there. But all those non sequiturs are there for effect.

You let the reader put it together. Listen to this passage near the end: "One story goes that federal agents came in one day to question Pilla about some of his diners. Now it is in the mob manual somewhere that the first item a connected guy buys is the most expensive hand-tooled, imported shoes he can find."

That sounds like real Philadelphia lingo to me.

Yeah, yeah. It's also as much mob lore as Philadelphia. And, without saying so, it's also Italian. Very important, the kind of shoes you have.

If you look at all the lead obits I've written, maybe 1,500 of them, you would have a pretty detailed picture of Philadelphia from about 1920 to the present: lemonade, lemon ice vendors at night, sitting on the steps, sleeping with windows open at night in the old days, how guys hung out on the corner, the turfs. It may only be a graph in each obit, but that's enough.

Let's look at Ace Clark, the ice man. Listen to the dialect in this passage: "We used to say that if *us kids had of been horses,* we'd have been the best-raised kids in the neighborhood because Dad knew more about horses than he did kids."

That's atrocious, but that's how he talked.

What's atrocious about it?

Well, any English teacher or your average copy desk would take one look at that and say, "You know, this is awful; let's paraphrase." But this is how it came out of the guy's mouth.

But when reporters quote in dialect, they often get letters objecting, "You shouldn't have quoted me in dialect, because people will think I'm stupid." Do you get objections to people being quoted verbatim?

No, and I'll tell you why: they are so delighted with the obit in total. Now, I'm sure that many people have said, "My God, I wish he hadn't quoted me on that!" But the sum total evidently overrides all objections.

Shall we talk about "Boss Hog"?

Yeah. This one got a fantastic reaction inside my newspaper. I got stopped in the hallway by people who commented on this one. A lot of my readers are closet readers. They won't admit to reading my page, even out in public, but they'll write me about it.

Why is that? Is it considered un-chic to read your paper, or just your page?

The page, and with some people, the paper. If they're under the age of 50, people don't like to be caught reading an obit page. I got a letter yesterday that said, "I thought I was the only one hooked on reading your obituaries. Keep writing them, except mine."

I'm struck by this loaded phrase at the start of the third paragraph: "But beyond his outstanding record as a custodian...."

Yeah, that's intentional. I believe that if you're a pro, you're a pro. These people who do some of these so-called menial jobs, if we were put next to them, in 10 years we couldn't come close. They are so good.

I wanted to lend dignity to what Boss Hog did as his regular job, beyond all this other stuff. And I just wanted to make a casual reference that he was a top pro custodian, and that's a given.

Jim, in any other newspaper or any other context, we might suspect condescension or irony, but there's not a bit here. You never seem to condescend to the people you write about, and that would be an easy trap to fall into.

Thank you. That's important. I've done most of
these jobs, and I didn't feel low class. I worked
for the county on the road and on the docks and
in oil fields and all this other stuff, with a college
degree. There's no way I can look down on them,
because I may be going back to that. But I hadn't
thought about that with that phrase. It was
almost a throwaway line, frankly.

**Well, somehow, you get away with it.
[Laughter] I like this quotation right in the
middle: " 'Cook?' said an incredulous William
Hodges. 'His roast beef melted in your mouth.
And fish and grits. His biscuits and
cornbread talked.' " Wow!**

Yeah. When I took that quote, I turned to Larry
McMullen, a columnist up there, and said,
"Larry, I couldn't invent stuff like this. I couldn't
make up quotes like this if I wanted to." There's
just no way you could improvise dialogue like
that.

**You didn't touch it up? That's exactly what
he said?**

Absolutely. This piece really got a reaction. I
didn't know a lot of people in my building were
reading me until this one came out, and then
they felt compelled to talk to me.

**Toward the end, you quote William Jackson,
who says, "He was a black Damon Runyon."
Any worries about that quotation?**

Some papers and maybe some reporters, worried
about racism, would have cut the word "black,"
but I don't worry about it. In view of my track
record and what I've done, I simply don't have
the kind of apprehensions I would have had
before. William Jackson is a high-placed black
official in the city of Philadelphia, a top man in
personnel, and a very sharp guy, and I could

hardly believe he was coming out with all of this, because this was more like something a guy on the corner would be telling me. His credibility, of course, was Triple-A.

Let's take a look at Marie Byrne, the Tasty-kake retiree. She is the least distinguished person here. She didn't do anything but be nice to children.

Yeah. But she's our reader. How many women have said, "Let's charge up all this on our charge account, because at the end of our lives, we won't have to pay for it?" Well, here's Marie Byrne telling you that, and the identification factor is important.

Newspapers complain today, Don, that their readers are leaving them. That's not the case. In most cases, the newspapers are leaving their readers. Take a look at your average big-city or even middle-sized newsroom. There's a collection of reporters who don't dress like, eat like, talk like, or act like the people they want to buy their newspapers. Now, how in the hell can they write a newspaper that's going to be bought by the people?

They also don't live like them, and they don't think like them.

Not at all, and how can they ask the right questions? And papers today, Don, are more accurate and have more integrity than ever in history, and yet they're farther removed from the people than they've ever been.

Do you think they're less human?

They're more governmental. All our lines that went into the neighborhoods have rusted apart from disuse. There's not a handful of reporters in Philadelphia who can go into the neighborhoods with sources on the corner, in the mob, or other places. We're putting out a paper by government action and reaction, by the movers and shakers.

Now, I understand the problems. You've got finite resources. You've got less news hole in some cases. You've got more things you're trying to do. But the great issues of today that concern a guy in a row house don't take place at the conference table in Geneva. They take place at his kitchen table. Now, if you can't get enough of those supper table issues in your paper, and you've got too many of the mayor's conference room table, or Geneva table issues, that guy isn't going to buy your paper. Where is the median, where is the balance?

Maybe it's having real people write about real people. Well, who's going to write your obit? Have you written it already?

No, no. I like to joke and say my obit will be written by whoever is the second-greatest obit writer in the world. [Laughter] But that wouldn't look good in print, being as modest as I am.

You may be too prominent for your type of obituary.

Yeah, maybe I couldn't make my own page. I'm not concerned about my obit. Very simply, my name is on all these things, and the sum total of these obits is my obit, and I believe that.

That would be quite an obituary.

Well, thank you very much, Don. I just love talking about this, because there aren't many people to talk to about obits.

St.Petersburg Times

Florida's Best Newspaper

Tom French
Finalist, Non-Deadline Writing

Tom French, 29, was born in Columbus, Ohio, and lived all over Indiana. He graduated in journalism from Indiana University in 1980. He joined the *St. Petersburg Times* in 1981 as a police reporter. Later he covered courts and politics. In 1985, he moved to the newsfeatures section, where he serves as a general assignment reporter.

The *St. Petersburg Times* grants its star writers time and space, and French's stories justify the investment. He reports in great depth, and selects his materials carefully. His stories succeed largely because of profound empathy and electric storytelling.

This prize-winning series, "A Cry in the Night," earned the legendary endorsement of readers: they met the delivery trucks to read the first copies.

A cry in the night
Part 1: The murder

SEPTEMBER 28, 1986

Much later, after nearly two years of searching for her killer, after the interviews at the station and the re-enactments in the dark and the lie-detector tests and the growing list of blind alleys and one sudden moment of stupid good luck— long after all of that, they finally arrested a man and charged him with rape and first-degree murder.

An investigator asked a neighbor:
Does he look like a murderer to you?
The neighbor said:
What does a murderer look like?

***

May 22, 1984, was a Tuesday. That evening, it was warm, and it was raining. Karen Gregory, a 36-year-old graphic artist, was moving some belongings from her apartment on the beach to a house in Gulfport.

The house was white and had a couple of big shady oak trees in the yard. It sat on the north-west corner of 27th Avenue S. and Upton Street, facing 27th Avenue. It was surrounded by a quiet neighborhood that had a citizens' crime watch program and that was filled largely with people in their 50s and older.

The house was owned by Karen Gregory's boyfriend, David Mackey. After dating David for a year, Karen was moving in with him. David was an administrator of a counseling program for Vietnam veterans. That night, as Karen moved some of her belongings into his house, he was in Providence, R.I., speaking at a training conference for other counselors.

Karen had been invited for dinner with a close friend, Neverne Covington. At about 8 p.m., after Karen finished moving for the night, she went to Neverne's house, and the two women ate. Afterward, they drank white wine. Neverne remembers the brand—Robert Mondavi Muscadet D'Oro—because she has not been able to bring herself to buy a bottle since.

The two women talked for hours. They talked about how much Karen liked her job, how excited she was about moving in with David, how she felt things were going right in her life. They talked about going windsurfing. They cracked silly jokes.

"We were very happy," Neverne remembered later. "We were laughing a lot."

Finally, sometime roughly between midnight and 1 a.m., Karen left for her new home in Gulfport.

A short while later, neighbors heard a cry.

Arthur Kuiper, who lived up the street, behind Karen and David's house, was reading in bed when he heard a short, single, agonizing scream. He looked at a clock. It was exactly 1:15 a.m. He got out of bed, turned off the light, and looked out the window. He didn't see anything, but just to make sure, he stood there for another 15 minutes or so, waiting to hear anything else. The neighborhood was quiet.

Martha Borkowski, who lived across the street from the house, was having trouble sleeping when she heard the scream and, immediately afterward, the slamming of a door. The scream was loud and clear, but to Mrs. Borkowski it did not sound like the cry of someone in trouble.

"When I heard it, it just went through my mind that that girl does not smoke because her lungs were so incredible," she said.

Glenda Harness, who lived on the southeast corner of 27th Avenue and Upton Street, was asleep. She heard the scream, looked out the window, and saw an old man, one of her neighbors, standing across the street in his doorway, looking out. Glenda went to the kitchen and looked out behind her house toward the garage, where George Lewis, her live-in boyfriend and a firefighter for the city of St. Petersburg, often worked late into the night.

The garage light was off, and Glenda couldn't see George. Thinking he might have gone out to check on the scream, Glenda grew frightened and sat at a table with her arms around her knees, waiting for George to come back. She was so afraid, she couldn't move. About 20 minutes later, George walked in. He said he'd heard the scream, too, and they talked about it, then went to bed.

Since it was a warm night, many of the neighbors had their windows open. More than a dozen of them heard the scream. None called the police.

Some of them, as they heard it, explained it away. They decided it was animals fighting, or people fighting, or a neighborhood nuisance, or kids getting rowdy.

"But it really wasn't that type of scream," one recalled. "It was—well—I'll never forget it, anyhow."

One man stepped into his front doorway to see what was wrong—he was the one Glenda Harness saw from her window—but his wife, police learned, apparently grabbed him and made him go back inside.

***

Early the next evening, more than 15 hours after the scream, Martha Borkowski, the neighbor from across the street, returned home from work. She noticed that the front door of David and Karen's house—a jalousie door that led onto a porch—was open. She didn't think anything of it, though. That door was often open.

An hour or so later, Peter Kumble drove up to the house in a van. Peter was a draftsman who in his spare time was host of a weekly bluegrass show on WMNF-FM. He was an acquaintance of Karen and David's. He had spoken to Karen a week or so before, he said, and she had invited him over for dinner that night. Peter had the impression David was going to be there as well.

Peter saw both David's and Karen's cars, but no one seemed to be home. He went to the front jalousie door, which was still ajar, as he later recalled. He knocked. When no one answered, he stepped onto the porch and knocked on the inside door. No one answered.

Peter waited for a few minutes, then left a note on the windshield of David's car and drove away. The note said: *Karen and David, Hello. Stopped by about 7:15 or so but saw no signs of life. Many to do tonight so I probably won't be back but I have something you wanted. Will be home not too late...Peter.*

***

That same evening, David Mackey tried to reach Karen. David was still in Rhode Island, and when he finished with the day's work, he tried calling Karen at home. There was no answer. He called again later, several times. Still there was no answer.

By midnight David was worried. He called Anita Kilpatrick, the woman with whom Karen had shared the apartment on the beach, and asked her if she'd seen Karen. Anita said no. She said maybe Karen had gone up to see her sister Kim, who lived in Dunedin.

David called Kim's home. Karen wasn't there.

***

The next morning, Thursday, David called Karen again. He phoned early, around 7:30, so he wouldn't miss her before she left for work. No answer. He called again. No answer.

At about 8 a.m., David called Datacom Associates, the firm where Karen worked. Karen's boss told him Karen hadn't shown up for work that day, nor the day before.

David called Anita Kilpatrick again. He was upset now. Anita also knew something wasn't right. Karen was not the type to skip work. David told Anita he was going to call one of the neighbors to see if anything was wrong. He'd call back.

Anita started calling police departments and hospitals to find out if there'd been an accident. None knew anything about a Karen Gregory. Anita waited for David to call back. She sat down on her couch, and suddenly these pictures entered her mind. She saw Karen struggling with a man, pushing and fighting with a man who was taller than she. Then she saw Karen lying on the floor. Anita pushed the pictures out of her mind, told herself she was dreaming. She tried to read the paper but couldn't keep her mind on it. She kept reading the same sentence over and over. She got up from the couch and started pacing.

David, meanwhile, was calling Amy Bressler, a neighbor who lived just up the street from his house. He asked Ms. Bressler if she could look out the window and tell if Karen's car—a white VW Rabbit—was there in the yard. Ms. Bressler looked over and saw the Rabbit in the driveway.

David was sure something was terribly wrong. He asked Ms. Bressler if she would go over and check on the house. He wanted to stay on the line.

Ms. Bressler went over to the house and knocked on a side door. No answer. She walked around to the front jalousie door, where she noticed broken glass that had been busted out of the door and scattered along the walkway. She knocked on that door. No answer.

She walked around toward the back and noticed that a bedroom window was open. She called out.

"Karen?"

No answer. There was a small slit in the screen—it had been there as long as David had owned the house—and Ms. Bressler put her hand through the slit and pushed back the curtains. She saw that the bed was unmade. She looked to the right and saw a woman lying on the floor in the hallway. The angle allowed her to see only the lower half of the woman's body, but she assumed it was Karen. She saw what looked like dried blood on the body.

"Karen?"

The woman didn't move. Ms. Bressler ran back to her house and picked up the phone. She was crying.

"Something really horrible has happened," she told David. "I don't know what it is."

She said she had to call the police. David hung up. He waited a few minutes, as long as his patience would let him, then dialed the number at his house. A Gulfport police officer answered the phone. David asked what had happened to Karen. The officer hesitated, then said:

"She's dead, sir."

***

After her murder, Karen Gregory's father wrote a letter to a judge.

"I will never understand," he said, "why this savage violation of her small body had to happen."

Karen had thick brown hair, olive skin, and eyes of such a penetrating blue that one friend describes them as being "crystalline clear... unadulterated by any other color." She wasn't really that small—she was about 5 feet 5 and trim. She wore little or no makeup. She liked to call some of her friends "sweetheart" or "honey" in a half-affectionate, half-silly way.

She was a vegetarian. She made a mean batch of *baklava*. She would not miss the film *Black Orpheus* if it played anywhere within driving distance. She had a fondness for socks, possibly because she'd lived before in the cold of New England. She loved to talk long-distance with her friends and would rack up phone bills that rivaled her rent checks. She liked to begin outlandish stories with declarations.

"Honey," she'd say, "you're not going to believe this."

Though she was born Karen Marshall, she had long since changed her name. In her 20s, after she was married and divorced, she decided to exchange her former husband's last name for another. She chose Gregory, her mother's maiden name.

Raised in Albany, N.Y., Karen was the oldest of four children. She had two brothers, one sister, and a habit of looking out for all of them in a maternal sort of way. "When she died," remembers Mark, the youngest of the four, "the feeling I kept getting was, 'Karen should be here. She'd know what to do.'"

The Marshall kids were extremely close. When they were younger, they talked about what they'd do if one of them died. Usually the answer was that such a thing would be unbearable, that there would be no reason to go on.

Not that they were always having such serious conversations. The four of them were all experienced storytellers who understood the fine art of embellishment. Roy, the older of the two brothers, was especially good at spinning wild accounts of childhood folly. He'd get rolling, and Karen would laugh so hard she would have to beg him to stop.

Karen was an artist. She had majored in art education in college, and later, while she was married, had taught art to elementary schoolchildren. After that, she had worked as a potter with a boyfriend in New Hampshire.

By January 1983, though, she was ready to move. She was still close friends with her boyfriend, but she wanted a change of scenery. So she left the snow of New England and moved with her brother Mark to Pinellas County. Mark later moved back north, but Karen stayed, eventually moving into an apartment with Anita on Pass-a-Grille Beach. To make ends meet, Karen waited tables at The Garden, a restaurant and bar in downtown St. Petersburg.

Karen had some fun with the job. On Halloween 1983, she showed up at work dressed as a frowsy, dime-store waitress straight out of the '50s. She'd made a little white apron and a little white cap, smeared on some red lipstick, stuffed a wad of gum in her mouth, and put on some of the strangest earrings to ever grace the planet.

"They looked like Sputnik," says her friend Neverne Covington.

But the best touch was the hair. Karen had sprayed it with this black gunk—gunk so fierce it stayed on the walls of her bathroom for months—and had piled her hair into a towering beehive. She had accidentally knocked it against her car when she was getting in, and this caused the beehive to lean at a 45-degree angle.

After she got off work, Karen—still in costume, still with the tilting beehive—went to a restaurant where Neverne and some other friends were eating. She strolled up to their table, snapping her fingers, chewing her gum, asking for their orders. Her friends did one of those cartoon double takes. Says Neverne: "We didn't even recognize her."

That was Karen. She had this animated, exaggerated way about her. She could run rings around people just talking to them. She'd slow down, speed up, go into reverse, then bulldoze straight ahead with the punch line. Her style was so distinctive that Anita Kilpatrick, her roommate, could do an imitation of her. Anita, remembers Neverne, would put her hands on her hips, throw her shoulders forward, and make one of those declarations:

"Now listen to this."

It was perfect. It was Karen.

***

Karen liked it in Pinellas County. She loved the beach, loved the sun, could ride her bicycle for miles in the heat as if it were nothing. She was crazy about reggae music, and at night, she'd pop a tape into a little portable cassette player and dance through the rooms of her apartment. Some nights, she lived on the phone, talking long-distance for hours with her friends up north, making GTE rich.

After she moved down here, the friends sent her a present: a sleek, black telephone. It was well-made. It could weather epic conversations. She loved it.

Karen was something of a specialist in the art of friendship. She was loyal, she was intense, she was not afraid of looking foolish in the pursuit of a good laugh. Once she got close to someone, she worked hard to see that nothing—not distance, not a difference of opinion—came between them. She didn't own many things, didn't have a lot of money. What she cared about were her family and friends.

One of the people Karen cared most about was David Mackey. She liked him right from the start. The day she met David, back in March 1983, she went home and told her brother Mark all about him. She debated aloud whether or not to call him. She was like a schoolgirl, Mark says.

Finally Karen decided to call. She left a message on David's answering machine, and they had a date. Soon the two of them were going out regularly. They were a certified couple.

"Have you seen David?" people were saying. "David's in love."

They were both in love. They talked about going abroad together. They talked about the possibility of marriage. "We had plans," says David, now 32, "to make a life together."

The two of them were always doing special things for each other. For Christmas 1983, Karen spent weeks making David a jacket. This was no ordinary jacket. It was reversible and had a patchwork of different colors and all sorts of zippers and pockets. Karen had no pattern; she just plowed ahead and hoped for the best. She worked on a table in her apartment. She wouldn't let David come over for fear he'd see. Often, she sewed past midnight, and time and again, she had to rip up the seams and start over. It gave Anita a headache just to watch.

In March 1984, David threw Karen a surprise party for her 36th birthday. As it happened, Anita had also been planning a birthday party, and she was disappointed when she didn't get to surprise Karen. That was how strongly people felt about her.

It was a happy time. Karen quit her job at The Garden, and in May, she started working as a graphic artist at Datacom. The job was challenging, and Karen loved it. Her relationship with David, meanwhile, was getting even more serious. They'd recently decided she should move into his house in Gulfport. She'd begun loading her things into the Rabbit and making trips from the apartment to the house, moving in bit by bit.

On the evening of May 22, 1984, Karen was almost finished. She went to the apartment, loaded up the car again, then left Anita a note. The note, which Anita would later save and keep in her wallet, ended like this:

See you soon. Love, K.

One of the things Karen was moving that night was her plant collection. She'd complained that David did not have any plants in his house, did not have anything living or growing there. She wanted to fix that, straight from the start.

***

At first, on that Thursday morning in May 1984, the police did not know there had been a murder. When neighbor Amy Bressler peered through the bedroom window, she could not tell for certain whether the woman lying on the floor was dead. At 8:39 a.m., approximately 31 hours after the neighbors had heard the scream, she called the Gulfport police dispatcher and reported what is referred to as a "nonresponsive person."

Ms. Bressler was waiting in the street in front of her house when an officer drove up a few minutes later. The paramedics arrived at almost the same moment. They went around to the back bedroom window, saw the body, and removed the screen. The officer crawled inside, walked through the living room and onto the front porch. She unlocked and opened the front jalousie door for the others.

Karen was lying on her left side in the hallway. She had been stabbed repeatedly in the neck. Her head had been either beaten with or shoved against a hard object. There were handprints, marked in blood, on her lower back and one of her legs.

From that moment, things happened quickly. The officer called her supervisor. The house was closed off with yellow police tape. A line of law enforcement officials started arriving. There were uniformed officers and detectives and the chief of police and a couple of people from the State Attorney's office and a couple more from the Medical Examiner's office. Some of them looked through the three-bedroom house, trying to find out what had happened.

All the lights were off. But in the northwest bedroom, the one in the back into which Amy Bressler and the officer had peered, a box fan was sitting on the floor. It was still blowing.

Blood was found in much of the house. In the northwest bedroom, there was some on the bed and on the sill and curtains of the window the officer had crawled through. In the hallway where Karen's body had been found, there was some on the walls and in the carpet. In the bathroom, there was some on the tile floor. On that floor, in the blood, was a bare footprint.

Out on the front porch, there were a few drops on the floor. There was a hole in the panes of the jalousie door, and around the hole were some brown hairs. The broken glass from the door was strewn along the front walkway, all the way to the curb. Not far away, the note left by Peter Kumble was still sitting on the windshield of David Mackey's car.

One of the people who looked inside the house was Dr. Joan Wood, the county's medical examiner. Dr. Wood is what many people would call a coroner, and when she arrived, it was her opinion that the officers of the Gulfport Police Department needed help. She didn't think they had the experience to handle this murder alone.

Dr. Wood knew Gulfport pretty well. She had once lived in this neighborhood, not far from the house. She knew it had been a long time since the city's police department had been faced with a murder such as this one, a murder where the killer was unknown. She told Herman Golliner, the chief of police, that as far as she could remember, the last time Gulfport had had such a murder was back in 1961. Chief Golliner, who was 57 and had been with the department for almost 25 years, said yes, he remembered that case. He'd been a patrol officer then.

Dr. Wood said she wanted to call in the FDLE, the Florida Department of Law Enforcement. The FDLE had a blood-spatter expert, someone who can study the patterns and shapes blood makes as it spills during an attack and then offer a theory as to what has happened. Dr. Wood told Lt. Frank Hanson, who was in charge of the investigation, that she wanted the FDLE to take over what's known as "processing the crime scene"—collecting evidence from the house.

Lt. Hanson, who had been with the Gulfport police more than 20 years himself, wasn't thrilled with the idea. "Call somebody else if you want to," he said. "But, hell, I can take fingerprints just like anybody else can."

Realistically, Hanson knew Gulfport was a small department, with only about 20 officers. He knew they'd be busy enough starting the door-to-door interviews with neighbors, not to mention the normal duties of the department.

So the FDLE office in Tampa was called, and two crime scene analysts came over and started work—taking photographs, dusting for fingerprints, searching for hairs, gathering items from around the house.

***

Outside the house, neighbors and others were standing around, watching the police work. Among them was Anita Kilpatrick, Karen's roommate from the apartment on the beach.

That morning, after she'd heard from David Mackey and had called hospitals and police stations trying to find Karen, Anita had waited anxiously for David to call again.

The phone had finally rung at about 9 a.m. It was David. He sounded strange. He was struggling to speak. He said Anita's name, then repeated it. When Anita heard him, heard that sound in his voice, she felt as if something in her stomach was swallowing her from inside. She wanted to hang up and pretend the phone had never rung.

David said: "Karen...is...dead."

Anita began screaming at David. She demanded to know why would he say such a thing, why was he telling her that. David tried to calm her. He asked her—and two years later, Anita would remember these words and their kindness—if there was someone who could be with her.

Anita called Michaela Jarvis, a friend of hers and an acquaintance of Karen's. Anita and Michaela worked together—they were both freelance writers for the *St. Petersburg Times*—and they were neighbors. One of them called the police station, and the dispatcher said that if they wanted any information, they would have to go to Karen's house, where the investigating officers were working. So Anita and Michaela drove over.

It was a warm, sunny day. As they drove, Anita had the sense that everything around her was floating, that nothing was fixed. She had the sense that time had begun to flip-flop and play games on her.

"God," she said as they waited for a stoplight. "Haven't we been on this road for hours?"

When they pulled up to Karen's house, they saw the police officers and the yellow tape. Anita didn't know what to do. She and Michaela sat on the curb, got up, walked around. They cried in each other's arms.

Anita saw one of the neighbors, a man with a dog. He seemed to be trying to find out what was going on. Anita asked him if he'd heard anything the night of the murder. The man said yes, he'd heard a scream.

"And you called the police, right?" said Anita.

The man said no. He'd only heard the one scream and had not known what it was. What was he supposed to do, he said, call the police and report a single cry in the night?

Anita heard people laughing inside the house. They were laughing so hard that to her it seemed the walls were shaking. Anita knew that people who deal regularly with tragedy sometimes protect themselves from it in odd ways. After all, she worked at a newspaper, and she'd heard the jokes some journalists make about horrible events. But that morning, when she heard the people laughing uproariously as they stood close to Karen's body, Anita wondered what could be so funny.

She overheard one of the officers say that Kim, Karen's sister, was coming to the house to identify the body. Anita knew Kim lived in Dunedin. Anita volunteered to identify the body instead, so Kim would not have to make a long drive. The police said no, Kim was already on the way.

A short while later, Kim and her husband arrived. Kim walked toward the house. She looked numb. In a flat, emotionless voice, she told an officer she was Karen's sister.

"The best thing you can do," the officer said, "is to go home and wait to hear from us."

Kim explained to him that the police had called and asked her to come down to identify her sister's body.

"The best thing you can do," the officer repeated, "is to go home and wait to hear from us."

Kim turned around, got back in the car with her husband, and drove away.

At some point in the day, two men drove up in a gray station wagon and got out with a stretcher. Anita and Michaela realized they knew who the men were. The previous night, a plane had crashed off the beach where the women lived. The pilot and a passenger had been killed, and Anita and Michaela had seen two men wheeling away the bodies on stretchers.

These were the same two men. Only now, they had come to take away Karen.

A few minutes later, the two men wheeled out Karen's body. It was in a bag, but as the stretcher jiggled, Anita saw movement inside the bag and suddenly had the notion that if she could just hug Karen and take her away from there, everything would be all right.

Eventually, one of the FDLE analysts came out of the house. She asked Anita and Michaela if they'd known Karen. The analyst told them she'd been able to get a sense of what Karen had been like from the way the house was decorated. She told them that even though Karen had been murdered, she'd looked as if she were only sleeping there on the carpet. There were tears in the analyst's eyes.

Anita asked who was going to clean up the house. The analyst, Anita said, explained that she and her partner were done, and they weren't going to do it. Neither were the police. Whoever owned the house would probably clean up, she said.

Anita was stunned. She knew David was flying back that afternoon from Rhode Island. She did not want him to have to see such a thing. She decided to clean the house herself.

***

Anita and Michaela drove to Anita's apartment, gathered some paper towels and spray cleaner and headed back to Gulfport. When they arrived, it was around midafternoon. The police were taking down the yellow tape and getting ready to leave. Lt. Hanson was standing in the front doorway.

Anita asked him if she and Michaela could go inside and clean. He motioned with his hand.

Go ahead, he said.

Anita and Michaela knew Karen had been murdered. But they did not know how prolonged and violent the struggle had been. When they stepped inside and saw what Karen had gone through, they began sobbing. Still crying, they began to clean their friend's blood from the walls. As she worked, Anita kept thinking about Karen and how her body had lain there after the murder, alone in the dark for two nights.

By this time, children were running up to the house, trying to look in. Cars were driving by slowly. Every time they heard one, Anita and Michaela stopped and looked up. They were by themselves in the house. They were afraid. Karen's murderer was still out there. How could they be sure he wouldn't come back? They closed all the windows, locked the front door, and went back to work.

Not long after that, some police officers came in. Anita had the impression these officers were there not on business, but to gawk. They walked through the house, speculating about the murder. They talked about how the attacker had probably "finished her off" in the hallway. They looked through photos of Karen and her friends. They did not speak to Anita or Michaela. They acted, Anita felt, as if the two women weren't there. And like almost everyone else that day, they kept referring to "the body" or "the victim." Anita heard them and thought Karen was neither one of those things. She was Karen.

After the officers left, Michaela had to stop cleaning. She told Anita she was sorry, but she couldn't do it anymore. She went out to the porch. Shortly afterward, she called out that a car had arrived. It was David Mackey and his brother, who had picked him up at the airport.

Anita stopped working. She'd done what she could, but there hadn't been enough time to clean up all the blood. She went outside and hugged David on the steps. She told him what she'd done, tried to prepare him for how bad things looked inside. David thanked Anita and said he was glad she was there. Then he went inside.

David looked around the house without saying a word. He stood there for a few moments, wrapped in solitude, taking everything in. Then he collected some clean clothes and left for the police station. Detectives needed to talk with him.

Anita and Michaela also left. They went back to Anita's apartment, the apartment that had once been Karen's. They were still afraid, and when the sun went down, their fear grew. They pulled a foldout bed out of the couch and spent the night awake, crying and holding each other tight and listening for sounds outside.

***

That Thursday, as they questioned neighbors, the Gulfport police officers soon realized how many people had heard Karen scream. A detective told one neighbor from across the street that she was the sixth person they'd talked with already who had heard the cry and who had not called the police. The neighbor said she was sorry.

The police officers already knew one of Karen's neighbors. George Lewis, the St. Petersburg firefighter who lived catty-corner across from her house, was also a volunteer firefighter for Gulfport.

When the police went to his house, George was at work. He went to the police station later that day and wrote out his recollection of what had happened the night of the murder.

He'd been working in the garage, he said, listening to the radio. He'd heard the scream. He'd looked up and down the street and had not seen anything suspicious. Late the next day, though, he had seen someone in a van—it turned out to be Peter Kumble—pull up to Karen's house.

The police were still trying to understand what had happened inside the house. With the assistance of the FDLE expert, they soon developed some theories about the path of the struggle. One was that Karen had gone to the front door, let someone in, and then fought with him from the porch to the bedroom and finally into the hall where her body was found. Another was that someone had been waiting for Karen inside the house when she came home.

Though there was never total agreement on any one theory, the Gulfport detectives eventually decided it was most likely that Karen had been stabbed first in the bedroom, then had escaped her attacker and had run onto the front porch, where she fell or was pushed against the jalousie door, knocking her head through the glass. Then, according to this theory, her attacker had forced her back inside, struggled with her further, and then stabbed her again in the hallway.

The detectives thought they knew how the attacker had left the house. The blood on the windowsill and curtains in the back bedroom told them he'd probably left through that window.

They weren't certain how he'd entered the house. They doubted it was the window. After all, the screen had been found in place, latched at the top. Sgt. Larry Tosi, one of the detectives on the case, explained later that it would have been awkward for the attacker to crawl through there, with the screen dragging along his back. They thought he might have forced his way through the door to the living room. But they weren't sure.

Something else confused Tosi and the other detectives. There had been a terrible struggle, late at night, with two people moving from one end of the house to the other. But the police had found nothing knocked over. There was a telephone and a fan on the floor in the back bedroom, and a nightstand with a lamp next to the bed, and stacks of records in the living room. All were in place.

Yet the police had found the lights turned off, suggesting that the struggle might have taken place in the dark. That didn't seem logical. Fighting with Karen in total darkness, the attacker would have had a hard time not knocking anything over.

Thursday night, after Karen's body was found, Tosi and another detective went back to the house, turned off all the lights, let their eyes adjust to the dark, then looked around to see if there was enough visibility to move without bumping into things. There was a streetlight on the corner outside, but that didn't shine much light inside. Without the lights, the house was extremely dark.

A light had to have been on, Tosi decided.

But that also seemed unusual to the detectives. It would seem unusual to anyone who saw the houses in that neighborhood and how close together they are. If someone were going to commit a murder in there, chasing through the house after a victim, why would he leave a light on and risk giving the neighbors a view of what was happening?

There was one more thing. On Wednesday, after Karen had been killed but before her body had been found, Mrs. Borkowski had noticed that the front door was open. It had still been open— or at least unlocked—when Peter Kumble had stopped by an hour or so later. Yet when the police arrived the next morning, the door was closed and locked.

The murderer, it appeared, had been back.

***

The same night, another detective, William Brinkworth, went to the house to search through Karen's belongings for names, addresses, any kind of lead. He had just opened a drawer in one of the bedrooms, he said, when the phone rang.

Brinkworth picked it up. It was Peter Kumble. He wanted to speak to Karen.

Brinkworth identified himself and said, as he later recalled, that there had been an "occurrence." He said the police were investigating a crime and Karen was unable to come to the phone. He took down Peter's name and address, hung up, and went back to searching through Karen's belongings.

Peter was shaken. He called his girlfriend.

Make sure your doors are locked, he said.

A cry in the night
Part 2: Fear, frustration

SEPTEMBER 29, 1986

The man said: Is this Karen Gregory?

Anita Kilpatrick, Karen's friend and former roommate, looked at the pale face before her. She knew she was expected to give an answer. She could not speak. Finally she said yes and began to cry. Standing beside her, Peter Kumble also said yes.

It was Friday, May 25, 1984, the day after Karen's body had been discovered. Peter, an acquaintance of Anita's, had called her after he'd learned about the murder. He had mentioned to her he was leaving later that day for a two-week vacation in the Northeast, and Anita had asked if she could ride with him.

Karen's funeral was going to be held in Albany, N.Y., and Anita wanted to be there. So she asked Peter to give her a lift. Peter said all right. Before they left that day, Peter and Anita stopped at the Medical Examiner's office in Largo. Anita had already agreed to identify Karen's body, and the office said a second person was needed as well. Peter was hesitant to accept such a responsibility, but he agreed to do it.

Making the identification was upsetting for both of them. Until that moment, Peter said, he had not known Karen had been stabbed.

After they were done, Anita and Peter talked with Sgt. Larry Tosi, a Gulfport detective. They sat at a table. As they spoke, Tosi noticed a scratch on Peter's right hand. Tosi didn't know if Peter saw him looking at the scratch, but Peter took his hand off the table, then put it back. Tosi asked him to check in with the police after he got back from his vacation. Peter said sure.

Then he and Anita left for the drive up north. It took one and a half days. Anita was a nervous

wreck. She hadn't slept. She was afraid. Every
time she closed her eyes, she saw someone hurting Karen. Anita did not know who had killed
her friend. She was looking at the men around
her in a way she never had before.

I'm a little jumpy, she told Peter.

I understand, he said.

***

Over the years, Gulfport police officers have
dealt with their share of speeders, burglars, and
neighborhood nuisances. But when it comes to
finding murderers, they are not the most
experienced officers in the world. That's because
in Gulfport, murders are relatively rare. St.
Petersburg averages about 20 or 22 homicides
every year. Karen Gregory's case, as far as Lt.
Frank Hanson could recall, was only the fourth
homicide in Gulfport in more than 20 years.

Lt. Hanson was supervising the Gregory case.
He, Sgt. Tosi, and the other detectives doubted
that the motive in Karen's murder had been
burglary. It had been raining hard the night
Karen was killed, and it seemed unlikely any
burglars would be out prowling. Moreover,
nothing appeared to be missing from the house.
During the autopsy, however, Dr. Joan Wood, the
county's medical examiner, had determined that
intercourse had occurred about the time Karen
was killed.

The detectives worked on the assumption
Karen had been raped. Since they had found no
definite signs of anyone breaking into the house,
they also believed the attacker might have been
someone she knew.

Sgt. Tosi, meanwhile, was hearing about the
case both at work and at home. He and his wife
were friends with George Lewis and Glenda
Harness, the couple who lived catty-corner across
the street from Karen Gregory's house. George
was a St. Petersburg firefighter who also worked
as a volunteer for the Gulfport Fire Department.

On the night of the murder, George had explained to the police, he had been working in his garage and had heard a scream and looked outside for anything suspicious. Glenda had heard the scream too, and shortly after the body had been found, she was over at Tosi's house, talking to Mrs. Tosi about what had happened.

Glenda had heard the scream while she was in bed. She had gotten up and looked outside toward the garage for George. She hadn't been able to see him, and she'd grown worried, wondering if George had gone out to check on the sound. Glenda told Mrs. Tosi that George had been gone for the longest time, and while she waited for him, she said, she'd seen a silhouette in the backyard by her window. Tosi, who occasionally stopped by George's house to chat, later asked him about the silhouette. George told him Glenda had mentioned it, but that the silhouette hadn't been his.

A week after the investigation began, Tosi left for a month-long vacation. He went to the Smoky Mountains in Tennessee and tried to get his mind off the murder. Lt. Hanson left the case largely in the hands of another detective, William Brinkworth. Brinkworth had been a police officer for years, but he had only recently become a detective. He had never investigated a homicide. He thought he needed help.

"It was my first one, and I was kind of stumbling through it," he said. "But I was trying the best I could."

Brinkworth was reluctant to ask Hanson for guidance with the investigation. To Brinkworth, the lieutenant seemed wrapped up in other cases and duties and did not seem to want to give him too much advice. So Brinkworth turned to two homicide detectives with the St. Petersburg police. They walked with him through Karen Gregory's house, theorizing on what could be learned from the evidence. And at one point, when Brinkworth was interviewing someone, one of the detectives sat in and asked questions.

From the start, there had been no shortage of suspects. Karen Gregory was a charismatic woman with many friends and acquaintances, and that had increased the number of men who knew her and could conceivably have been her murderer. In the weeks that followed her death, fingerprints—and sometimes palm prints and hair samples—were taken from at least 10 men.

Among the suspects:

• A man who had regularly cut the lawn at the house Karen had shared with her boyfriend, David Mackey. The police did a background check on the lawn man and found that he had a record of violence. When the police interviewed him, the man said he'd mowed the lawn at that house about a week before the murder but had not talked with Karen.

• A man who had once threatened someone with a knife at the Bay Pines Veterans Administration Medical Center. David Mackey was an administrator of a counseling program for Vietnam veterans at Bay Pines, and several years before, David had counseled this man. Once David had been called out to a house where the man was threatening to kill himself. David told the police that the man had not even known Karen and that he didn't think he had anything to do with the murder.

• A man who knew Karen from when she was a waitress at The Garden, a restaurant in downtown St. Petersburg. The man had expressed a romantic interest in Karen. An engineer who was part-owner of a woodworking shop, the man said he had once invited her to the shop to listen to some speakers. But during the week of Karen's murder, he said, he'd been working on the East Coast. The police checked and found that was correct.

• A man who was accused of abducting and raping a woman in the Tyrone area. According to the St. Petersburg police, who had arrested him, the man also had carried a knife and had stabbed the woman repeatedly. The man told the police he did not know Karen, and when Brinkworth saw the knife used in the Tyrone assault, he didn't believe its dimensions matched the kind of wounds found on Karen's body.

***

The person who attracted the most attention, however, was Peter Kumble, Karen's acquaintance and the man who had given Anita Kilpatrick a ride up north for the funeral.

Months later, the police would decide that Peter was innocent and no longer a suspect. But in the early days of the investigation, several things made the detectives consider him. To begin with, they knew Peter was the one whom George Lewis had seen drive up to Karen's house after she was murdered but before her body had been discovered. That evening, Peter had stepped across the broken glass that was scattered on the front walkway and walked onto the front porch. Hadn't he noticed the glass, the detectives wondered. Didn't he have a clue something was wrong?

Then there were those phrases in the note he had left on David Mackey's car: *Stopped by... saw no signs of life... I have something you wanted.*

Peter also had that scratch on his hand, a scratch that might have been made during a struggle. In addition, he had helped Anita Kilpatrick identify Karen's body at the Medical Examiner's office. Peter had not been eager to identify the body. He had been asked to do it. But for some reason, Brinkworth had the impression that Peter had offered to do it.

"To me," said Brinkworth, "that is a little out of the ordinary."

***

On the Monday following the murder, after Anita had arrived in Albany, N.Y., for the funeral, she had gone to the house of Karen's brothers, Roy and Mark. They were just leaving for Karen's wake when the phone rang. It was Sgt. Tosi. He wanted to speak to Anita.

Tosi, who had not yet left for his vacation, asked Anita if Peter Kumble was there. She said no. He asked where Peter was. Boston. Had she noticed the scratch on his hand? Yes.

Anita, as she would later recall the conversation, asked Tosi why he was going through these questions. She paused, then asked if Peter was a suspect.

Tosi sort of mumbled something.

Anita said: *Is Peter a suspect?*

Tosi said: Yes.

Anita began to tremble. She felt as though she'd been slapped. She had made a long trip, alone in a van, with a murder suspect. She thought about how Peter had seemed impatient with her on the trip when she'd taken the time to call friends. She thought about how they'd stopped for several hours one night at a rest stop, about how she'd sat there, shaking with fear in the dark while Peter slept.

Anita could not know that Peter would eventually be dropped as a suspect. That was months away. So when Tosi called, she thought back on those details of the trip and suddenly they took on new significance. She passed her observations along to the police.

Two weeks later, when Peter returned to Pinellas County from his vacation, he found that the police were investigating him. Officers had been asking ominous questions about him at the firm where he worked as a draftsman. Why had Peter suddenly left town? He hadn't, said his co-workers, explaining that Peter had been planning his vacation for some time. Was he a violent man? No, they said.

Similar questions were asked of Peter's housemate and his girlfriend. Both said Peter was a calm, loving person, someone who was not at all violent.

Does he ever get mad, a detective asked.

Well, yes, said Peter's housemate. Doesn't everybody?

Peter was asked to go to the Gulfport police station to give his fingerprints and to talk with Brinkworth and another detective. They asked where he'd gotten the scratch on his hand. Working on his van, Peter said. What was the "something" he wanted to give Karen and had mentioned in his note? It was a reggae tape—Peter Tosh's *Bush Doctor*—that he'd borrowed from her. Where had he been the Tuesday night Karen was murdered? He'd worked on his van at home, then gone to bed at about 11.

Why had he gone to Karen's house the next evening? He'd had a dinner invitation from her, and he'd had the impression David would be there as well. Had he noticed the broken glass on the front walkway? No.

Brinkworth found it hard to believe that Peter had not noticed the glass. It would have almost certainly crunched under his feet. Brinkworth didn't know if Peter had any romantic intentions toward Karen, but he did believe Peter liked her as more than a friend.

As Peter sat there in the station, he felt as if Brinkworth and the other detective were asking loaded questions, then watching him to gauge his reactions. They seemed to be fishing. Peter was confused. He wasn't sure, he later explained, that he was seriously being considered as a suspect. He had explained to the police why he'd gone over to the house. He had explained where he'd been the night of the murder.

After the detectives let him go, Peter told his girlfriend the kinds of questions they'd asked. Surely, he said, they didn't really think he had killed Karen?

Stop being so naive, said his girlfriend. Get a lawyer.

***

One week after Karen's body was found, the *Gulfport Gabber*, the local newspaper, reported that the police were looking for leads in the case. Anyone with a tip was asked to call Sgt. Tosi or Detective Brinkworth at the station. In the same issue, the newspaper also ran "Gulfport Gabs," one of those columns where a question is posed to several people on the street and then their pictures and answers are published.

The question in this issue was: "Do you think Neighborhood Crime Watch is effective?"

The answer from the people on the street was "Yes."

"People watch their neighbors' homes and will contact the police if anything is wrong," said one woman. "I know I would and expect others to do it for me."

As it happened, there was such a program in the neighborhood where Karen had been killed. There was even a sign across the street from her house, in George Lewis's yard. It said: *Warning. This is a citizens' crime watch area.*

None of that had helped Karen. Neighbors all around the house had heard a scream, but not one had called the police. Shortly afterward, Neverne Covington, one of Karen's closest friends, wrote a letter to the *St. Petersburg Times.* In the letter, Neverne explained how Karen had screamed and no one had done anything about it. Neverne said she was screaming now for Karen, who no longer had a voice. Neverne said she was screaming at the apathy of the neighbors. She said she was screaming at the injustice of what had happened.

The letter was never published, though. Neverne was afraid of having her name printed.

Neverne had been in Boston for a wedding immediately after the murder, and she had not found out for several days what had happened. David Mackey had waited until after the wedding to tell her. He'd called her on that following Sunday, when Neverne was at a brunch at the house of the bride's parents. When David told her Karen had been killed, Neverne collapsed to the floor. Her body crumpled, she later described it, like an empty paper bag.

Afterward, Neverne—like others—was afraid of many things. At night, she would not drive by herself, would not go alone into her backyard to carry out the garbage. She took a self-defense class. After going to bed she got up repeatedly to make sure the doors were locked.

Neverne was a 33-year-old artist. She was not the type of person to scare easily. But Karen had come over to her house the night she was killed, and with the murderer not found, Neverne was forced to think in ways she had never thought before. No longer did she assume that the people around her meant no harm. No longer did she take it for granted that she would survive to see the end of the day.

One night, Neverne had a dream about Karen. In the dream, Karen was alive. Neverne saw her outside the pier in Gulfport and could not believe it. She told Karen she was supposed to be dead. Karen said no, she had gone to Texas to heal. She said she'd had to leave Gulfport, had to get away from everyone and everything, or she would have never gotten better. She showed where the wounds on her neck had begun to heal. Then Karen began walking away. When Neverne said she wanted to go with her, Karen said no.

"I'm sorry," she said. "But you can't come with me. You can't come here."

In her waking hours, Neverne was frustrated because she did not have the words to describe the feelings of fear and grief inside her. It was as if such words were part of another language. That summer, she painted a picture of an empty chair. She didn't think about it at the time, but weeks later, she realized that the chair in the picture was Karen's. Karen should have been sitting there.

Neverne also painted a picture of David Mackey, who was then staying with her and her boyfriend. The picture showed David sitting in front of a window. He was surrounded by bright, vibrant colors—sunshine was pushing through the blinds on the window—but his face had the weary look of someone in prolonged pain.

***

David, too, was dreaming about Karen. Many times the same thing happened. He and Karen would be near each other, but would not be able to communicate. Something—one time it was a wall of glass—kept coming between them.

Like Neverne, David was living in a new world. He became extremely concerned, sometimes obsessive, about the safety of his friends. He had trouble eating. He had trouble sleeping. At times, he doubted he would recover the ability to enjoy life.

David was 29. He had lost Karen. He had lost their future together. And he had lost the home they had planned to share. Karen had been murdered while he was out of town. When David returned and saw his house and how Karen had died, he had been overwhelmed by a sense of violation.

"It felt like the house had ceased to be my home," he said, "but was rather a house that simply contained some of my belongings."

David went back to the house occasionally, did some chores, tried to see if he could get used to being there. It was no good. He lived with friends for a while, then got an apartment in St. Petersburg. Eventually, he sold the Gulfport house.

***

Then there was Anita Kilpatrick. Anita, also 29, was afraid of the dark because Karen had died at night. She was afraid that the murderer might be hunting her because she knew the police thought Karen might have known the man who had killed her. For weeks after the murder, Anita stayed out of town, moving from Albany, N.Y., to Providence, R.I., to Montreal, hoping the detectives would find the killer and arrest him. One day, staying in someone's house in Providence, she heard footsteps in the hall—heavy footsteps, as if the person were wearing boots. Anita got down on her hands and knees and looked through the crack at the bottom of the door. She could see someone's feet outside.

Anita moved away from the door. She crawled under a bed and hid and waited until the person left. Later, she learned that it had probably been a woman who lived downstairs. The woman, she was told, wore clogs. That did not end the fear. The man who had killed Karen had not been arrested.

Eventually, Anita came back to Pinellas County. But the day she returned, something happened to upset her all over again. She had gone to the newsroom of the *St. Petersburg Times*, where she worked as a free-lance writer. A reporter saw her and walked up. The reporter said she was working on an article about Karen's case. She said the police had arrested a man but weren't giving out his name. She said she had the man's initials. She asked Anita if she could tell her the full name. Anita was stunned. She hadn't heard anything about an arrest. She called the Gulfport police and asked if it were true. The police said no. The reporter, Anita realized, had probably been bluffing to get information.

That night, Anita did not stay in her apartment. She called some friends who lived on the 18th floor of the Bayfront Tower, a high-rise in downtown St. Petersburg, and asked if she could stay with them. The building had a guard at the front door, and she felt safer there. But as the days passed, Anita remained terrified. She felt as if she were sinking. She called a friend who was living in Costa Rica and told him about her fear and paranoia. She asked if he thought she was crazy. The friend said no. He understood. He thought Anita should come to Costa Rica, where she'd be safe and could relax.

Anita stayed in Costa Rica for more than a month. She and the friend lived in a remote cabin. Anita knew there was almost no way anyone could have followed her there, but still that did not stop the fear. At night, she awoke screaming from dreams in which she saw Karen being killed, over and over.

It went on like that for weeks. Then, one night, Anita had a different dream, one that was similar to Neverne's. Karen came to Anita in this dream and assured her she was all right. Karen called her "honey," just as she had in real life. She said she wanted Anita to see that she'd healed, to stop worrying about her. Karen said she couldn't stay. Someone was with her. They had to go.

***

On June 1, 1984, when he left for his month-long vacation, Sgt. Tosi thought Karen's murder would be solved by the time he came back to work. Then the weeks rolled by, and June turned into July, and when Tosi returned there had been no arrest, despite the efforts of Detective Brinkworth.

Tosi was not pleased. The investigation, he felt, was disorganized. Peter Kumble had been a suspect before; he still was. Plus, other suspects were being considered.

Lt. Hanson wanted Tosi to take over the investigation. Tosi had been a detective for more than a decade; Brinkworth had been one for only a few months. In early July, Hanson told Brinkworth he was off the case.

Brinkworth had been working 12 or 14 hours a day on the investigation. He recognized that he was inexperienced, but that was why he'd sought the advice of the two St. Petersburg detectives. David Mackey and Karen's other friends were regularly calling in, asking questions, making sure Karen was not forgotten. But as far as Brinkworth knew, David was not unhappy with his work. David, in fact, did think highly of Brinkworth. David and Neverne Covington both felt he had worked hard on the case. They felt he had recognized their pain and had shown them compassion. David, Brinkworth knew, was also pleased that he had gone to the St. Petersburg police for help.

Inside the department, meanwhile, no one had told Brinkworth he was doing poorly. So when Hanson ordered him off the case, Brinkworth asked why. The lieutenant, Brinkworth said, told him not to ask any questions. The case was Tosi's.

While David Mackey and Neverne Covington had thought highly of Brinkworth, they liked Tosi, too. They thought he also treated them like human beings and was dedicated to finding the killer. They thought that he, like Brinkworth, cared about Karen.

At the time, Lawrence C. Tosi had been with the Gulfport police for 13 years. He was 39. He had brown eyes, a brown mustache, and brown hair that swept across his forehead. He was fairly short—"5-foot-6½ without shoes," he'd once said. He had a low voice that seemed to rumble from somewhere far away. His middle name was Constant. As he'd explain it, years later, he had become a police officer "to protect the innocent from aggression."

"The average person," Tosi said, "is just not aware of what actually goes on out here in the world.... People just don't know, they don't see as we do what human beings can do to one another. Especially in terms of physical violence."

By May 1984, when Karen Gregory was murdered, Tosi was one of the most experienced detectives in the department. He had spent many long nights looking after the innocent. He had even investigated a few homicides.

As he began working on the Gregory case again, though, Tosi felt there were more problems with the investigation than those he'd noticed within the Gulfport Police Department. He was also dissatisfied with the job the FDLE, the Florida Department of Law Enforcement, had done when Karen's body had been discovered. The FDLE had been given responsibility that day for processing the crime scene—collecting fingerprints, hairs, and other physical evidence from around the house. The Gulfport police had been ready to do it, but FDLE analysts had taken over the job after it had been suggested that they had expertise—specifically, in the study of bloodstains—the Gulfport police lacked.

Now, more than a month after the murder, Tosi felt the experts had messed up. He did not feel they'd been thorough enough.

Tosi was unhappy that the FDLE analysts had not vacuumed the house for hairs, fibers, and other evidence. Later that same day, the analysts had announced they were done and left. Since that presumedly meant that all the necessary evidence had been collected, the police had then allowed Anita Kilpatrick and a friend to clean up some of Karen's blood. By the time Tosi realized that the FDLE analysts had not done all they could have, then, the scene could no longer be returned to its original state. It had already been disturbed.

Lt. Hanson was also less than pleased with the FDLE's work. He told Tosi the analysts had found a good set of prints on the screen of the back bedroom window and had then seemed to slack off, apparently assuming the prints were from the intruder and were good enough to make an identification. The fact was, Hanson wished Gulfport—not the FDLE—had processed the scene.

(The FDLE analyst who was in charge of the processing that day in 1984 doesn't want to talk about such complaints while the court case is still pending. He does say, however, that he and his partner did collect important evidence at the scene.)

Another difficulty, one for which the FDLE could not be blamed, was that Karen Gregory's body had lain in the house for 31 hours before it had been discovered. The detectives didn't know if anyone could have arrived quickly enough to have saved Karen if the neighbors had called when they'd heard the scream. But if the police had arrived minutes after the murder, and not 31 hours, it would have been easier to find the killer. For one thing, he would not have had so much time to get away. He might even have still been there at the house. Then there were the bloody handprints that had been found on Karen's body. By the time the body was found, it was no longer possible to identify who had made the prints, no longer possible to see the distinguishing ridges that make every individual unique.

Tosi did know that the FDLE analysts had photographed a bare, bloody footprint on the tile floor of the bathroom. Shortly after he got back from vacation, Tosi said, he called the FDLE laboratory in Tampa and asked if it were possible to make a life-size photo from the negative, then see if it showed any visible ridges. According to Tosi, the FDLE lab told him to forget it, that the negative only showed a blotch of blood.

There is some disagreement over this account. Tosi says he spoke with a serologist—a blood expert—that day. The serologist says she does not remember the conversation. Further, she says, she would not have been the one to consider his request.

In any case, the photograph of the footprint was not made. Tosi pushed on. He talked to Karen Gregory's friends and ran down more leads. He and another detective also interviewed Peter Kumble again. By now, Peter realized how serious the situation was and had hired a lawyer. He did not like the questions the Gulfport detectives had been asking about him. He did not like the fact that they considered him a suspect in a brutal rape and murder. Still, he wanted to clear his name. So when he was asked to meet with Tosi and the other detective for another interview, Peter said yes. This time, though, his lawyer came with him.

The detectives asked Peter the same questions he'd been asked before. They got him to give them hairs from his head, chest, and pubic area. Finally, they told him once again that he could go.

The fingerprints and hairs that had been taken from the suspects were sent to the FDLE to be compared with the evidence collected at the house. But as the months passed, the laboratory comparisons still had not identified anyone as the murderer.

***

Unlike the police, Neverne Covington did not suspect Peter Kumble. From the start, Neverne had thought the killer was someone who lived in Karen's neighborhood. The police knew that whoever had done it had probably been covered with blood when he left the house. Neverne reasoned that only someone who didn't have far to go could escape undetected. Furthermore, she was troubled when the police told her that one of the neighbors had seen Peter Kumble stop by Karen's house the evening after the murder, before the body was discovered.

Neverne had a question. Who was paying such close attention to the house, she wondered, that he had noticed Peter? And if this neighbor was so attentive, why hadn't he called the police the night before when Karen had screamed in vain for her life?

A cry in the night
Part 3: Breakthrough

It was the fall of 1984. Months had passed, and still the police did not know who had killed Karen.

When the investigation began, Gulfport detectives had asked David Mackey, Karen's boyfriend, if he knew anyone who would have wanted to hurt her. David had said no. David also did not know anyone who would have wanted to hurt him by hurting Karen. Nor did he know of anyone who stood to gain much from Karen's death. She had not had a lot of money. She'd owned relatively few possessions. David had tried to think of any reason why someone would have wanted to harm her, and he had found none.

After the murder, it occurred to David that there are people in the world—more than he cared to think about—who have a capacity for terrible violence. It occurred to him that he could not simply look at these people and see that capacity in their faces. It occurred to him that he could not keep such people from hurting those he loved.

David, who had moved out of the house in Gulfport, often thought about Karen's murderer. He tried to imagine how the man lived with himself, tried to comprehend what this person had inside that allowed him to get through a day, knowing what he'd done. David wondered if the man would ever be caught.

Anita Kilpatrick, Karen's former roommate, had moved back into her apartment on the beach and had put a chain on the door. She was still afraid, especially when the sun went down. She was trying to get past her fear, but she still worried that the same man who had killed Karen might come for her, too. She felt helpless. She felt as if the man had taken Karen's life and was now controlling hers.

Neverne Covington, who had been a close friend of Karen's, was still afraid as well. Like David, it bothered her that she could not tell which people around her were capable of such violence. It bothered Neverne, as she put it, that her radar was broken. She did not feel protected anymore. She felt as though she were suffocating. She wondered if the world was a place of random, unpredictable acts.

Karen's death was changing other lives as well. In the neighborhood where Karen had been killed, one man now kept a gun close to his side. Another neighbor, a woman who had not really known Karen, turned around her sense of priorities. She decided to treat each day as if it might be her last. She sold her fast sports car. She bought a piece of island property she had always wanted.

In one of the houses across the street from where the murder had occurred, meanwhile, Martha Borkowski wrestled with her conscience. Mrs. Borkowski, a 48-year-old secretary, was among those who had heard Karen scream and had not called the police. To Mrs. Borkowski, the scream had not sounded like the cry of someone in trouble. Immediately afterward she'd heard a door slam, and she'd thought maybe someone had been fighting in a car.

Once the body was discovered, Mrs. Borkowski asked herself if she could have saved Karen's life by calling the police. She told herself the answer was no. She had thought the scream had come from behind her house, and if she had called the police, she would have sent the officers in the wrong direction. Still, she could not help thinking about how Karen must have looked across the street during the struggle and seen the lights of Mrs. Borkowski's house.

At one point, Mrs. Borkowski's feelings of guilt and fear were so strong she moved out of her home and stayed with her sister-in-law for a few days. Even after she came back, though, she avoided looking at the small white house across the street.

"Every time I stepped out the front door," she said, "I saw that house staring me in the face."

After the murder, Mrs. Borkowski had new locks put on her door. She had a burglar alarm installed. She acquired a .38-caliber revolver. She began, she said, to feel close to Karen. Though Mrs. Borkowski had not known her, she wondered if Karen had ever been married or had any children. She wondered if Karen had been happy.

***

Sgt. Tosi was still trying to learn more about what had happened on that night in May 1984. Repeatedly he drifted back into the neighborhood, talking to people about what they'd seen or heard, picking their memories for stray details.

Mrs. Borkowski told Tosi about hearing the door slam. She said that although it had sounded like a car door, she had not heard any car start up or drive away. Tosi had an idea. He thought the slam might have occurred when Karen had escaped to the front porch before being forced back inside. Maybe the slam had come from the door between the front porch and the living room.

One night Tosi told Mrs. Borkowski to go into the bedroom where she'd heard the scream and the slam. He went across to Karen's house, slammed the door, then went back to Mrs. Borkowski and asked her if she'd heard anything. She said she'd heard a door slam and that it could have been the same sound she'd heard the night of the murder.

Tosi was also talking with George Lewis, the St. Petersburg firefighter who lived in the house on the opposite corner from Karen's. Lewis and Tosi were friends. Lots of police officers knew George. He was in his early 20s, friendly, good at rebuilding engines and other mechanical tasks. Aside from putting out fires for the city of St. Petersburg, he was also a volunteer firefighter for Gulfport. So he was around the police station from time to time, enough that people recognized him. Tosi's wife knew George's live-in girlfriend, Glenda Harness. Tosi had been to George's house for cookouts, and they'd been out together. George had even worked on Tosi's car.

George was an important witness in the Gregory case. All the other neighbors had been inside their homes the night Karen had been killed. George, as he'd explained when the investigation began, had been working in his garage that night. He said he'd walked outside, heard the scream, and looked up and down the street. He said he had not seen anyone suspicious then, but the next evening had noticed a man— Peter Kumble—drive up to the house in a van.

Occasionally, Tosi would stop by George's house and talk with him about the night of the murder. During one of these conversations, George said that after he heard the scream he had walked over to Karen's lawn. That didn't match what George had said in another conversation—he had not said anything about going onto the lawn—but Tosi didn't think much about it.

* * *

Thanksgiving arrived, and Neverne Covington found herself thinking about Karen. Neverne also thought about the murderer. She wondered what he was eating for his holiday dinner. She wondered if he was having sweet potatoes with his turkey.

* * *

By December, Tosi still had made no real progress on the case. He took a little time out to attend to another duty. Tosi was a notary as well as a detective, and on Dec. 15, he performed the marriage ceremony of George Lewis and Glenda Harness. In keeping with George's career, George and Glenda were married on a fire truck. It was a ladder truck, actually. George wore a black tux with a red rose in the lapel. Glenda wore a gown and veil and carried a bouquet.

***

Christmas arrived. Neverne thought back to Christmas the year before, when Karen had made a jacket for David. Neverne recalled how hard Karen had worked, how she'd sewed for weeks. That year, David had been out of town visiting his family on Christmas Day, and Karen had gone to Neverne's house. Neverne had cooked a goose, and Karen had made *baklava*.

Neverne wondered what kinds of presents Karen would have received this year if she'd still been alive. She wondered what kinds of presents the killer was getting. She wondered if he was opening them in front of a family. She wondered if he ever thought about what he'd done to Karen.

***

Around the end of December, there was a farewell party at Gulfport's City Hall for the city manager, who was resigning to take a job in another city. Marie Messervey, a Gulfport bus driver, was at the party, talking with a Gulfport police sergeant. They were having a casual conversation when Mrs. Messervey mentioned that she, too, had heard a scream the night in May when Karen Gregory had been killed.

The sergeant passed this on to Tosi and Lt. Frank Hanson, the detective overseeing the investigation.

They were surprised.

Mrs. Messervey lived on 46th Street S., three blocks east and one block south of Karen's house. Tosi and Hanson did not know the scream had been that loud—the police hadn't talked to neighbors who lived that distance from the house. Hanson couldn't believe that the scream had carried that far.

Tosi went and talked to Mrs. Messervey, and then he and Hanson reviewed some of the details and information that had been gathered over the months. When they got to George Lewis's original statement, the handwritten one he'd given the day Karen's body was found, the detectives stopped. George, they noted, had been outside that night. George had been the only neighbor outside.

If somebody as far away as Mrs. Messervey had heard Karen scream, they thought, then maybe George had heard something from across the street that he hadn't mentioned before. They thought it would be good to talk to George again. There was one problem, though. Tosi didn't think he should talk to George. Tosi was a friend of George's. He thought Hanson should do the interview. He thought Hanson could be more objective.

Hanson tried to arrange the interview. He got George on the phone, and they set up a couple of times for him to come to the station to talk.

George didn't show up.

***

New Year's Day came and went. In mid-January 1985, there was a fire in Gulfport. Hanson and another detective went to check it out in case it was arson. There were fire trucks and hoses all over the street, and Hanson was walking up when he saw George, working the fire.

George was leaning over, hooking up a hose. He glanced up, saw Hanson, and this expression came over his face. Hanson didn't think much about it then, but later he would describe the expression as one of sheer fright, as if George were afraid the lieutenant was going to haul him to jail right there.

"Hi, George," said Hanson.

George apologized for not making it to the interviews. He said he'd had to lay some carpet, but that he could come to the station to talk the following week. Hanson said no problem.

This time, George showed up. He and Hanson went over what had happened the night of the murder. George said he'd been in the garage, working on a motorcycle, doing some welding, listening to the radio. It was late. He saw some kids go by on a bicycle. He walked out of his garage and then heard a scream. He didn't hear it too well, though, because the radio was on—exactly what he'd said the first time. He turned out the garage light, waited for his eyes to adjust to the dark, went out to the street, and looked around. He didn't see anybody suspicious. George also brought up again the fact that the next day, before the body was discovered, he'd seen a man drive up in a van.

Hanson listened, comparing what George was saying now to what he'd said in his original handwritten statement in May 1984. Something didn't sound quite right. For one thing, George said he hadn't heard the glass breaking as Karen had hit the jalousie door during the struggle. A woman several blocks away had heard Karen scream, and George had been across the street and not heard the glass?

At this point, Hanson was thinking: he was an acquaintance of George's himself. Shouldn't the Gulfport police get somebody who didn't know George at all to go over this? Hanson told George something wasn't adding up. Hanson said he wanted to get the truth.

"George," he said. "Would you mind taking a polygraph test?"

George agreed to do it. The test was Feb. 7, and Hanson hired an examiner from ESP Investigators—Executive Security Professionals—to conduct the test at the station. George and the examiner went into a room by themselves. When they were done, the examiner walked out and asked Tosi to come inside. The detective looked at his friend. George had been crying.

"George has something else to tell you," said the examiner. "He saw somebody that night."

***

This time George said he'd heard the scream and had been standing outside his garage when he'd looked toward Karen's house and had seen a man. The man was moving across Karen's lawn, moving toward the back between the house and a big oak tree that stands beside it. George said the man stopped and stared back at him.

"What did the guy look like?" said Tosi.

George said the man was big. He was white, about 6 foot 3, with a trimmed red beard. He had stocky shoulders and what looked like a weight-lifter's arms. He wore a loose-fitting green shirt with short sleeves and gray or black dress pants. George didn't notice whether the man was wearing shoes.

"Did the shirt have a collar on it?" said Tosi.

No collar, George said. It was open in front, with no buttons. It looked like one of those surgical scrub shirts.

George said he and the man stood there, looking at each other. As George went back inside his house, he watched the man walk toward Karen's driveway. He didn't hear a car start up. He didn't actually see the man leave.

George hadn't told Glenda about the man, he said, because he hadn't wanted to worry her. He said he hadn't told the police because the man had seen him, seen where he lived, and he was afraid for his wife and baby.

Tosi knew that at the time of the murder, George had had neither a wife nor a baby. He and Glenda weren't married yet. Glenda had become pregnant around that time, but the baby's birth had been months away. In fact, as George sat there giving the detectives this new account, Glenda was still expecting, due to deliver shortly.

George's vivid description of the intruder also didn't make a lot of sense. The murder had happened at about 1:15 a.m. It had been raining. George had been standing by his garage; the man had been standing all the way over in Karen's yard. How could George have seen him in such detail?

The detectives asked George if he'd be willing to do a re-enactment. George said all right.

They did it at about 9:30 one night. Tosi picked up Detective William Brinkworth and dropped him off with a radio about a block away from the two houses. Then Tosi went to George's house and waited for Lt. Hanson to arrive.

When Hanson got there, he and Tosi and George stood outside the garage, where George said he'd been the night of the murder. Tosi told George they had positioned a man not far from Karen's house, that they were going to have him walk onto Karen's lawn and that George should let them know when the man reached the point where the intruder had been.

Tosi picked up his radio and told Brinkworth to start moving. When George said stop, Tosi told Brinkworth to hold it.

Tosi asked George to describe the man in the yard.

"Well," George said, "he's wearing some kind of a jacket."

The man was.

"Can you tell me what color it is?" said Tosi. "No."

Tosi asked George if he could describe the man any further, the color of his hair or anything else. George said no. Tosi asked George if he could identify the man on the lawn. George said no.

Something wasn't right. George had known Brinkworth for years. But standing there, in the same place where he'd supposedly seen the intruder in such detail, George could not tell it was Brinkworth across the street.

Hanson asked George how that could be.

"Frank," George said. "Something is wrong with the lighting."

George said the night of the murder had been different. That night in May it had been raining. George pointed out that there was a street light on the corner of his lawn, the corner closest to Karen's house. Maybe, he said, the light had reflected off the wet street and had cast more light onto Karen's lawn. Maybe, he said, the moon had been brighter.

Tosi knew it had been overcast the night of the murder. He also knew that the street had not been lit as well as it was now. Tosi had checked. Mrs. Borkowski, the neighbor who lived across

from Karen's house, had said that she might
have had a small porch light on during the night
of the murder. But there had also been three tall
evergreens in her yard that night, cutting down
on the light from the house. Since then, Mrs.
Borkowski had gotten rid of the bushes.

Obviously, Tosi thought, George could not
have stood outside his garage and seen the
intruder so vividly. He had to have been closer
to Karen's house.

The detectives asked him, and George said
yes, he may have been a little closer, maybe over
in his yard, near a For Sale sign that was standing there.

"But I know I didn't go off of my property,"
George said. "I know I never left my property."

That didn't sound right either. In his original
written statement, George had explained that
he'd walked out on the street and looked around.

There were more contradictions. At one point
before, George had said that he had never seen
Karen Gregory on the day or night of the murder.
Now, after the re-enactment, they asked him
again if he'd seen her, and this time he said yes.
It had been about 7:30 that evening, he said.
Karen had been in the kitchen, washing dishes
in front of the window.

Tosi and Hanson thought George was lying.
They thought maybe George had seen a man that
night and was now keeping something to himself
because he was afraid. But they didn't consider
him a suspect. They called it a night and went
home.

***

After the re-enactment, Tosi continued to stop
at George's house to talk about the case. One
night when Tosi came by, George was out
working in the garage again. They talked, and
George brought up some more details he'd never
mentioned before. This time, according to Tosi,
George said that not only had he seen Karen
doing the dishes that night, but had heard the
dishes rattling.

That was the way it was going. As the weeks passed, George was giving one story after another.

Hanson reminded George he was a firefighter. He told George he was obstructing the investigation. He said if George was holding back because he was afraid of somebody on the loose out there, not to worry, they would catch him.

Hanson said he wanted the truth. All of it.

George denied he was holding anything back.

***

On Feb. 24, 1985, George became a father. According to the announcement in the paper, Glenda Lewis delivered at Bayfront Medical Center, at 7:02 p.m. The baby weighed seven pounds, 12 ounces. Her name was Tiffany.

***

On March 7, George went to the police station for another polygraph test.

When the test was over, the examiner had more news. Now, he said, George was saying he'd talked with the intruder in Karen's yard.

This time, George said he had not stayed on his property that night. He said he'd been working in the garage, had heard the scream, walked outside, waited for his eyes to adjust to the dark, then walked up and down the street. He said he was walking past Karen Gregory's house, rounding the corner, when he saw a man standing in the yard. The man was only about three feet away. George asked him what was the matter. The man told him to get the hell out of there. The man said if George told anyone about seeing him, he'd come back and kill him.

George's stories kept changing. At one point he had said he'd been in his driveway. Then he'd been on his lawn. Now he said he'd been out in the street, next to Karen's house. The next thing that was going to happen, Hanson said, was that George was going to say he had been inside Karen's house.

George said no, he had not been inside the house.

Had he walked up to a window and looked inside?

George said no. He said he had not gotten any closer to the house than the street.

The story wasn't washing. George was still failing the polygraph. Hanson told him he was lying. He told George he was now considered a suspect and would have to be advised of his Miranda rights.

George looked disgusted. Go ahead, he said.

Hanson advised George of his rights and asked him if he'd sign a written waiver of them. George signed it. Then they had him tested again on the polygraph. Now the examiner focused his questions on the murder itself. He asked George if he'd been inside Karen's house when she was killed.

George said no.

Had he stabbed Karen?

George said no.

Had he killed her?

George said no.

The examiner told George he still wasn't passing the polygraph. George said he was a little nervous. The examiner explained how the test worked, explained that it was natural to be nervous. He said he'd already been accounting for George's nerves.

They went on. George's voice was rising.

He said: "I didn't do it...I can't believe you're accusing me of this."

Though George was now officially considered a suspect, the detectives had nothing to prove he'd been in the house that night. When they were through talking to him, they told George he could go.

***

Tosi was running through all the stories George had told them. There were so many inconsistencies. George had said before that he hadn't noticed whether the man on the lawn was wearing anything on his feet. Now George was saying the man had worn dress sandals. Then, in this newest account, George was saying he had not noticed any blood on the man. But Tosi knew there'd been blood on the curtains where the killer had left the house. He knew the killer had to have been covered with blood when he had walked outside. George said the man had stood only a few feet away, had stood there and stared at him. Why, Tosi wondered, would a murderer allow a witness to look him over so thoroughly? There had been a scream. Glass had shattered. For all the killer knew, a neighbor had called 911. The police could have been coming around the corner any second.

Why would this stranger stand there waiting to be caught? Why, Tosi thought, wouldn't the man have killed George?

Tosi didn't know what to think.

"The whole thing didn't make any sense," he would later explain. "At that point in time, I was still trying to believe George. I wanted to believe him, although I realized that it was just unbelievable."

***

In the months that followed, the Gulfport police searched for proof that would confirm their suspicions. They took George's fingerprints. They took his palm prints and footprints. They took samples of his head, chest, and pubic hairs.

Hanson went and talked to Glenda Lewis. Shortly after Karen's body had been found, Glenda had told Mrs. Tosi that she'd seen a silhouette in her backyard on the night of the murder. Hanson asked Glenda about that now, and Glenda said she hadn't seen anyone in the yard except for George. Hanson asked her what George had been wearing that night. She said he usually wore old shirts and shorts, but that she could not remember if he'd had a shirt on that night. She said George had probably been barefoot.

Hanson asked her if George had explained why the detectives kept calling him over to the station. Glenda said George had told her they were asking him about the man he'd seen that night. When George had told her this, she said, he'd looked scared. He'd had tears in his eyes.

Tosi, meanwhile, was checking George's story, trying to find out if there indeed had been a man on Karen's lawn that night. George went over his description of the man—how he'd had red hair and a beard and so forth—and he and Tosi put together a composite drawing. Tosi took the drawing to several people who had known Karen. They all said they couldn't think of anyone who looked like that.

Tosi did, though. Tosi thought it looked like George. George had red hair, and he had once worn a beard.

A cry in the night
Part 4: The arrest

OCTOBER 1, 1986

George Lewis has many friends. They say:
He loves babies.
He loves being a firefighter.
He enjoys baking chocolate chip cookies.
He could not have murdered Karen Gregory.

***

Sgt. Tosi was also a friend of George Lewis. But in the spring of 1985, Tosi was having trouble with his friend's latest explanation of what had happened the night of Karen Gregory's murder. Now Lewis was saying that he'd seen a man on Karen's lawn and that the man had threatened to kill him if he mentioned having seen anyone. Tosi was still trying to believe Lewis, but to the sergeant, the story didn't make any sense.

When he tried to find the stranger, Tosi got nowhere. Tosi and Lewis had put together a composite drawing of the man. None of Karen's friends recognized him. Tosi gathered photos of people who had been suspects and asked Lewis if any of them was the man. Lewis said no.

Then there were the phone calls. During his March 7 interview at the police station, Lewis told the detectives someone was calling his house repeatedly in the evening and after midnight, then hanging up without saying a word. Tosi got General Telephone to put what's called a "trap" on Lewis's phone. General Telephone's computer kept track of every phone call to the house. Lewis was instructed to write down the time and date he got these calls and to tell his wife Glenda and his sister, who was living with them at the time, to do the same.

General Telephone started the trap on March 8, the day after the interview. Suddenly, Lewis said he wasn't getting any more of the calls. He said Glenda and his sister had gotten a couple, but they hadn't marked down the times. Lewis said he'd told them to keep track, but that he'd tell them again. On April 12, more than four weeks later, when Lewis said he still wasn't getting any more of the calls, General Telephone took the trap off his phone.

Through all of this, Lewis remained a suspect. As far as Lt. Hanson was concerned, Lewis was the prime suspect. But the police hadn't matched his fingerprints with any of those found inside Karen's house. They hadn't found any physical evidence to prove he'd been there the night of the murder.

The months rolled by. Karen's birthday had been March 29, and that date came and went. Then, in May, the first anniversary of her murder came and went. Summer came and went.

***

Karen's friends were trying to move on with their lives.

David Mackey, who had been Karen's boyfriend, quit his job as an administrator of a counseling program for Vietnam veterans that summer and went to the University of Miami to work on a doctoral degree in psychology. David was unhappy in Miami. He found he could not stop thinking about Karen and how the police still had not found her killer. It was difficult for him to be so far away when the case was unresolved. After one semester at the university, he left, moved to Tampa, and found another job counseling veterans. He found it was not enough to deal with Karen's death day by day. He had to deal with it, he said, moment by moment.

David turned to his friends and family for help and comfort. Though he was a counselor and had long known that life was fragile, he understood that now in a way he never had before. At work he looked at the veterans around him, and he was astounded at the strength and resiliency they had found inside themselves to survive their pain. Like Karen's other friends, David also understood now that nothing in the world is guaranteed. When he left home in the morning, he never assumed he would return at the end of the day.

Anita Kilpatrick, who had been Karen's roommate, had spent more than a year trying to deal with her fear. She still did not like to go anywhere at night by herself. Before she went to sleep, she would make sure the new chain on her door was latched. In her wallet, she carried the last note she'd received from Karen. *See you soon. Love, K.*

Neverne Covington, who had been one of Karen's closest friends, also thought of Karen. Neverne remembered Halloween the year before, when Karen had dressed up like a frowsy dime-store waitress and had piled her hair into a towering beehive. Like Anita, Neverne was also slowly finding ways to deal with her fear. At first after the murder, she would not take the garbage into her backyard at night alone. Now she was beginning to drive in the evenings by herself. She was trying to learn to trust the people around her again. She knew, though, that she would never feel as safe as she had before. It was as though she had lost an innocence that could not be regained.

***

One day in October 1985, Neverne was standing in a line at a bank in Gulfport when she was struck by the feeling that someone was staring at her. She turned around and saw George Lewis, who was in line not six feet away. Neverne knew who Lewis was. She knew he had been a suspect in Karen's murder, and that the detectives still had not been able to prove or disprove their suspicions.

Neverne also suspected Lewis. Before the murder, she had been over at Karen and David's house, and she had seen Lewis across the street, getting into a pickup truck with tinted windows and driving away. The truck had scared her. Later, after Karen was killed, Neverne had concluded that the murderer had to be one of the neighbors. Detectives had told her that on the day after the murder Lewis had noticed a man in a van drive up to Karen's house. Who was this neighbor, Neverne had asked, who had been so attentive? Why had he not been so attentive the night before? They had told her it was Lewis, a firefighter.

Neverne knew that people are raised to trust firefighters. But she did not trust George Lewis.

Now, standing a few feet away from her at the bank, Lewis was staring at Neverne. He was staring so hard, she said, he seemed to be boring a hole through her.

After she left the bank, Neverne went to Eckerd College, where she was an artist in residence. She was driving toward Eckerd, she said, when she noticed Lewis was driving behind her. Neverne tried to tell herself Lewis was not following her. She had worked so hard for so many months to get past her fear, and she did not want to be afraid all over again. She saw Lewis in her rearview mirror, and she tried to think of logical explanations for his driving behind her. Maybe he knew someone at Eckerd. Maybe he had just happened to pick the same stretch of road. Lewis drove behind her for several miles. Finally, just as Neverne reached the Eckerd campus, he drove off in a different direction.

Later that month, when Halloween arrived, Neverne gave a card to Sgt. Tosi. She'd taken a copy of a painting she'd done of David Mackey—a painting from after the murder, one that showed the pain in his face—and written a message to the sergeant on the back.

In the message, Neverne told Tosi about the incident with Lewis. But that wasn't the main reason she'd written him. She wanted to remind him that on Halloween two years before, she and Karen had been together, laughing. She told Tosi she knew that a long time had gone by since Karen's murder. She told him she was still waiting for the prompt resolution of the case.

**

It was January 1986. Karen Gregory had been dead for more than 19 months. George Lewis had been a suspect for 10 months. But Sgt. Tosi and Lt. Hanson still hadn't found any evidence to place him in the house the night of the murder.

Tosi was thinking about the bare footprint that the police had found in blood on the tile floor of her bathroom. The Florida Department of Law Enforcement (FDLE) had photographed the footprint and still had the negatives. In the summer of 1984, Tosi had called the FDLE's Tampa laboratory and asked if it would be possible to enlarge the photo and see if the ridges in the footprint were distinct enough to make an identification. According to Tosi, he was told that the photo showed only a blotch of blood and not enough detail to make an identification.

In 1985, Tosi had called the FDLE lab and asked again if it were possible to enlarge the photo of the footprint. Again, Tosi said, he had been given the same answer. A lab supervisor had told him that there was nothing in the photo, that trying to make an ID from the photo would be a waste of time.

Tosi was not convinced. He was determined to see that photo. So on Jan. 6, 1986, he went to Tampa and got the negatives.

(The supervisor disputes this account. He says Tosi did call and ask for the negatives, but did not ask him about enlarging the photo.)

Once Tosi got the negatives, he brought them back to the station, and a Gulfport technician made a photo. On the day the photo was taken, a ruler had been placed beside the footprint for measurement. Now, almost two years later, the Gulfport technician enlarged the photo to life-size.

Tosi looked at the photo. He could see the ridges in the footprint.

Then Tosi sent the negative and the photo to the Pinellas County Sheriff's Department. Using what Tosi describes as a high-intensity, black-and-white lens, the sheriff's department made another copy of the photo, this time with a sharper definition.

Then one of the sheriff's print technicians was handed the photo of the footprint from Karen's house, handed the footprint George Lewis had given after he became a suspect, and asked to determine whether the two matched.

The answer was no.

Negative on that print, said the technician.

Tosi still wasn't convinced. The Gulfport detectives had been sending prints to the sheriff's department for a long time, asking for comparisons, and several technicians had done it for them. This particular technician had been doing it for roughly a year. It seemed to Tosi and the other detectives that, over and over, this technician was telling them there was no match, even in cases where the detectives were sure they had the right man and that the prints had to match.

Now here was the same technician saying the footprint on the bathroom floor was not from Lewis.

Tosi decided to get a second opinion. He sent the photo and George's footprint to the FBI in Washington, D.C.

On March 11, Tosi got an answer. John Saunders, an FBI print specialist, called Gulfport.

George Lewis, he said, had made the footprint in the blood.

Saunders said it had been hard to make the comparison. It had taken several hours. But he said he'd found more than 30 points of comparison. He said he could keep looking for more if they wanted him to, but he didn't think there was any need for that. The footprint, he said, definitely belonged to Lewis.

Tosi and Hanson talked to the State Attorney's office about the footprint. It was time, they decided, to arrest Lewis.

***

Later, Larry Tosi was asked if he'd ever known George Lewis to be the kind of person who could kill another human being.

"Well," said Tosi, "how well do you know someone? I mean, I knew him. I mean, he's not a brother."

On Oct. 4, this Saturday, George Lewis will be 25 years old. He has red hair and a red mustache. His eyes are brown. His face is dotted with freckles. He stands 5 foot 8. He has a wife. He has a young daughter named Tiffany. He has friends who trust him. Before the Gregory case, he had never been arrested before.

"He's not a violent type of kid," says Pam Hackett, a friend who has known Lewis for several years. "He's a real sweet guy."

Lewis's father worked for the postal department in St. Petersburg. His mother worked for the local Roman Catholic diocese. Together, they reared a big family—in one employment application, Lewis mentions three brothers and three sisters. Lewis attended grammar school at St. Jude's and went to high school at Boca Ciega. His senior yearbook says he was known as "Big Red."

By all accounts, Lewis is extremely mechanical and good with his hands, the kind of guy who loves to work in his garage until 2 or 3 a.m., rebuilding engines. After he graduated from Boca Ciega, in fact, he worked as a welder and machine operator.

But what Lewis really wanted to do with his life was become a firefighter.

"It was his goal," says Mike Blank, a friend who met Lewis after the two became volunteer firefighters for Gulfport. "He didn't want to do anything else but that."

Blank felt about the same. He and Lewis were the kind of kids who never grew out of chas-

ing after fire trucks. As teenagers, they'd hear
the sirens, jump on their bikes or into their cars,
and take off in pursuit of that wailing sound. The
two of them didn't know each other then, but
Blank still remembers racing along with this red-
haired kid beside him.

Lewis became a volunteer firefighter in
Gulfport in March 1980. Two years later, he went
through the basic firefighting course at the
Pinellas Fire Academy. Herb Johnson, the head
of the academy, remembers him as a friendly,
hard-working cadet.

"I like George," says Johnson. "He's one of
the best.... Never violent, always had a good,
level disposition. A fun-loving guy."

A few days after he was graduated from the
fire academy, while he was still working as a
welder and putting out fires for Gulfport in his
spare time, Lewis applied to be a full-time
firefighter and emergency medical technician
with the city of St. Petersburg. The following
August, the city hired him.

"When he became a St. Petersburg fireman,"
says Blank, "that was his bread and butter."

Lewis did fine in the department. His first
annual evaluation noted that he was hard-
working, polite, and patient.

His personal life, meanwhile, had seen some
turmoil. He'd already been divorced once. His
first wife's name was Denise. She lived in Pennsylvania, and Lewis met her on a blind date in
1980 while she was vacationing in Florida. When
her vacation ended, Lewis quit his job as a welder
and went back with her to Pennsylvania. They
were married soon afterward and moved to
Florida. It didn't work out. For one thing, Denise
didn't like how George was always working in
the garage. They were divorced in July 1982, a
few months before he entered the academy.

Though some of his friends describe Lewis as
a calm, easy-going man, the detectives have
spoken with others who say he can be argumen-
tative and hot-tempered. Denise told police that

while they were married George had struck her several times and once even tried to strangle her.

When George began going out with Glenda Harness, their relationship had its own ups and downs. Though they got along well enough for her to move in with him, at least one friend later told the police that the two of them had argued quite a bit.

＊

There was some pressure on Lewis around the time of the murder in May 1984. Glenda had become pregnant. Friends disagree on whether he wanted to marry Glenda. Some say he wanted to stay single and see other women. One friend noted that Lewis was acting strangely around then. The friend says Lewis was going out with other women, drinking more than usual, trying to arrange orgies.

Some friends have also said that Lewis was not blind to the fact that a young woman was living across the street. One friend recalled a day in 1984 when he and Lewis had both seen a woman in a bikini—the friend wasn't sure whether it was Karen Gregory—at the house. Lewis, the friend said, remarked on the woman. Another friend said that he and Lewis had once seen two women sitting in lounge chairs over at Karen's house. The friend told the police that he had made some comment about them and that Lewis had said he'd already "checked it out."

As he and Tosi investigated Lewis, Hanson kept in mind that there was a faucet and hose in the backyard of Lewis's house, between the garage and the kitchen. It was Lt. Hanson's opinion that, after the murder, Lewis could have washed the blood off himself with that hose and thrown any bloodstained clothes in a nearby trash can. The trash can was not searched immediately after the murder. Lewis was not yet a suspect.

＊

On March 15, 1986, four days after they got the call from the FBI, Sgt. Tosi and Lt. Hanson went to see Lewis at the St. Petersburg fire station where he worked, Station No. 9. It was a Saturday, and it was the first day Lewis was due back at work since the call from Washington. Tosi and Hanson had decided to wait until he was at work, to wait until they knew where he was going to be.

So that morning, they went over to Station No. 9, at 475 66th St. N., and got Lewis. He was in his uniform. They didn't tell him he was under arrest. There were other firefighters around, and Tosi and Hanson didn't want to embarrass him.

"I do have some compassion," Hanson later explained. "I don't have to come down like the Raiders of the Lost Ark on people."

Tosi and Hanson told Lewis they needed to talk to him some more and asked if he'd come back to the station in Gulfport. Again, so as not to embarrass him, they let him drive behind them. As they drove, the detectives watched Lewis in their rearview mirror.

When they arrived, Hanson advised Lewis of his rights, and once again they went over what had happened the night of Karen's murder. A tape recorder was running.

Lewis went through it all—how he'd been working in the garage, had heard the scream, gone out onto the street and seen the man on Karen's lawn, how he'd gotten scared because the man had pointed at him and warned him not to tell anybody what he'd seen. Lewis said there had been no lights on in Karen's house and that he had not been able to see inside. Lewis said he had not gone on Karen's lawn, her sidewalk, or into her house.

Then Tosi told Lewis that the FBI had matched his footprint with the print found in the house.

"There's no way," Lewis said. "I wasn't even barefoot that night."

Hanson asked Lewis how his footprint had gotten in the house. Lewis said he didn't know.

"Well, with that," he said, "I'd like to talk to a lawyer because that's not right. There's something wrong."

Tosi asked Lewis if that meant he wanted to end the interview. Lewis said yes. Tosi told him the interview was over. Tosi said they'd simply been giving Lewis a chance to explain how his footprint was found in Karen's house.

"Wait a minute," said Lewis. "I still don't believe this. I definitely want to find out why that's like that."

Tosi had the impression Lewis wanted to say something else. When he didn't, Tosi told him he was under arrest for the murder of Karen Gregory.

Lewis said he hadn't killed Karen Gregory. Tosi said all the indications were that he had.

Then Lewis began talking.

"I saw the guy," he said. "I went in the house. I heard Karen scream. I had never seen anything like that before. I didn't see the guy do it, OK. I saw the guy outside. I went in after that real quick. I still don't believe it. I didn't kill her, Larry. I saw her laying there with her throat cut open. The guy had seen me. When he left I ran back in the house, OK, but I didn't kill her. I saw her laying there in blood. I panicked. I didn't know what to do. The guy had seen me. To this day I still have bad dreams about that. When he left I walked back over to the garage. I ran back over there 'cause I wanted to see. I wasn't sure if David or somebody was there, too. There wasn't any lights on in the house, and when I went in, I went in through the back window 'cause I ran around the back bedroom. I looked and I saw her laying on the floor. That's it. I didn't do anything else. I was scared. 'Cause when I saw what that guy did to her, he saw me. He knows what I look like right now. I would never do anything like that to a human being ever. Frank, I didn't kill her. I should have just told you the whole thing to begin with and worried about the guy coming back earlier. I can't even prove my innocence now. I was so afraid to tell you guys I was in there, but I wasn't sure if that guy was gonna come back."

Tosi took Lewis back to the booking section of the Gulfport police station. Tosi photographed him and fingerprinted him, and Hanson went and got Glenda and brought her to the station to see her husband before he was taken away.

Then Tosi and another officer drove Lewis to the Pinellas County jail. It was raining, and Lewis sat in the back seat with his head against the window. He appeared to be falling asleep. Tosi asked him if he was all right.

"Yeah," said Lewis.

They arrived at the jail, and Tosi handed the paperwork on the arrest to a booking officer. Tosi walked over to Lewis, his friend, the man whose wedding he'd performed, the man whom he was now charging with first-degree murder. Lewis, as he later recalled, spoke to him one last time.

"Thanks, Larry," Lewis said. "Just if you could see to it that, you know, my wife is taken care of."

***

That Saturday morning, Sgt. Tosi called David Mackey. When the phone rang, David was fixing breakfast. After Tosi told him about the arrest, David felt relieved. But it was an empty kind of relief. He thought about the long court case ahead, about how there were going to be hearings and questions and a trial. He began calling Karen's family and friends.

That same day, as the word of the arrest spread, an editor from the *St. Petersburg Times* called Anita Kilpatrick at her apartment on the beach and gave her the news. Over the past two years, as she'd waited for an arrest, Anita had imagined this moment and had expected to have a strong reaction. But when she heard about the arrest, she felt almost nothing. She felt limp. She had never met George Lewis. She only knew his name. It seemed unreal.

Anita called Neverne Covington and told her what had happened. Neverne was at home, talking with her boyfriend and some of his family, and when she heard the words, she felt chills and broke into a sweat. She felt nauseous. She had waited so long for an arrest, it had become only a concept to her, something abstract. Now it was something tangible. They had arrested a man. They had arrested a human being. It was almost incomprehensible.

Neverne walked up to her boyfriend.

"They've arrested George. They've arrested him."

***

Today, George Lewis is being held in the Pinellas County jail. He has been indicted on one count of involuntary sexual battery and one count of first-degree murder. The prosecution says it will seek the death penalty. The trial is set for Nov. 12.

Lewis has not wavered from his insistence that he did not kill Karen Gregory. He has hired Joseph Ciarciaglino and Robert Paver. Though the two attorneys will not discuss the case in detail, their comments indicate it's likely they will argue at trial that the footprint from the bathroom was not made by Lewis. Lewis, they say, is innocent.

"He did not do it," says Ciarciaglino.

So far, Lewis has neither lost his job nor been suspended. He is still a firefighter with the city of St. Petersburg and draws a paycheck. Since the arrest, he has received two pay raises. One was an annual raise. Another, which only became effective on Monday, was a general wage increase all firefighters received. His biweekly salary is now $759.62.

Though his vacation time ran out long ago, dozens of other firefighters and paramedics have donated their vacation and holiday time to Lewis so he can support his family. Since his arrest, in other words, he has technically been on vacation.

Glenda and Tiffany Lewis have moved out of the house in Gulfport and are living elsewhere in the county. Like many of her husband's friends, Glenda does not believe George killed Karen Gregory. One friend says that Tiffany,

who was born in February 1985, just as Lewis
was becoming a suspect in the murder, does not
understand what has happened. Not long ago, the
friend says, Tiffany was at a restaurant when she
saw a man wearing a red cap, mistook him for
her father, and began crying.

The house where the Lewis family lived is
now being sold to some friends. A neighborhood
crime watch sign still stands in the yard.

Sgt. Tosi continues to work at the Gulfport
Police Department. Since the arrest, David
Mackey and Neverne Covington have personally
thanked him for his efforts. They have also
thanked Detective William Brinkworth, who was
initially assigned to the case.

Peter Kumble, the acquaintance of Karen's
who was initially a suspect in the case, has
moved to Tucson and is working on a master's
degree at the University of Arizona.

Martha Borkowski, the neighbor who lived
across the street from Karen, lives in the same
house and continues to ask herself whether she
should have called the police. When she steps
outside, she still avoids looking at the house
where Karen was killed.

Karen's family is waiting for the trial.
Karen's brother Mark wonders what he would
say to Lewis if he met him. Karen's mother,
Mark says, still cries when she hears Karen's
name.

David Mackey has sold the house in Gulfport
and now lives in Tampa.

Anita Kilpatrick lives in the apartment she
once shared with Karen.

Neverne Covington lives in the house where
she and Karen had dinner the night of the
murder. Since then, Neverne says, she has
learned how precious her friends and family are.
She has learned, she says, that those you love
are gifts. She has learned, as she puts it, that it
takes an act of faith to get through every single
day.

Chicago Tribune

Cheryl Lavin
Finalist, Non-Deadline Writing

Cheryl Lavin, 41, was born in Chicago, where she grew up. She graduated from the University of Wisconsin in 1967 and received a master's degree from Northwestern University in 1973. She joined the *Chicago Tribune* in 1981, where she writes mostly for the Sunday magazine and *Tempo*. She has started two syndicated columns, "Fast Track" and "Tales from the Front," the latter about romance in the 1980s. Cheryl has won awards for her profiles, including the Scher and Lisagor prizes for investigative reporting, and the Lisagor and UPI awards for features.

Lavin writes with Mark Fineman's eye for detail and Don Marsh's instinct for the absurd. Her considerable interviewing skills produce wicked quotations, but she knows when to let her subjects just talk away. And she can deliver a Dave Barry zinger without batting an eyelash; who else would describe George Burns as looking "like an organ grinder's monkey"?

George Burns: From has-been to superstar

FEBRUARY 2, 1986

LAS VEGAS—It's a slow Tuesday night on the Strip, but Circus Maximus, the show room at Caesar's Palace, is packed. The opening-night crowd has stood in line for hours for these $30 seats, and now, halfway into the 10 o'clock show, they're happily, noisily knocking back their two-drink minimum. The opening act, singer Gloria Loring, shimmies off the stage leaving the middle-aged audience with a faint tingle and a warm glow. And then the band strikes up a nice, lazy version of "Ain't Misbehavin'." A buzz goes through the crowd. They put down their drinks, rise to their feet, and clap their hands.

From stage right walks a little old man, stooped over, wearing a tuxedo in a size that would fit a bar mitzvah boy. There's a neat little gray toupee on his suntanned head, shiny black shoes on his tiny feet, a perky red silk hanky in his breast pocket. His eyes are sparkling behind his round black-rimmed glasses; his ears are huge. He looks like an organ grinder's monkey.

When he gets to center stage—he's taking his time about it—he turns to the audience and says what they're all thinking: "Look at that! And he walks, too!" Then he carefully flicks the ashes off his big, smelly El Producto, waits for the laugh, gets it, and rolls right on to the next bit. His timing, as ever, is impeccable.

"Usually a performer gets a standing ovation at the *end* of his act," he says, his head engulfed in a cloud of smoke. "I get mine at the beginning. You're afraid I won't make it."

There's no need to worry. George Burns makes it. He's 90, but he's not going to die. "Why should I die?" he asks, a wicked little smile on his lips. "I already died. I died in Altoona, I died in Schenectady...."

A funny thing happened to George Burns on his way to oblivion: He became a superstar. At 79, at the age when most men are retired—scratch that—at the age where most men are *dead*, he got his second wind via a part in the movie of Neil Simon's *The Sunshine Boys*, and he's been floating along with full sails ever since. There have been three *Oh, God!* movies (a fourth is being planned), three albums, a yearly TV special, six books (including *Dr. Burns' Prescription for Happiness*, which spent 18 weeks on *The New York Times* best-seller list), and endorsements for everything from World Airways to Pollenex air purifiers. He's a multimillion-dollar-a-year conglomerate.

And now, less than a week after his birthday special on CBS (which was No. 1 in its time slot, thanks to a media blanket of interviews and promotions), he's playing Vegas, as part of his five-year contract with Caesar's Palace. "They wanted to make it 10 years," Burns said when he signed in 1983, "but how do I know the hotel will last that long?"

To show their appreciation, Caesar's gave Burns a reception the night before he opened and invited the other performers on the Strip to drop in at the Bacchanal Room, where the girls wear togas while they pass the vino. Red Skelton, Norm Crosby, Rich Little, some singers, some dancers, all showed up. Burns sat on a chaise longue on the tiny stage, a six-foot Cleopatra on one side, a curly haired, bare-chested Caesar on the other. He refused to wear the laurel leaves the hotel provided.

Each of the guests made a little speech. Burns stood up to welcome each one, stood up again to say goodbye. Up, down, up, down, up, down (35 minutes of calisthenics every morning keeps him limber). Norm Crosby said, "It's a pleasure to pay tribute to a man who is physically incapable of a sex scandal." Burns just kept

puffing and smiling. Rich Little pulled out a cigar
and did his George Burns imitation. "He sounds
like me with a cold," said Burns. The McGuire
Sisters paid their respects. "Did you see them?"
Burns asked after the party in his well-known
gravelly voice. "They still dress alike." He
chuckles to himself and then mumbles, "Nice
girls, nice girls." *Girls* comes out *goils*.

After the reception, Burns led a little group
back to his suite at the hotel and played host.
"Do you want some booze, kid?" he asked a
middle-aged woman. "Some coffee? How 'bout a
nice old man?" He was only kidding. He's already
taken. For the last five years he's been keeping
steady company with a 40-ish divorcee from
Dallas named Cathy Carr. She had read one of
his books and sent him a funny and flattering
fan letter that he responded to. Now, he visits
her in Dallas, and she visits him at his $2.5
million Beverly Hills estate that he bought 50
years ago for $59,000. "I love her love, but I'll
never marry her," says Burns. "If I was 20 years
younger, maybe.... " Even though he won't make
the relationship binding, he keeps a tight rein
on Carr when they're together.

Burns fixed himself a martini, got comfortable on the couch, and started talking show biz.
He reads *Variety* and the *Hollywood Reporter*
every day and he knows who's playing where. He
spends two hours a day at his office working on
new material with his full-time writer. He was
asked who his all-time favorite comedian is, and
he said, "Charlie Chaplin. To me he was the
greatest." "Not Milton Berle?" asked his
manager, Irving Fein. "Now you're making me
think," Burns shot back, his face deadpan.

With Fein and Little, and a few other cronies
as his audience, Burns launched into a selection
of his favorite stories. There was the one about
Gracie Allen, his wife and partner for nearly four
decades: "I said to her, 'How's your brother?' and
she talked for 38 years." The one about his
mother: "We were having breakfast one morn-

ing, and she said, 'You know you come from a very nice family.' I said, 'Really?' She said, 'Yes, you have seven sisters and they were all virgins when they married.' I said, 'Mama, the reason they were all virgins when they married was they were all ugly.' She said, 'Pass the salt.' " The one about his secret for longevity: "I like my food hot, I exercise, I smoke 15 to 20 cigars a day, and I dance very close."

And then he led them all off to dinner at the Palace Court, graciously giving his guests the best view of the restaurant. He had a couple more martinis, a steak doused in ketchup (when the waiter asked how he'd like it, he answered, "Who the hell cares?"), and a strawberry ice cream sundae. He refused to touch the vegetables and turned down the sushi appetizer: "A Jew has enough trouble. He doesn't need to eat raw fish."

George Burns, who was originally named Nathan Birnbaum, was the ninth of 12 children in his family on the Lower East Side of New York. He has been performing since he was 7, smoking cigars since he was 14. "From 7 to 27, I had jobs, but they were lousy jobs," he says. "I was very fortunate because they had theaters that were worse than I was." And then he met Gracie, an out-of-work Irish actress. At first, Burns was the comic, Gracie, the straight man. That didn't last. Whatever Gracie said, she got the laughs, and Burns, who wrote the act, quickly reversed their roles, if not their billing.

"My big lines were 'Really?' 'No kidding?' and 'Is that so?' " says Burns. "At the end of the act I used to point to her feet and she'd do an Irish jig. It got so I could point with either hand. The audiences loved her. I used to have to test which way the draft was coming from and stand downwind of Gracie. If I blew cigar smoke in her face, they wanted to kill me." Three years after they began working together, they got married.

"It was a great marriage," says Burns, whose face and hands are remarkably smooth and unspotted, thanks, he says, to Eterna 27. "I was never a great lover, but marriage is what you do out of bed, not in bed. The marriage was a by-product of what we were doing for a living: show business. We never worked at our marriage. We were married, we stayed married. If the soup was hot, it was a great marriage. If the audiences were good, it was a great marriage."

When Gracie Allen died in 1964, several years after she retired, Burns had a hard time adjusting. "But I did something that worked for me," he says. "We were sleeping in twin beds by then—we'd been married a long time—and about two weeks after she left me, I started to sleep in Gracie's bed, and it worked. I didn't feel so alone." He visits her once a month at Forest Lawn cemetery and talks to her: "I'll tell her we talked about her today. I'll tell her how I did in Vegas. That they gave me a little party. It makes me feel good."

Burns had another adjustment to make after Gracie. Not only did he lose his wife and partner, his career went on the skids, too. "Before *The Sunshine Boys,* he was doing very little," says Fein, who was representing Burns's best friend, Jack Benny, at the time. "He'd do a guest spot once in a while. We always had him on the Jack Benny specials; that was about it." As a favor to Benny, Fein agreed to manage Burns, too. When Benny, who was signed to do *The Sunshine Boys,* died, Fein got Burns a reading for the part. "Everyone was after the role," says Fein. "Danny Kaye, Milton Berle, Art Carney, Jack Albertson, who had done it on Broadway. But I worked with George on the script and he got the part." And he got an Academy Award as best supporting actor, as well.

Fein, who is Burns's agent and publicist as well as manager, and the one who ultimately decides how much Burns will work, parlayed the part into a whole new career for the comedian. "We played London and then I took ads in the trades: 'London Loves George Burns.' We played Carnegie Hall, and I did the same thing. Little by little we broke down the resistance. People thought without Gracie he was nothing, you know? He was a second banana. Gracie was the star of the show. Like with Abbott and Costello. Costello was the funny guy, Abbott just asked the questions. And the more work he got, the more confidence he got. When he first started playing nightclubs as a single, he'd have to take two or three shots of scotch in order to get out on the stage. Then he found out he could do it without her."

***

Burns's 54-minute act is moving along nicely. He sings a couple of songs. "I Wish I Was 18 Again" was a big hit for him, although he swears he really doesn't want to relive his youth. "Why should I?" he asks. "When I was 18 I couldn't get a job." He does a couple of shuffling dance steps. He tells a few of his Dirty Old Man jokes, poking fun at his penchant for young women. "When I'm on a date, I go to a restaurant and I ask for a nice quiet corner so the girls can do their homework." Then he moves along to his Oye, Am I Old! jokes. "That Burt Reynolds, I hear he has three or four girls a night. I'm lucky if I can hold on to my hair when the wind's blowing." And finally, "Why should I retire? If I quit, who'd support my mother and father?" And then he sings "Young at Heart."

He makes a false exit and gets a standing ovation, comes back, and exits again to another standing ovation. "He always gets three," says Fein. "You can bet on it. The audiences love him. He'll work until he can't stand up anymore. When they play 'Ain't Misbehavin' ' and he can't walk out, then he'll quit. And maybe we'll wheel him out in a wheelchair. Show business is his life. It keeps him alive."

At 90, Burns refuses to live in the past. He keeps no memorabilia, no scrapbooks, or old notices. "I'm not interested in yesterday," he says in an interview. "I'm interested in today. Now. Now I'm talking to you and tonight I'll do a show.

I'm not looking back, and I'm not looking ahead. Let me tell you something. Years ago, in vaudeville, everyone carried their own pictures and the theater manager would hang them up. If the manager didn't like you, he canceled you after the first show. And the way he canceled you was he gave you your pictures back. Life's like that, too. They gave Jack Benny his pictures back. Jolson got his pictures back. Gracie. But, I'll tell you, if the guy knocks on my door with my pictures, I'm not going to answer."

Burns puffs quietly on his cigar. "I have no regrets. I've had a nice life, I *still* have a nice life. If I had to do it again, I'd do it the same way.... What's it all about? You mean life? I'm sitting here, there are all kinds of flowers and cigars and candy that people sent me. They gave me a party and everybody said I was a nice man. That's it. It's nice."

The performance is over. A few of Burns's cronies from Hillcrest Country Club in Los Angeles have flown in for opening night, and they stop backstage to congratulate him. Burns sips a martini and enjoys the praise. "I *was* good, wasn't I, Irving?" he asks. "You were great, George," Fein answers. "It went over very well."

"Someone asked me if I ever get nervous before I perform," Burns says to a reporter. "I said only people who have talent get nervous." He chuckles. It was the same reporter who had asked him that question a few hours earlier. Over the course of two days, he has told the same jokes, the same stories, over and over again. And yet, when he and Fein are trying to remember the name of the band leader, it's Burns who comes up with it.

And then it's time to call it a night. Burns leaves his dressing room to head back to his suite. But he's too high from his ovations to turn in yet, even though it's well past midnight. As he walks through the casino, he stops. "Wait, wait," he says to Fein. "I feel like playing a little blackjack."

Burns pulls two fresh hundred-dollar bills out of a gold money clip. ("Money means nothing to me," says the man who has recently donated a million dollars to Cedars-Sinai Medical Center and a million dollars to the Motion Picture and Television retirement home.) He plays two hands, betting $10 and $15 on each one. He's on a lucky streak. He wins, and wins again, and again, letting his money ride. "Last hand," he says. He gets a jack and 10 on one hand, two eights on the other. He takes another card on the eights, pulls a five. Two more winners. He cashes in his chips, counts his cash—he's made a couple of hundred dollars in 10 minutes—tips the dealer, and heads for bed.

Sydney Barrows: Happy hooking to major booking

OCTOBER 16, 1986

Now here's where all that breeding really shows. Sydney Biddle Barrows, much better known as the Mayflower Madam, is riding up a freight elevator to film a segment of NBC's news magazine, *Fast Copy*, and the show's producer tells her that her interview is actually part of a bigger story. One on "Best-selling Books by Crooks." And her answers will be edited in next to Jean Harris's and R. Foster Winans's.

And the tight, correct little smile on her face never flinches. "I'm in good company," says the convicted promoter of prostitution of her place in TV history, right next to a convicted murderer and a convicted stock swindler.

Sydney Barrows, 34, is promoting her best-seller, *Mayflower Madam* (Arbor House, $17.95), dressed in a hooker's version of classy: a blue silk dress, flesh-colored stockings, classic black pumps, pearls, subdued makeup, sedate pageboy. You could call the look Updated Pilgrim. This particular dress has white cuffs. Its detachable white collar is at the cleaners but will catch up with Barrows at the next stop on her tour. The only sexy thing about this woman, who ran a high-priced Manhattan call-girl service for five and a half years, is her low, throaty laugh.

And that's no accident. Barrows has written a Golden Books version of prostitution and positioned herself somewhere between Lee Iacocca and Goldilocks, between a struggling entrepreneur and a wide-eyed innocent—"naive" is her word—who took a job answering the phones of an escort service barely knowing what the heck an escort service was. A hard-working gal trying to make it on her own in the big city who just happened to "fall into" running a kind of a

dating service that linked men willing to pay
$200 an hour for companionship with girls who
owned matching bras, panties, and garter belts.

Barrows paints a picture of prostitution that
makes it sound better than dating. "It was fun,"
she says over and over. "We were making a lot
of people happy without hurting anyone." In
place of the myth of the hooker with a heart of
gold, she substitutes the call girl who's putting
herself through med school. Or law school, or
working as a broker on Wall Street, or a lawyer,
or a business trainee, or spending her afternoons
on auditions, or taking advanced classes in
"music, dance, art, or acting." They came from
the finest of families: "Margot's father was a
judge; Alexia's father was a diplomat; Paige was
an heiress."

And the tricks and johns, whom she
scrupulously refers to as clients, included CEOs
and Arab princes, a judge, several law-
enforcement officials, many doctors and lawyers,
bankers, brokers, deal makers, consultants, a
dope-smoking Catholic priest, an Orthodox rab-
bi, a "famous hockey player," a "prominent
television personality," a "well-known British
rock musician," a "film producer from California," and a "professional opera singer." All
unnamed, of course.

They took the girls to premieres, to formal
dinners hosted by Henry Kissinger, to weddings,
to bar mitzvahs, to Broadway shows, to fabulous
restaurants, and, only incidentally, to bed.
Almost to a man, they were "so attractive and
successful that most single women in Manhattan would have killed to go out with them."

A bad guy in Barrows's book is one who
doesn't keep a couple of cans of diet soda in his
fridge for her thirsty girls. Or one who didn't
change his cat litter often enough. Or one who
needed new towels. But far more common are the
men who gave the girls Cabbage Patch dolls,
dresses, ski parkas, $100 tips, and career advice.
And then they handed over their Visa or Master-

Card. (The girls carried miniature imprinters in their briefcases—a good disguise to get them past hotel security in the middle of the night.)

The "dates" were so pleasant the girls sometimes threw in an hour for free or refused to go back because they were having so much fun it didn't seem right to take money. "Many girls came back from their first call saying, 'I can't believe I'm getting paid for this!' " Barrows writes.

In nearly 300 ghost-written pages (William Novak did the deed between *Iacocca* and Tip O'Neill's autobiography), not one girl gets slapped around. Not one girl has sex with a 300-pound "client." Not one girl has to work on an 80-year-old man.

"It didn't happen," says Barrows, shrugging her shoulders. "The American public has been fed so many lies. People think the girls are degraded. That's not true. The girls who worked for me never were. I made sure of it.

"In point of fact, our clients worked as hard as the girls. They had to give the girls a glamorous and fun and exciting experience or they couldn't be clients. Believe it or not, that's true. And it's not true that the girls didn't enjoy it. The majority enjoyed it the majority of the time. They're just ordinary girls, articulate, fun, warm, very honest. Nice people with goals in life who just needed a little extra money.

"It's very difficult for people to believe that girls could do this and have fun and not have anything terrible happen to them.

"I know this isn't for everyone, but ethics are in the eye of the beholder. I couldn't smoke— that's a disgusting habit; I don't gamble. Those are my personal moral choices." (In the course of the day, Barrows repeatedly will compare prostitution to smoking, drinking, gambling, and once to writing a gossip column, but more about that later.)

"A girlfriend of mine who works in public relations got a big promotion. She called me up and said, 'Sydney, I'm so excited! I've been offered this fabulous account: Stolichnaya (the Russian vodka)!' I said, 'You're not going to take it, are you? You're not seriously considering it?' She said, 'Of course, why wouldn't I?'

"I said, 'You're talking about a communist product. Trying to con people into buying a product where the money goes back to a country that's trying to destroy us. How could you possibly do that?' She didn't see it that way at all. But I would never have taken that job in a billion years. I don't care if they had offered me four times as much money as I was making. People have different values."

It was her values that led Barrows into prostitution in the first place. This daughter of not one, but two, descendants of the Mayflower pilgrims, this child of boarding schools, this debutante, was working in New York as a buyer for a company that shipped merchandise to boutiques all over the country. As Barrows tells it, she was asked to unload some unfashionable handbags because her boss was "on the take."

"I was horrified and scared," writes Barrows. "It was a real dilemma: if I didn't distribute the handbags, I'd lose my job. But if I did, I'd lose my reputation. It took me about four seconds to decide."

It was while she was out of work, her reputation intact, that Barrows learned that a friend was making $50 a night "off the books" answering phones for an escort service. She told her friend to let her know if another job came up. "I think anyone in my position would have done the same thing," says Barrows.

When a job did come up, Barrows said, "What the hell," and grabbed it. She learned so much about the call-girl business that she and her friend decided to open their own. "The idea of running an escort service—and doing it right—became enormously appealing."

And that's how Barrows got into the sex-for-money biz. No big moral dilemma, no soul-searching, no sleepless nights, nothing.

"It really wasn't a big decision," says Barrows. "We just got so into 'Let's do this.' 'Yeah.' 'And let's do that.' And then we went out and got some phones and that was it. I'm sorry if I'm disappointing you, I get the feeling you're looking at me like I'm lying to you, but that's really how it was."

Barrows was in psychotherapy for five years, working on "liking myself better." The issue of what she did for a living rarely came up. "My therapist didn't have any problems with the business I was in because it didn't upset me. It didn't bother me. I didn't feel I was doing anything wrong. I was rather proud of it. ("Rather" rhymes with "father.") I was getting a lot out of it both personally and professionally."

There comes a point when most readers of Barrows's book must stop and ask a very rude question: "Why should I believe this?" Not one name is mentioned. Barrows refers to her clients as the *creme* of New York and international society, but a spokesman for Manhattan District Attorney Robert Morgenthau says they've been through her little black books and "not one name leapt off the pages." When asked about the discrepancy, Barrows says, "He's lying."

Why should he lie?

"I don't know," she says, "...and I don't care if people believe me. There's nothing that I can do about it. If people believe I worked as a hooker, I can't help it (she denies that she herself ever turned a trick). I'm not going to beat my head against the wall. Therapy helped me realize it's unrealistic to expect everyone to like you. As long as you have high standards and values for yourself, that's all anyone can expect from you. There will always be people who don't like me and write snide, catty things about me and laugh at me behind my back. There's nothing I can do about it.... I know I conducted my business more honestly, and with more integrity, than anyone else.

"Show me another business run as well. Cigarettes kill people. Other businesses don't care about their employees. I'm not ashamed of what I did. I have nothing to be ashamed of. I'm proud of it."

(While Barrows is waiting to be interviewed by Drew Hayes of WMAQ-AM, she asks for the sound to be turned up on her favorite soap opera. "There's probably one thing I do that I am a little ashamed of," she confides. "I love *All My Children*. I'm not real proud of that.")

"She seems to feel no guilt," co-author William Novak said by telephone. "I would feel guilt. You and I wouldn't run this kind of business."

Before Arbor House sent Sydney Biddle Barrows on the road, marketing director Michael Carter advised her not to wear red. "We thought it was a little hotter than we wanted her to be," says Carter. "She was already a madam that middle America could accept. We didn't want to ruin that. She's the girl next door. That's why this is so fascinating."

Then he sent her to media coach Dorothy Sarnoff, who has also worked with Novak and Alexandra Penney, author of *Great Sex*. "I told her to just be who she already is," Sarnoff says. "She has a kind of an unsophisticated look that works for her. It's casting against type, isn't it? She's a brilliant woman. I just wish she had been in another industry."

Soon she will be. She's co-producer of the CBS-TV movie based on her book, and she'll play a cameo role in the production. (Cybill Shepherd might portray her, she says.) But Barrows knows she can't be the Mayflower Madam all her life, so she hired manager Terry Whatley to move her into some other areas.

Says Whatley: "I'm setting her up with licensing groups, endorsement groups. We're working on a TV talk show for her, another book—a work of fiction—several different lecture circuits, a syndicated column. She's certainly

well-qualified to give advice to both men and
women. Some people want her to represent a
restaurant in New York.... The hook is, first of
all, that she comes from the equivalent of
American royalty—the Mayflower descendants—
and then that she ran something so slimy and
dirty in a proper and dignified way."

Barrows sees herself as the next Diane von
Furstenberg or Gloria Vanderbilt with her
name—Sydney Barrows—on everything from
lingerie to perfume to sheets to sportswear. But
there is one major difference between her and
those women: They never ran a call-girl operation. Does it matter? Is America ready to buy a
procurer's jeans or cologne?

"Who knows?" says Whatley. "This country
is nuts."

As her manager, Whatley intends to hang onto the Mayflower Madam label until Barrows's
own name catches on, but Barrows feels differently. She doesn't want to be associated with it anymore.

"You can't write INC. your whole life, right?"
she said to her interviewer, who until a year ago
was one of the writers of *The Tribune*'s INC. column. "You don't want to be known as this sort
of snide, catty person. You've got to move forward, too. You're trying to write more seriously, to be accepted as a serious interviewer. You
want people to say, 'She's a fine journalist,' not
'Oh, my God, don't let her near you, she only
writes dirt about people.'

"Well, I'm trying to get away from my bad
reputation and into something I can be more
proud of, too. It's the same thing. We're both trying to better ourselves. At least our reputations."

Don't think for a moment that because Barrows is trying to put her past behind her that she
in any way regrets even the bust that led to her
arrest in 1984 and her $5,000 fine.

Would she do it all over again?

"Sure. Who wouldn't? Why would I turn
down the opportunities? What happened that was

so bad? I got busted? So what? Am I dead? Blind? Don't I still have both my arms? Have I lost any friends? Doesn't my family still love me? Don't I have a wonderful future ahead of me? I can't find one negative thing about it."

What about the front-page pictures of yourself in handcuffs? What about going to jail, sharing a cell with street-corner whores?

"That was a very interesting experience. How many people get to have an experience like that? It was fascinating. And you know so much of it was luck. I just got caught in the middle of a circulation war between the *New York Daily News* and the *New York Post*. On the Friday before Labor Day weekend, the *Daily News*—the biggest paper in the biggest city in the country—puts 'Madam Talks Between the Covers' across the whole front page. Talk about a public-relations dream. I've just been so lucky. You can't buy this kind of luck."

It's about the only thing you can't buy.

At home with the Angels

NOVEMBER 19, 1986

NEW YORK—The mister is in his undershirt, vacuuming the hovel. The missus is out.

"Where is she?" he yells. "What's she doin'? Drinkin' a cappuccino? Figures. Figures she'd go off to some coffee house and do some yuppie thing like that. She better not bring any of the yup 'n' prep stuff in here!"

Welcome to Chez Sliwa, home of Mr. and Mrs. Guardian Angel, Curtis and Lisa, subway patrollers, authors, lecturers, personalities-for-hire.

We're on Avenue A in the Lower East Side. The east East Village. New Yorkers call it Alphabet City and avoid it. Chicness is several long, bum-lined blocks away.

We're in a tenement. Not a cute, funky tenement, a real tenement. It reeks of urine. The neighbors are dopers, dealers, muggers, hookers, and elderly Poles scared to leave their locked doors.

And now we're in the Sliwa apartment. A combination slum and media center. Squalor and sequins.

Let's take a little tour. First there's the bathroom. The floor in front of the toilet is caving in and a rag has been stuffed in the hole. "That's where the rats come through," says Curtis, who needs a shave. A sheet of plastic keeps one rotting wall from falling into the bathtub. There's no sink. No hot water. Lisa, a sometimes Elite model, star of her own self-defense video, and head-turner in any crowd, has to heat water on the stove to wash her hair. But when she does, it's with Pantene shampoo. And she keeps her imported Evian mineral water spritz right next to the Black Flag roach spray.

Then there's the kitchen. A rat is dying behind the refrigerator. Curtis says he can smell him. Toothbrushes are sitting in a glass over the sink. The cups are chipped. But there's a Braun coffee maker and a microwave oven, even though the missus is not much for cooking.

There's a combination dressing room/office. The tools of all their trades are here: makeup, a map of the New York subway system, a photocopier, and two boxes of index cards listing all of their local and national media appearances, the date of every interview they've ever given going back to 1979 when Curtis began the Guardian Angels, and the name of every reporter they've ever spoken to. Curtis intends to computerize all this information some day, the better to control his little empire with its 5,000 members and 60 chapters.

Then there's the living room. The walls were painted white sometime during the Depression. The furniture is mismatched, misshapen, broken. There's a crate for a bookcase. Only two of the five lightbulbs in the ceiling fixture are working. The room smells like frying fish, courtesy of some neighbor across the way.

There are bars on the windows. A thief recently ripped off their VCR, but he charitably left them their color TV. He also left the latest issue of *Variety* and a long, sexy, red-sequined dress, a designer original. It's the dress Lisa wore to her recent book-signing party. *Attitude: Commonsense Defense For Women* (Crown Publishers, Inc., $9.95) was introduced like a rock album at a Manhattan cabaret.

And then there's the bedroom. The bed takes up most of the room and it's not a big bed. There's a baseball bat propped in the corner. Curtis says it's for those rats. A single, naked lightbulb is plugged into the ceiling. Lisa's shoes are lined up along one wall, including her pink Reeboks.

"You know how embarrassing it is for me to walk down the street with her in those things?" asks Curtis. "Jeez. The missus sure likes her fluff and puff. What a princess!"

If you stuck a red beret on Ralph Kramden and booked him on *Donahue* a couple of times, he'd come out pretty much like Curtis Sliwa, 32. He's nicknamed "The Rock," and he walks loudly and carries a big *shtick*. His basic routine: "Yo! I'm just a poor street kid and all of a sudden I got myself this hotsy-totsy wife and ain't we got fun!"

So much for Curtis. But what's Lisa doing here, stepping over bums and showering in cold water? She's a 1975 graduate of Lake Forest College, with a degree in economics and a minor in 17th century French literature. A former pom-pon girl, cheerleader, and Girl Scout. She once worked in an art gallery. How did she get herself into this mess?

"I always wanted new experiences," says Lisa, early 30s, sitting in a coffee shop, eating a Swiss cheese omelet and drinking that cappuccino. "I always had a desire to really do something with my life, not just stand on the sidelines. And I always knew I could depend on myself to get out of whatever I got into."

Lisa is wearing the kind of black leather jacket that when you buy it they don't give you change back from your $500, skinny black jeans, red socks scrunched down over penny loafers, a Guardian Angel T-shirt, a red leather belt, and a red beret decorated with buttons and pins. She's skinny, with cheekbones that could double as lethal weapons and enough teeth to make a mugger think twice, especially if he's read the section of her book on biting. "Anywhere, anything, anytime!"

Right now she's running on about three hours sleep. She took a middle-of-the-night cheapo flight back from Houston where she lectured and tended to Angel business, grabbed a couple of hours rest, and then spent the morning promoting her book on a two-hour radio show.

On the air she sounds like a miniature Curtis, *wid a reel Noo Yawk akksent.* (Rather unusual considering she's from Hinsdale, Ill., the fourth safest community in America, according to *USA Today*.)

She's introduced as the national director of the Guardian Angels and then she goes into her Dirty Harriet spiel: "...it's time to quit giving creeps and mutants carte blanche...ya gotta deal with the slime factor...." She's so hip at hype that when a segment is taped to be played in San Francisco, she automatically drops "the Bay Area" and "the Golden Gate Bridge" into her patter.

But away from a microphone, when she's telling about how she came to New York in 1979, rented this $125-a-month apartment, and stayed —even though six people had been machine-gunned to death on her corner—she sounds like a nice girl from the Midwest.

"I was scared out of my mind," she says. "But I've always felt that if something scares you, you have to face it down. I didn't stay out of courage; I did it out of stubbornness, to prove I could survive."

Lisa was stubborn, but she wasn't stupid. She knew if she was going to last, she'd need some protection, so she took a martial arts class. Then she had all this muscle and no one to use it on. That's what led her to the bombed-out Guardian Angels headquarters in the Bronx.

"I never thought I'd survive the subway ride," she says. "Curtis was there. He was very egotistical, very cold. The police were arresting Angels every night and he was like a general in battle, no time for small talk or emotions or jokes. He was very sarcastic toward me, like I was some kind of debutante, which I wasn't. I was wearing a leather jacket, boots, jeans, your basic New York outfit that you can go anywhere in."

Curtis remembers the outfit a little differently: "It was like some black sequin jumpsuit. To me she looked like she just got off the dance floor at Studio 54 and someone whispered to her, 'Gee, wouldn't it be a kick to join the Guardian Angels and slum a little bit?'

The last thing I needed was a chick who was looking for a vicarious thrill. She looked like a good gust of wind could have knocked her over. We had some women members, but they had nicknames like 'Little Man' and 'Crusher,' so I just brushed her off. I treated her like I'd treat any new recruit, which is like dirt."

Lisa stuck out the training and earned her beret and she slowly became fond of Curtis. Very slowly. He keeps his charms well hidden. When exactly did he become a human being to her? "He never became a human being," says Lisa, sipping her second cappuccino.

But they got married anyway, on Christmas Eve, 1981, in a church in Greenwich Village, attended by 400 Guardian Angels. And five years later, she's happy.

"There are so few things you can do in life and really feel challenged on every level—emotionally, physically, mentally—and have the chance to grow. If it happens once in a lifetime you're lucky. I get it thrown at me every day.... If I weren't a Guardian Angel, I'd probably be a yuppie, an unfulfilled yuppie, with a nice car and a nice apartment, wondering if there's more to life. The only thing that's really appealing to me about that lifestyle is a nice bathroom. But even that's not worth it. Curtis and I made a commitment to help people when we got married. It keeps us together because we're completely different. We disagree on everything."

"I like to watch educational TV; they're doing a thing on Africa," says Curtis. "Lisa will want to watch *The Lifestyles of the Rich and Famous*." He spits out the words like he's shaking goo off his hand. "She likes to go to parties; I can't stand them; they make me uncomfortable. It's not like I'm a computer nerd whiz-kid, but I have very little in common with those people, and sometimes they're a little voyeuristic, like I'm part of a freak show.

"We just come from entirely different backgrounds. This was brought home to me this weekend. I was driving to Milwaukee with a couple of the Angels and I said, 'Guys, the missus tells us she had a basically middle-class upbringing; so let's just cru-u-u-uise through Hinsdale; we've got half an hour to spare. People were playing cricket!' "

Curtis does not feel badly that he has taken Lisa from cricket to cockroaches. "Absolutely not," he bellows. "It's about time she took the escalator down the ramp instead of up. She's been fluffed and puffed enough. Her brothers—I call them the yuppies supreme—told me all about Miss Sally Suburban Princess. This (he waves his arm around the living room) sort of balances things out. It keeps our heads in place with all the things we've got in development (a Guardian Angel film with John Avildsen, the director of *Rocky* and both *Karate Kid* movies, and future chapters in Paris and London). It's easy to do what I call the Jane Fonda-Tom Hayden trip, trying to appear to be part of the quote-unquote movement when you live in palatial surroundings in the People's Republic of Santa Monica."

For all his macho posturing, Curtis is the first to admit that he lives off his wife. It's her modeling, writing, and lecturing that pays their bills and some of the Angels' expenses as well. Neither of them draws a salary. Her income is so important to them that when a call comes in from her modeling agency, he goes tearing out of the apartment, leaving the door open, to find her. But the money has been coming in slowly. Lisa is a "personality" model, which sounds great but pays poorly. Corporate America does not want her hawking their hamburgers.

"This is the first year we've been able to start paying off our debts," says Lisa. "We borrowed money the first couple of years just to exist. A year and a half ago we took out a $6,000 loan from a little local Polish bank. They just gave us the money. We didn't have any collateral."

The hard-luck lifestyle might end when and if the Sliwas become parents. Lisa had one miscarriage, an experience she says made her feel like "a real failure." But, she says, "we'll cross that bridge when we come to it."

Meanwhile, back on Avenue A, the mister is still holding court in the living room. He can talk all day about the Guardian Angels, about Lisa, about their "we come from opposite-sides-of-the-subway-tracks" marriage. But finally he hears the door open.

"Well, who have we here?" he says. "It's little Miss Puff and Fluff herself. So you finally decided to come home!"

"I got your meat," says Lisa, holding out a bloody package wrapped in butcher paper. "Some veal chops."

"Veal chops! You can't cook veal chops! All you can cook is tofu! Or brie! You better call my mother...."

The phone interrupts Curtis's act. He answers it.

"Good afternoon, Guardian Angels.... Very good, and where are you?.... You have all the paperwork?... Now, you're going to take the double L train to the last stop in Brooklyn, Rockaway Parkway, and then call me from there...."

The *shtick* and the veal chops will wait.

Tomlin and Wagner are a team—just ask Lily

NOVEMBER 30, 1986

A lot of people who think they love Lily Tomlin really love Jane Wagner. Jane puts the words in Lily's mouth. She writes her material, she creates her characters, she makes her sound smart, she makes her sound funny. She works with her, she lives in a Spanish-style house in the Hollywood Hills with her, she protects her, she mothers her, she fusses over her, she finishes her sentences, she even reads her mind.

The two are huddled over breakfast at the Mayfair Regent Hotel. They're talking about the cult following inspired by Wagner's play, "The Search for Signs of Intelligent Life in the Universe." Tomlin starred in the one-woman show for a sold-out year on Broadway and recently moved it to L.A. She calls it "the *Saturday Night Fever* of the theater" because the die-hards come back to see it over and over again.

Says Lily: "People have come to see it five, six times, even mo..."

"...one woman told us she had seen it 17 times!" says Jane.

"Well, she was a little over the edge," says Lily. "She also had 'Jane' tattooed on her arm. Uh..." She catches herself and stops.

"What were you going to say?" a reporter asks.

She shakes her head. "Nothing."

"She's afraid this all sounds so self-serving," says Jane, interpreting the "uh" and the shake of Lily's head. "She doesn't like that."

"That's right," says Lily, "but I can say it because it's Jane's material. When the play is working, it's so affirming, so dense intellectually and verbally, so emotional, and very, very funny. People just want to see it again and again."

The two are putting away lumberjack
breakfasts. Eggs, toast, sausage, coffee, and
tomato juice for Jane. Oatmeal, eggs, toast,
coffee, and tomato juice for Lily. "Maybe I should
have the Belgian waffle," says Lily. "No, have
the eggs, you need the protein," says Jane. Later
she'll insist that Lily not pose outdoors for a
photographer. "She worries about my voice,"
says Lily. Every time the film *Nashville* is
mentioned, Wagner will remind everyone that
Lily won an Academy Award nomination for it.
On her part, Tomlin will make sure that Wagner
is included in every interview.

Lily is the tall, bony one with the map of the
Appalachians carved on her long, pale, hang-dog
face. (Her family is from Kentucky.) Jane is the
smaller, rounder, softer one who looks like pecan
pie and mint juleps. (She was raised in
Tennessee.) They're both in their mid-to-late 40s.

Lily is wearing a red leather jumpsuit,
enormous red sunglasses, strange, flowered red
pumps, red stockings, and not a single piece of
jewelry. She's got a dark blue coat that looks like
it was designed by Dow Chemical and a cap with
ear flaps. Jane is wearing layers and layers of
chic black leather—a fur-lined leather coat over
a leather kimono over leather slacks, high heels,
and wrists full of silver and rhinestone bracelets.
Lily's hair is black. Jane's is frosted blond.

They're both here to promote Wagner's book,
*The Search for Signs of Intelligent Life in the
Universe* (Harper & Row, $15.95). It's basically
the script of the play. They've got a non-stop day
of interviews that includes *The Oprah Winfrey
Show*; Chicago's gay and lesbian newspaper, the
Windy City Times; and a book-signing at Kroch's
& Brentano's. Wagner, the worrier, is afraid the
rain will cut down the crowds at the bookstore.
Tomlin, the rock, assures her it will be OK.

Tomlin has no financial interest in the book;
she gets no credit for it. And the fact that she's
here is about as strong a testimony to friendship
as you can get. She's putting herself on the line,

exposing herself to reporters, who are bound to ask personal questions. She hates to really talk about herself, refuses to reveal anything. Her interviews are filled with the same set pieces, recycled over and over again: growing up in Detroit, making the rounds in New York, working as a waitress at Howard Johnson's.

Only rarely does she let her guard down. In a 1973 interview with *The New York Times*, she scoffed over the likelihood of marriage and instructed the reporter to write "that I've had 50 women and 20 men." Tomlin later told *Newsweek*, "The truth is that you should love anyone, man or woman."

There's nothing nearly as controversial going on today, but Tomlin's defenses are raised anyway. "Your career has really been a roller coaster with some pretty big successes and some pretty big failures," one TV reporter says. Tomlin stares at him with contempt, takes a few seconds to compose herself before she deigns to answer.

She recently appeared on *The Late Show with Joan Rivers* and was introduced in a very funny staged bit that picked her up in her dressing room and followed her as she walked out on stage, supposedly in a huff because Rivers had stocked the dressing room with roses and she's allergic to them.

In the bit, Tomlin walked out mumbling to herself: "All those years of heartache and sacrifice for this... She's going to tell me to be myself. If I wanted to be myself would I have invented 37 characters?... She's going to say 'Lily, you've got to need people.' Would I do a one-woman show if I wanted to need people?"

When asked if any of that was true, that she had sacrificed to get where she is, that she does sometimes hide behind her characters, that she doesn't like to rely on others, she answers abruptly, "No. They just wrote those lines for me."

Then why is she here? She has a show to do tonight in L.A., which she'll miss because her plane doesn't leave on time. "She'll be furious," says Jane. "We'll have to refund all those tickets." (Tomlin is known for being tight-fisted and the two women have put up all the money for the show themselves.)

The answer is simple: She's here for Jane. "Lily's the commercial drawing power and she wanted to help launch the book," says Wagner's editor at Harper & Row, Craig Nelson. "Lily wants Jane to get the credit she deserves. It was the same with the play. Jane's name on the marquee was almost as big as Lily's. Part of the reason to publish the book was to continue getting Jane more professional credit."

Tomlin and Wagner have a professional and personal relationship that goes back 15 years, to when Tomlin saw a Peabody-winning TV show that Wagner had written called *J.T.* about a southern black boy living in Harlem. She recognized a certain heart in the writing, and she wanted her to write for her Edith Ann character, the outrageous little girl in the oversized rocking chair that the country fell in love with on *Laugh-In*.

It was a meeting that Wagner calls "providential." Since then they've worked on Grammy-winning albums together, Emmy-winning TV specials, the Tony-award winning Broadway play "Appearing Nitely," and a couple of not-so-successful movies: the underrated *The Incredible Shrinking Woman* and the notorious *Moment by Moment*.

A lot of people make stinko films. Did you see Meryl Streep and Robert DeNiro in *Falling in Love*? Happen to catch Robin Williams in *Club Paradise*? Or Goldie Hawn in *Protocol*? John Belushi in *1941*? Dan Aykroyd and Chevy Chase in *Spies Likes Us*? Dudley Moore in *Santa Claus, The Movie*? What about Barbra Streisand and Gene Hackman in *All Night Long*? But none of those films was met with the full-out derision that greeted Tomlin and John Travolta in *Moment by Moment*, an older woman/younger man movie both written and directed by Wagner.

Travolta was about the hottest thing in the country at that time, riding high on *Saturday Night Fever* and *Grease*. No one wanted to blame him too much. And Tomlin is a beloved star. She's Ernestine, the arrogant telephone operator; Edith Ann; Bobbi Jeanine, the lounge pianist; Judith Beasley, the ultimate consumer. There was a limit to how much the press wanted to criticize her. Mostly they attacked her for giving her "good friend" Jane so much power. The snickering could be heard from L.A. to New York.

"The hostility was all out of proportion to the film," says Wagner later in the day, after Tomlin has left for O'Hare and her aborted flight back to L.A. ("I hope it wasn't raining when she left. She hates to fly in the rain.") "If it's a bad movie, so it's a bad movie. There are a great many talented people who make bad movies. It's funny how ill-prepared we were for that."

It was the flat-out failure of *Moment by Moment* that has made the success of "Search" all the sweeter. It's a loving play—really a tapestry of 16 characters from Trudy, the crazy bag lady whose umbrella hat picks up signals from outer space, to Kate, the snobby Manhattanite who's got rich people's burn-out. Wagner updates the lion lying down with the lamb when these two unlikely characters come together at the end of the play.

"The success has been affirming and validating," says Wagner. "Maybe I wouldn't have needed it so much if it hadn't have been for the other. In some ways you never recover from that. You think you'll never work again; you think no one will ever want you to work again. I said to Lily, 'The terrible thing about the bad reviews we got is that all those doubts that you have about yourself, suddenly everyone has them.' Lily could have blamed me and cut me loose, but she didn't. Even so, I didn't work for a while. I didn't want to.

"The ups and downs are so unrealistic in this business. It's manic-depressive at best. You can hardly enjoy the good times, thinking about what will happen next. It's like you have to top yourself every time. Everything costs so much— to mount a production, to produce a book—it's like everything has to be a success on all levels, or you've failed."

Tomlin and Wagner raised the money for "Appearing Nitely" from investors. They financed " Search" themselves. "Our accountants went crazy. But so much of the money on 'Nitely' went to other people. This time we decided to do the whole thing ourselves. If it had failed, we would have lost a fortune. We really did everything wrong, it just happened to turn out right."

Together they made the decision to move the play to Los Angeles. "Maybe that was stupid, too," says Wagner. "We left while we were selling out. But Lily's agent felt it was very impactful for her to come to L.A. so the movie people would see her. And we live there."

Wagner is the writer-director of the show. Tomlin is the star-producer. "Lily is a wonderful producer," says Wagner. "We have a general manager who's supposed to take care of the money, and he's good, but he can't touch Lily. I'd say she's like an accountant, but I've never known an accountant who's that good. She amazes the accountants. She remembers figures. She's able to calculate things in her head. She remembers telephone numbers, too. She's that kind of person. I can't even remember who I'm supposed to call. That's the kind of mind I have.

"She was the older child in her family and she was very responsible. She took care of things. She tells this story about how her mother bought a vacuum cleaner on time. She was vulnerable to salesmen and he talked her into it. Lily felt they couldn't afford it so she called up and demanded that they take it back. They gave her a hard time but she badgered them until they took it. She was only in her early teens. To this day, I see that part of her. I'm more like Lily's mother. I'd keep the vacuum. But she's strong and takes charge."

Lily is the take-charge partner at home, too. "She's more reality-based" is the way Wagner describes her. "I'm more of a dreamer. She allows me to be to a certain extent."

Since they met 15 years ago, Wagner has written exclusively for Tomlin, although Tomlin has performed other people's work, including the films *All of Me* with Steve Martin and *Nine to Five* with Jane Fonda and Dolly Parton. She'll film a sequel to it this spring.

"It would be a good career move for me if the next thing I do is not for Lily," says Wagner. "A lot of people have put that idea out. From a practical standpoint it's a wise thing, but I'm spoiled. To work with Lily is very safe for me. It's secure. Maybe I lack courage. It's safe for her, too, though. Maybe that's at the heart of any collaboration.

"If I'm protective of Lily, it's because I feel she's vulnerable. And she's so giving to me. I never would have asked for my name on the marquee. She wanted to give me some recognition. She thought I deserved it. She probably thought I needed it, too. I did."

But all this is later in the day, after the books are signed and the interviews are given. Back at breakfast, Tomlin and Wagner are asked about their next project.

"It's too early to think about it," says Lily.

"For me, too," says Jane. "I've got a lot of ideas, just snatches of conversation, bits of dialogue...."

"Jane makes a lot of notes and then suddenly sits down one day and writes a draft," says Lily, "and then I go back and I search through the notes and she hasn't used a thing and I say, 'What about this?' 'What about that?' I'm the curator of her work."

"When something's good I know it intuitively," says Jane. "More and more I'm beginning to trust my intuition. Both of us are very intuitive and I think a lot of our mistakes come from taking too much advice. Don't you agree, Lily?"

"Mmmmmm," says Lily.

"That's what's nice about having a success. It's not power, I'll never feel powerful, but I'll feel more confident."

Someone mentions an old monologue Lily had performed on the Joan Rivers show.

"Why don't you practice it in case Oprah asks you to do it?" Jane suggests.

"Right now?" asks Lily, looking around the restaurant.

"I always love those old monologues," says Jane.

But there's no time; they're running late. They'll run late all day long. As they leave, Jane turns to Lily and says, "Public humiliation is just around the corner."

Author meets video,
takes Manhattan

DECEMBER 11, 1986

PRINCETON, N.J.—If Ernest Hemingway were alive today, he'd make a video to promote his new book, *The Sun Also Rises After the Bell Tolls on Kilimanjaro.*

It would open with a shot of Papa Hemingway in wrinkled khaki, stampeding elephants behind him. And then there'd be a fast cut to a bullfight. Papa with a cape, making a couple of passes at a frisky bull. Ava Gardner next to him, clicking her heels. Ingrid Bergman throwing kisses.

And then Harry's Bar in Paris. Papa drinking too many scotches and telling too many tales. "We were young. We drank wine. We made love. We wrote. And it was good."

And then Papa fishing off Key West. The sun setting behind him, making a halo around his mighty head. And a final shot of the cover of his book and a voice-over, saying, "You love the man, now buy the book...."

But Hemingway, a writer who knew quite a bit about self-promotion, is dead.

So we have Tama Janowitz, instead.

Janowitz is the author of *Slaves of New York* (Crown, $15.95), a hot, hip, best-selling collection of short stories about the East Village art scene. And she's also the star of the very first literary video. This is the first time in the history of Western civilization that a book has been sold on MTV. The first time since Johann Gutenberg invented the printing press that an author has been peddled like a rock star.

"I figured, what the hell," says Janowitz.

The video opens with the dust jacket of Janowitz's book, which is a portrait of her lounging against silk pillows, her little Yorkshire terrier in her lap, a gardenia in her hair. And then the portrait dissolves to the real Tama, in the same odalisque pose, only this time dressed in stretch pants. A male voice is intoning: "*Slaves of New York*...the New York art scene...the color, the characters, the relationships."

And then there's Tama floating through the wholesale meat market of Manhattan wearing a strapless evening gown; and Tama giggling, sandwiched between Andy Warhol and Deborah Harry; and Tama hugging her knees, leaning her head on her computer (typing with her ear?); and Tama in a tutu discussing her art while she plays with her ruffles.

"Stories, like, ya know, just kinda throw themselves at me," she says, and then launches into one about a band of 6-foot-tall, ballerina-like transvestite prostitutes who camp outside her door and grab all the cute guys for themselves.

Slaves of New York: Coming soon to a bookstore near your house.

"The video was fun. I was doing the whole Tama Janowitz act. I was like George Plimpton pretending to be a football player," says Tama Janowitz.

It's a dreary, drizzly Sunday in Princeton, N.J., about as far from the East Village as you can get. Tama Janowitz is curled up on a burnt-orange sofa in a living room furnished in motel modern. She's wearing a short, torn black sweater over a long, torn black sweater over a long, brown skirt and black stockings.

She's fussing with her hair. She has massive amounts of hair. Long, full, ratted black hair. It rises high and wide over her forehead, hangs down past her shoulders. Small, furry things could nest in there. It's a look.

Janowitz is living in a faculty house for her year as an Alfred Hodder fellow. There is barely one personal item in the whole place. Just her computer sitting on the dinette table. She's discussing art, life, fame, and boyfriends. The four basic food groups.

"I spent years and years by myself in my room trying to write, living marginally and having just a really quiet life and now this is my 15 minutes," says Janowitz. "The video was a career move. It doesn't make me (pulp novelist) Judith Krantz."

Janowitz, 29, has been writing her whole life. Her mother is a poet—how many people can say that?—and she grew up watching her send out poems, get back rejection notices, apply for grants, barely scrape by. Janowitz seemed to be following in her mother's footsteps. She lived from grant to grant, fellowship to fellowship, in one dreary room after another, on one campus after another. Occasionally she'd sell a story, first to publications like the *Mississippi Review*, then to *The New Yorker*. The prestige was great. The money was lousy. Her first book, *American Dad*, was published when she was just 22, but it quickly disappeared. The next four wound up in a desk drawer. And then came a grant from the National Endowment for the Arts in 1982.

"I was so tired of being isolated," she says, "I thought, I'll go to New York and I'll be around people. But I just sat in my apartment day after day. The phone never rang. When I'd go out, I'd go to a bar and sit there. I'm terribly shy and I wasn't going to speak to anyone. I had been by myself from 9 in the morning till 8 at night, writing. Did I have any interesting gossip? Any interesting stories? No. I was totally asocial. I was just as isolated as I was in Provincetown or Virginia.

"And then I found out, almost by accident, that if you went into SoHo on a Saturday in the fall, there was an art opening taking place. And there'd be 300 people and they'd spill out on the street and someone would give you a cheap glass of white wine and then the next thing you know someone would say, 'Well, what do you think of the painting?' So the art scene was the one scene I could walk into. You'd just go in and join the crowd. So I went."

She went and she listened and she took notes and then she went home and put it all into her stories.

Or as Eleanor, one of her continuing characters, says: "So it's like this: for some time I've been hanging around at a lot of different places. And where I've been, it's mostly downtown. The things I've seen, while I was there, I kept my mouth shut. But later, when I got home, I wrote down what I saw."

The stories are basically about the apartment situation in New York. There aren't any.

They're about artists who don't talk about art: They talk about who's selling which picture and for how much. Who drink "Perrier and water" and work in new media such as ground bones and blood or mirrors and lemons, who depict Good and Evil in terms of Bullwinkle and Quick Draw McGraw and plan on constructing the Chapel of Jesus Christ as a Woman adjacent to the Vatican "complete with Her own Stations of the Cross: Washing the Dishes, Changing the Diapers, Self-Flagellation at the Mirror, Fixing the Picnic Lunch, et cetera." Who start conversations with their girlfriends with "What is it about you I hate the most?"

And then there are the girlfriends, the slaves who slave over the stove all day. Dinner is either "Cornish game hen with orange glaze, curried rice, and asparagus or it could be fettuccine alfredo with garlic bread and arugula salad." These are the girls who move to New York to make plastic James Bond doll earrings and find that other girls are already doing it so they switch to making belts from teeth and rhinestones and silver chunks. The ones who are scared to death their boyfriends will kick them out. "Well, it's his apartment, and if we have a fight or something I sometimes get this panicky feeling: Where the hell am I going to go?"

"They're all me, all the characters," says Janowitz. "Eleanor is me and all the women I knew. I had lots of relationships and I always felt powerless. What was interesting to me was women wanting boyfriends and then living with these guys. And the guys would stay out all night and then say they wouldn't do it again and then the next time they'd stay out for two nights. Or they'd come home drunk and beat them. I didn't think about themes when I was writing, but now I can see that the stories are about power. The men had all of it.

"I was around for years and years and there were all kinds of people who wouldn't even say hello to me and then, all of a sudden, I'm on the cover of *New York* magazine and I'm on *David Letterman* and they're like, 'Who is this bitch? Who does she think she is? Her book is boring.' I'm like, 'Give me a break. Where's *your* book?' There were a lot of patronizing remarks: 'She made a video. She sold out. She's so commercial.' The video and the publicity just means that I'll have an easier time getting my next book published."

"Tama was a natural," says Andrew Martin, managing director of publicity for Crown. "She looks like someone from a music video." Crown had been approached by Bob Becker, head of American Made Productions, about using a video to sell a book and when they looked through their stable of authors, Janowitz jumped out. "They could use me like a character from one of the stories," says Janowitz. That put the whole publicity machine in motion. As many interviews were done on the video as reviews were done on the book. And Janowitz cooperated to the hilt.

"Tama and I really maximized the press opportunities," says Susan Magrino, Crown publicist. "If there was something we thought we could get into a column, we called it in. We began with items. Then when *The New York Times* did a piece over the summer on how to keep cool, we got Tama in it saying she goes to the meat lockers. And then parodies of the book started. Once the parodies start, you've got it made."

For *New York* magazine and the video and Letterman, Janowitz trotted out the whole Tama Janowitz routine.

"I mean, let's face it, when I wake up in the morning and no one's here and I'm like staggering to the kitchen for my bowl of cereal, I wouldn't make the most fascinating interview. Before I went on David Letterman, I was sitting in that dressing room, waiting and waiting and waiting, and if I get too nervous, I get spaced out, so I had to make myself stay up, so I pretended to be Tama Janowitz.

"And I chew gum all the time, so I was chewing gum to make me calmer and I didn't realize what it would look like. And then when I saw it, I thought 'Oh, no!' But then I thought, 'Oh, well, that's part of the Tama Janowitz act. There she is on TV, chewing gum. Obviously she couldn't care less." The point is you have seven minutes to make people remember you and feel like buying the book the next day. I didn't consciously think 'I'll write a book and I'll model myself on Madonna.' It's not that deliberate. It just happens. And it's fun.

"I had the other part: You're broke, you live in one crummy room, you don't know how to meet people, you have no avenues to meet people, the day is interminable, you're sitting here and trying to write, and everything is tough and hard. I had that. That's the way most people live. You get up and you get dressed and you go to some dreary job and your biggest thrill is going to the shopping mall. You're trapped. Rich people have crummy problems, but with money or fame, you're not trapped. You fly to Miami for the weekend or someone says, 'Come on, we're going to this fabulous party.' In New York, there's a certain crowd that lives like they're not trapped. They go to the nightclubs and stuff. I never would have been able to be a part of it if I hadn't worked so damn hard....

"This stuff doesn't change your life. Like there I was on the cover of *New York* magazine and my phone wasn't ringing with people saying, 'Please come to Jacqueline Onassis's party.' And I went on TV, on a news show, as one of New

York's 10 most eligible women and I got two letters. One was from a chiropractor in Fort Lee, N.J., and the other was from a diamond cutter who said, 'I wonder how you'd feel about going out with a man who's appeared on the pages of *Playgirl* magazine.' What changes your life is like (at this point Janowitz goes into a sing-song) getting to be happier with yourself, feeling like you're growing as a writer, maturing as a person. All the regular, boring stuff. It's fun that the book is selling and that people are paying attention to me when nobody paid attention to me in my whole life, but it's not very important. Tomorrow I get up and hit the typewriter. That's where the real life is."

For her next book, Janowitz is reworking one of those four books in her desk drawer, *A Cannibal in Manhattan*, about a cannibal who marries an American heiress and gets involved in the drug trade and winds up eating his wife after she's been barbecued on a hibachi in Central Park. There is an outside chance that this book might not sell as well as *Slaves*.

"I'm totally prepared for it. Everyone is going to say give me more *Slaves*, but I love this book."

Besides *Cannibal*, Janowitz has a new edition of *American Dad* coming out, the paperback edition of *Slaves*, and she's working on a couple of screenplays, one based on the Eleanor stories.

In spite of it all, she says, "I don't feel successful. My life is quite boring. What do I want? I feel like if I answer this correctly, I'll get a crown. I want to write better. I don't want to be alone. I think life is a lonely process. If you're with someone, lots of times you're still just as lonesome—I don't expect much of relationships—but at least I'd have someone to watch TV with. I want some kids. If my next book gets rejected, it would be nice to have someone say, 'I still love you.' And then I'd like a leather jacket and an apartment and I'd like to get my furniture out of storage."

The Miami Herald

Belinda Brockman
Finalist, Obituary Writing

Belinda Brockman, 38, was born in Cedar Rapids, Iowa, and graduated in history from Iowa State University. She worked as a bartender, a secretary, and a food co-op manager before she joined *The Miami Herald* in 1982 as a city desk clerk, her first newspaper job. She now serves as obituary writer for the *Herald*.

Brockman's obituaries resemble Jim Nicholson's in their rich detail, multiple sources, and focus on personality. She also plays down organizations and formulas. Both succeed by reporting in depth.

Orange Bowl's Hal Fleming dies

JANUARY 29, 1986

Hal Fleming, the Orange Bowl's "Mr. Indispensable," whose nuts-and-bolts knowledge transformed Miami's New Year's celebration from a rolling rumble of floats into true majesty, died Tuesday of lymph gland cancer. He was 65.

In his 39 years with the festival, Mr. Fleming "literally developed into the closest thing that I've ever seen to an indispensable man," said Dan McNamara, executive director of the Orange Bowl Committee. "He was fantastic. My main man. We put out a lot of fires together."

Those fires were all part of turning others' creative dreams into the glitter and gold that parades down Biscayne Boulevard each New Year's Eve, or marches across the playing field each New Year's night, or races through the waterways and streets of Miami each Orange Bowl season.

Mr. Fleming was the all-around handyman who saw to it that everything went just right.

"He was a guy that worked doggedly at everything he did, with a great friendly attitude," McNamara said. "He was everything. He could bellow like a bull and be as gentle as a lamb, whatever was needed."

In the bigger-than-life atmosphere of the Orange Bowl, bigger-than-life stories abound about its central characters. Of Hal Fleming, most of those tales are true.

Take for instance when NBC was planning to cover for the first time a powerboat race from Watson Island. The producer pointed out that for ideal shooting a television camera tower must be moved, adding, facetiously, that half-a-dozen coconut palms seemed to be in the way. Mr. Fleming took the producer at his word.

"The next morning when we got over there, the tower was moved and about six or eight trees were transplanted," McNamara recalled.

For years afterward, Mr. Fleming stuck a few palm fronds on the edge of the bleachers along the parade route, just for the benefit of the cameramen.

Always amenable, he once offered to cut a hole through the MacArthur Causeway in aid of the Orange Bowl Regatta.

Born and raised in Stokes, N.C., Mr. Fleming played baseball in the minor leagues, until World War II broke out.

Stationed briefly on Miami Beach during the war, he vowed to return to the land of sunshine.

Suffering a leg injury while fighting in Germany, Mr. Fleming knew his chances at the major leagues were gone. He did, though, win a tryout at the New York Giants spring training camp in Miami.

He didn't make that team, but he made another, Earnie Seiler's Orange Bowl team.

Seiler, the "mad genius" creator of the festival, hired Mr. Fleming for odd jobs. He was to work for a month. He stayed 39 years.

Seiler and Mr. Fleming's relationship developed into one as close as father and son.

"He was one fantastic guy," said Seiler's son, Pete. "He worked you hard and took care of you and played hard with you."

When Mr. Fleming first went to work for the Orange Bowl in 1946, the festivities were a far cry from the pageantry of today.

That year, Mr. Fleming asked the festival's bookkeeper and ticket manager for money to buy tools.

"She gave me $5 to go get a hammer, screwdriver, a square, and a saw," he recalled. "She sent me to Woolworth five-and-dime on Flagler Street to get it. I think I spent $4.20. The first time I hit a nail, the hammer just—bffrrt!— disintegrated."

After that, he borrowed tools for 10 years.

But the years of year-round hard work were given with total love.

"You plan, plan, plan all year, and you see everything go off great," Mr. Fleming said in December from his National Children's Cardiac Hospital bed. "Then all of a sudden, it's all over with, and you start all over again.

"That," he said, "has been my whole life."

Survivors include his wife, Cindy, and four children, Gale, Rhonda, Leslie, and Ross.

Prayer services will be at 7 p.m. Thursday in Ahern-Plummer Bird Road Chapel, with graveside services at 11 a.m. Friday in Miami Memorial Park.

Laura Cushman dies at 99

APRIL 15, 1986

Laura Cushman, the egalitarian founder of the Cushman School, Miami's oldest private educational institution, died Sunday at the age of 99.

"She left a really beautiful heritage," said Norah Schaeffer, whose youngest child attended the Cushman School. "She left a wonderful school."

There were no "prize" students at Dr. Cushman's school, a Miami landmark for more than 60 years. For Dr. Cushman saw in each child a special trait. And it was through her guidance that the "specialness" was developed.

"Her basic philosophy was that every child has worth and should be given character development," said Joan Lutton, the school's current principal. "If you're doing all the things you're supposed to be doing to build character, you'll have a better student.

"Her philosophy is a strong one."

"I've always said as I pull out the weeds, it's just like taking all the troubles out of little children's lives," Dr. Cushman once said in an interview. "The good is in the child, and you just develop it."

Dr. Cushman's philosophy was also a noncompetitive one.

"If we can have all winners, then we'll have all winners," said Lutton.

Born in Iowa, the daughter of a far-sighted real estate man, Dr. Cushman moved to Miami with her family in 1913.

She had a degree from Morningside College in Sioux City, Iowa, but after moving to Miami furthered her education at Wheelock College in Boston, qualifying as a specialist in kindergarten education.

Looking for work, Dr. Cushman found a job as a second-grade teacher at Coconut Grove Elementary, where she also taught music and sewing to the older students.

The next year, she went to work as a kindergarten teacher at Riverside Elementary, teaching in the morning and running a normal school for potential teachers in the afternoon.

Then in 1922, under a severe financial strain, the school board pulled the rug out from under her. It canceled all kindergarten classes.

Though Dr. Cushman was offered the position of principal at Riverside, she turned it down.

Because she believed vehemently in the importance of early childhood guidance, Dr. Cushman began campaigning full time for the reinstatement of the kindergarten program.

"She tried to fight to keep the public kindergartens open," Lutton said. But when she was unsuccessful, "she decided to start her own school. And it worked—here we are."

From the screened-in porch of her parents' home, Dr. Cushman taught her first class.

Mary Frances Perner was in that inaugural 1922 kindergarten class.

"We had a very wonderful start in her school, which has let me pull through some good times and some bad times in my life," said Perner.

With $35,000 from her father, Dr. Cushman bought three tiny white frame buildings at 33 NE 38th St. in 1924, and set up school for real.

Two years later, she sold the property for a sizable profit to make room for Biscayne Boulevard.

With the money, she built a new school at 60th Street and Biscayne Boulevard.

Today, the Spanish-styled building, nestled among huge old oaks, remains basically the same as when it was built in 1926.

Students still sit at carved oak tables and are summoned to class by a bell once used to call the workers who built Vizcaya.

Last July, the school was named an historical site by Dade County.

But not only the physical aspects of the Cushman School have remained virtually unchanged through the years; so has the spiritual vitality that the tiny teacher, barely taller than some of her pupils, built 60 years ago.

There are still the weekly performances, the farewell handshakes, and the teaching techniques that Dr. Cushman innovated years ago—independent study, team teaching, and contract work.

"She was so far ahead of her times," Lutton said.

At the age of 87, Dr. Cushman stepped down as head of the school, but continued as chairman of the board and an adviser to the school until two years ago, when she suffered a stroke.

Sixty years ago, Dr. Cushman told a reporter: "My aim is to offer first-class scholastic training in a healthful and beautiful atmosphere. 'Everything for the children' is our motto and desire."

Survivors include a sister, Lucy Collins; a brother, Laurence Cushman; four nephews, Franklin, Robert, George, and Larry; and a niece, Elizabeth Nichols.

Memorial services will be at 4 p.m. Saturday at the First United Methodist Church of Miami, under the direction of the Lithgow Miami Chapel.

The Cushman School will also have a memorial service at 9 a.m. Wednesday at the school, which has established a memorial scholarship fund in honor of its founder.

Daniel Stampler, inventor of 'doggie bag,' dies

JUNE 12, 1986

Retired restaurateur Daniel Stampler, who at his famed Greenwich Village Steak Joint introduced a standard in dining out, the doggie bag, died Thursday at the age of 72.

With a pampered Scottie pooch at home, Mr. Stampler, a Miami resident since 1970, simply hated to see good food go to waste. A purveyor of enormous portions, he wanted to encourage his patrons to take home leftovers for a midnight snack, for their best friend, or whatever.

So in 1948, two years after opening his steakhouse, Mr. Stampler's waiters began offering diners the now classic red-and-white paper bags, embossed with a smiling mutt imploring, "Take Me Home and Enjoy."

A tall, elegant, mustachioed man, Mr. Stampler would personally greet customers of his 300-seat steakhouse, attired in European designed suits, custom-made shirts and shoes.

"That's the way he ran his whole life," said Mr. Stampler's son-in-law, Gerald Drogin. "It had to be perfect.

"I'd say he was best described as bon vivant."

Upon entering, Steak Joint patrons' eyes were treated to rich panelling and tufted furniture. "His theory was that he wanted you to be as comfortable in the restaurant as if you were in your own dining room," explained Drogin.

Then their palates were enticed with Mr. Stampler's special garlic steak and scrumptious "snowball" dessert—a ball of vanilla ice cream coated in chocolate and rolled in coconut.

"When he was in his prime, it was the largest steakhouse in New York," said Drogin.

For the amateur magician, Sundays were always very special occasions. On that day, Mr.

Stampler would perform his delightful magic for all the kids, said Drogin, who remembered many a special childhood birthday spent at the Steak Joint.

In 1970, the native New Yorker, who grew up in the saloon-keeping business, decided to close his restaurant and retire to the warmth of South Florida.

"He took a few years off and said, 'This isn't for me,' " Drogin said. So Mr. Stampler opened another Steak Joint in Hallandale in 1973. Drawing on the acclaim of the first restaurant and the number of retired New Yorkers living in South Florida, the Broward Steak Joint became a popular place in a hurry.

But Mr. Stampler became ill with cancer and was forced to close the steakhouse in 1975, rather than lend his name to a concern that he did not directly oversee.

"He was just especially nice, and people really loved him," said Drogin.

Survivors include three daughters, Suzen Drogin, Penni Schimel, and Julie Stampler; one son, Jonathan Stampler; and four grandchildren.

Graveside services will be at 11 a.m Sunday at Mount Hebron Cemetery in New York.

Plato Cox, 'Old Man of Miami River,' dies

JULY 3, 1986

Plato Cox, the fabled Old Man of the Miami River, died Tuesday at the age of 76.

For 52 years, Plato Cox sold and repaired diesel ship engines along the brown waters of the river, cultivating clientele and friends ranging from small-time fishermen to Caribbean political leaders at Auto-Marine Engineers Inc.

He was so much a part of the river that those friends sometimes wondered if that same brown water did not pulsate through his veins.

"He's been on the river ever since I can remember," said Tommy Curry Jr., whose late father and uncle established Tommy's Boat Yard, Miami's second oldest. "All along the river, you mention Plato Cox's name and he was well known.

"Anything you ever wanted that had anything to do with the river, he'd have an answer for you."

A bulwark of a man, with arms like bridge pilings, Mr. Cox would daily survey his four-acre Auto-Marine Engineers Inc., a massive collection of ship and engine parts. Dressed in baggy work clothes, he looked every bit the junkyard master.

"Most people thought it looked like junk," said Mr. Cox's daughter, Joy Hooper. "But he knew what it was worth and who would need it."

The office of the deep-voiced, tight-mouthed, shrewd businessman, who lived in ritzy Bay Point, told the tale. Its walls were paneled with photographs and paintings of his friends—Sir Roland Symonette, first colonial premier of the Bahamas; Roddy Burdine; former Dominican Republic dictator Rafael Trujillo—among others.

A crusty conservative, who couldn't abide Communists, unions, or whippersnapper Coast

Guard inspectors, Mr. Cox was a decidedly self-made man. He knew every inch of his property so well he could walk right into his warehouse and lay his hands on an obscure part that may have been sitting on the shelf for months. And when no one else could find an engine part, Plato Cox would track one down.

"He took pride in doing that," said Curry.

He also knew every inch of the Miami River and its history, for, as he told it, "Miami comes from the river."

An umpteenth-generation seafaring man, Mr. Cox was born in Morehead City, N.C. He came to Miami as a tot in 1911. His grandparents had already sailed their way to Miami from North Carolina in 1899. His father, Christian, worked for the company that dredged Government Cut.

Mr. Cox struck out on his own at the age of 14. He cruised the world as an engineer on yachts. Then in 1934, he opened Auto-Marine Engineers.

Once a big-time fisherman, he caught a world-record 638-pound blue marlin off the coast of Bimini in the 1940s. It was the last one he ever kept.

Years later, the Old Man of the River would liken the experience to that of Ernest Hemingway's *Old Man and the Sea*: "I knew what the man meant when he said he loved that fish."

But time has found the Miami River a far different place than Mr. Cox's river of old. Where thriving shipyards once stood now stands a developer's dream. Tommy's Boat Yard closed in April. Mr. Cox stopped working in January.

"Daddy is an end of an era on the river," said Hooper.

In addition to Hooper, survivors include his wife, Edna; one sister, Catherine Weidele; and two grandchildren.

Services will be at 11 a.m. today at the Church-By-The-Sea, under the direction of the Cofer Miami Shores Funeral Home.

Selected bibliography

By JO A. CATES

This bibliography describes the literature of newspaper writing, reporters, and reporting published in 1986, with the exception of William Zinsser's *On Writing Well*, which should be included in all bibliographies ever compiled on writing. I include articles on coaching writing as well as items on the teaching and mechanics of writing. I have also added some general items on writing.

BOOKS

Atchity, Kenneth John. *The Writer's Time: A Guide to the Creative Process from Vision Through Revision.* New York: Norton, 1986.

Atwan, Robert and Bruce Forer. *Why We Write: A Thematic Reader.* New York: Harper & Row, 1986.

Baker, Sheridan Warner and Robert E. Yarber. *The Practical Stylist with Readings.* 6th ed. New York: Harper & Row, 1986.

Berkow, Ira. *Red: A Biography of Red Smith.* New York: Times Books, 1986.

Best Newspaper Writing. Annual. Don Fry, ed. St. Petersburg, FL: The Poynter Institute for Media Studies, 1986.

Best of Pulitzer Prize News Writing. William David Sloan, Valarie McCrary, and Johanna Cleary, eds. Columbus, OH: Publishing Horizons, 1986.

Biagi, Shirley. *Interviews that Work: A Practical Guide for Journalists.* Belmont, CA: Wadsworth, 1986.

Born, Roscoe C. *The Suspended Sentence: A Guide for Writers.* New York: Scribner, 1986.

Burkett, Warren. *News Reporting: Science, Medicine and High Technology.* Ames: Iowa State Univ. Press, 1986.

Calkins, Lucy McCormick. *The Art of Teaching Writing.* Portsmouth, NH: Heinemann Educational Books, 1986.

Clark, Roy Peter. *Free to Write: A Journalist Teaches Young Writers.* Portsmouth, NH: Heinemann Educational Books, 1986.

Daiker, Donald A.; Andrew Kerek; and Max Morenberg. *The Writer's Options: Combining to Composing.* 3rd ed. New York: Harper & Row, 1986.

Foley, Stephen Merriam and Joseph Wayne Gordon. *Conventions and Choices: A Brief Book of Style and Usage.* Lexington, MA: D. C. Heath, 1986.

Ford, Richard. *The Sportswriter.* New York: Vintage Books, 1986. [novel]

Franklin, Jon. *Writing for Story: Craft Secrets of Dramatic Nonfiction.* New York: Atheneum, 1986.

How I Wrote the Story. 2nd ed. Christopher Scanlan, ed. Providence, RI: Providence Journal Co., 1986.

Keir, Gerry; Maxwell McCombs; and Donald L. Saw. *Advanced Reporting: Beyond News Events.* New York: Longman, 1986.

King, Larry L. *None But a Blockhead: On Being a Writer.* New York: Viking, 1986.

Leonard, Thomas C. *The Power of the Press: The Birth of American Political Reporting.* New York: Oxford Univ. Press, 1986.

McDonald, Daniel Lamont. *The Language of Argument.* 5th ed. New York: Harper & Row, 1986.

Mencher, Melvin. *Basic News Writing.* 2nd ed. Dubuque, IA: William C. Brown, 1986.

Metzler, Ken. *Newsgathering.* 2nd ed. Englewood Cliffs, NJ: Prentice-Hall, 1986.

Murray, Donald M. *Read to Write: A Writing Process Reader.* New York: Holt, Rinehart & Winston, 1986.

Patterson, Benton Rain. *Write to Be Read: A Practical Guide to Feature Writing.* Ames: Iowa State Univ. Press, 1986.

Patterson, Margaret Jones and Robert H. Russell. *Behind the Lines: Case Studies in Investigative Reporting.* New York: Columbia Univ. Press, 1986.

Reporting Science: The Case of Aggression. Jeffrey H. Goldstein, ed. Hillsdale, NJ: L. Erlbaum Assoc., 1986.

Reston, James. *Washington.* New York: Macmillan, 1986.

Rivers, William L. and Alison R. Work. *Freelancer and Staff Writer: Newspaper Features and Magazine Articles.* 4th ed. Belmont, CA: Wadsworth, 1986.

Safire, William. *Take My Word for It: More On Language.* New York: Times Books, 1986.

Schor, Sandra and Judith Summerfield. *The Random House Guide to Writing.* 3rd ed. New York: Random House, 1986.

Scientists and Journalists: Reporting Science as News. Sharon M. Friedman, Sharon Dunwoody, and Carrol L. Rogers, eds. New York: Free Press, 1986.

Stephens, Mitchell. *Writing and Reporting the News.* New York: Holt, Rinehart & Winston, 1986.

Stewart, Donald C. *The Versatile Writer.* Lexington, MA: D. C. Heath, 1986.

A Supplement to the Oxford English Dictionary. Vol. 4. R. W. Burchfield, ed. Oxford: Clarendon Press, 1986.

White, William S. *The Making of a Journalist.* Lexington: Univ. Press of Kentucky, 1986.

Writing Across the Disciplines: Research into Practice. Art Young and Toby Fulwiler, eds. Upper Montclair, NJ: Boynton Cook, 1986.

Writing Prose: Techniques and Purposes. 6th ed. Thomas S. Kane and Leonard J. Peters, eds. New York: Oxford Univ. Press, 1986.

Zinsser, William K. *On Writing Well: An Informal Guide to Writing Nonfiction.* 3rd ed. rev. and enl. New York: Harper & Row, 1985.

MAGAZINE AND PERIODICAL ARTICLES

Alexander, Roberta. "Four Techniques for Overcoming the Terror of the Blank Page." *Writer's Digest,* June 1986, pp. 32-33.

Andersen, Richard. "Let Formulas Be as Many, as Various, as Life Itself." *The Coaches' Corner,* Sept. 1986, pp. 8, 9.

Anderson, Peter. "Columnist Calumny." *feed/back*, Spring 1986, pp. 8-11.

Ausenbaugh, James D. "How Temporary Writing Coaches Can Help Writers." *The Coaches' Corner*, Sept. 1986, pp. 7, 9.

"Barbara King: Writing Coach, Will Travel." *The Coaches' Corner*, Dec. 1986, p. 2.

Benedict, Stewart. "Writing Coaches Should Stress Linguistic Consciousness." *Editor & Publisher*, 13 Sept. 1986, p. 64.

Berkheimer, Darrell E. "Quotes and the Credibility Gap." *Editor & Publisher*, 17 May 1986, p. 68.

Berner, Thomas R. "Literary Newswriting: The Death of an Oxymoron." *Journalism Monographs*, No. 99, Oct. 1986, pp.1-25.

"The Best of Journalism." *The Quill*, June 1986, pp. 14-16, 18, 20-22, 24-26, 28-33.

Blount, Roy Jr. "Humor by Roy Blount Jr.: A Whole New Generation of Tools for Writers, Kind Of." *Writer's Digest*, Nov. 1986, pp. 42-43.

Boot, William. "NASA and the Spellbound Press." *Columbia Journalism Review*, July/Aug. 1986, pp. 23-29.

Braden, Maria. "Stamping Out Automatons." *The Quill*, May 1986, pp. 26, 28.

Brown, Millard C. "A Few Jaded Reflections on Opinion-Writing Today." *The Masthead*, Summer 1986, pp. 18-22.

Buchanan, Edna. "Advice from One of the Best Police Reporters Around." *ASNE Bulletin*, April 1986, pp. 10-12.

Byler, Robert. "Ten Tips for Faster and Better Writing." *The Writer*, July 1986, pp. 15-17.

Clark, Roy Peter. "Feedback on Feedback..." *The Coaches' Corner*, March 1986, p. 2.

---- "On Writing, Coaching, and the Lamaze Method." *APME News*, Feb./March 1986, pp. 19-23.

"Coaches Can Help Erase Bias Against Minorities." *The Coaches' Corner*, Dec. 1986, pp. 4-8.

The Coaches' Corner. A Quarterly Exchange on Coaching Writers. Editors are Paul Salsini, *The Milwaukee Journal*, Box 661, Milwaukee, WI 53201, and Lucille deView, *Florida Today*, Gannett Plaza, P.O. Box 363000, Melbourne, FL 32936.

Cool, Lisa Collier. "How to Write Fast." *Writer's Digest*, Nov. 1986, pp. 28-31.

Coram, Robert. "Grizzard, Inc." *The Quill*, Nov. 1986, pp. 34-38.

deView, Lucille. "Reporters Care, Too; Let Them Say So." *The Coaches' Corner*, March 1986, p. 4.

"Distinguished Service Awards 1985." *The Quill*, April 1986, pp. 2-4.

Doe, John (pseud). "Anonymity Isn't So Bad." *The Quill*, Jan. 1986, pp. 23-24.

Dudas, Jim. "Outdoor Writers." *Editor & Publisher*, 25 Jan. 1986, pp. 26, 30.

Eason, David L. "On Journalistic Authority: The Janet Cooke Scandal." *Critical Studies in Mass Communication* 3 (1986): 429-447.

384

Elliott, Bud. "Clichegate!" *ASNE Bulletin*, March 1986, pp. 26-27.

Fitzgerald, Mark. "Was It or Wasn't It News?" *Editor & Publisher*, 8 March 1986, pp. 9, 15.

Fry, Don. "...And How to Coach Reporters to Write Good Endings." *The Coaches' Corner*, Sept. 1986, p. 5.

---- "Coaching Disorganized Middles." *The Coaches' Corner*, June 1986, p. 1.

---- "The Differences Between Editing and Coaching." *APME News*, Feb./March 1986, pp. 17-19.

---- "Good Writers Reveal the Essence of Winners, Sinners and Losers." *ASNE Bulletin*, July/Aug. 1986, pp. 12-15.

---- "Special Techniques Needed in Coaching Leads." *The Coaches' Corner*, Dec. 1986, p. 3.

Garton, Jane Dwyre. "The Road to Better Ag Stories." *The Quill*, Nov. 1986, pp. 30-32.

Genovese, Margaret. "AIDS. Reporting the Tragedy." *presstime*, Dec. 1986, pp. 26-28.

Gibson, Martin L. "Clean Up Excess Verbiage in Leads." *Publishers' Auxiliary*, 10 Feb. 1986, p. 8.

Glassman, Robin. "...And How Editors and Reporters Can Work Together." *The Coaches' Corner*, March 1986, p. 2.

Goldstein, Mark. "The Business of Business Writing." *The Writer*, Feb. 1986, pp. 20-22.

Hart, Jack. "Tactics for the Directed Rewrite." *The Coaches' Corner*, Sept. 1986, p. 7.

"Harvey Aronson: Working Together With Writers." *The Coaches' Corner*, Sept. 1986, p. 3.

Hess, Stephen. "Covering the Senate: Where Power Gets the Play." *Washington Journalism Review*, June 1986, pp. 41-42.

"How Words Work." Various authors. *Writer's Digest*, June 1986, pp. 34-40, 42, 44-46, 48-50, 52, 54-55.

Johnson, Daniel. "Business Writing Tips." *Content*, Jan./Feb. 1986, pp. 21-22.

Johnson, K. S. "The Portrayal of Lame-Duck Presidents by the National Print Media." *Presidential Studies Quarterly* 16 (Winter 1986): 50-65.

Johnson, Richard. "Some Winners Find the Pulitzer Is No Prize." *Washington Journalism Review*, May 1986, pp. 30-33.

"June Smith: The Invisible Writing Coach." *The Coaches' Corner*, June 1986, p. 3.

Kail, Harvey. "A Writing Teacher Writes About Writing Teachers Writing (About Writing)." *English Journal*, Feb. 1986, pp. 88-91.

Kamins, Morton. "Images of Jim Murray." *Writer's Digest*, June 1986, pp. 26-28.

King, Barbara. "On Translating High-Tech Language." *The Coaches' Corner*, March 1986, p. 7.

King, Stephen. "Everything You Need to Know About Writing Successfully—in Ten Minutes." *The Writer*, July 1986, pp. 7-10.

Kranhold, Kathryn. "Investigating Lawmakers: A Step-by-Step Plan." *The IRE Journal*, Fall 1986, pp. 3-7.

Laakaniemi, Ray. "Coaches Need Tact, Patience, Especially with Publishers." *Journalism Educator,* Summer 1986, pp.13-15.

Laermer, Richard. "Covering the 'AIDS Beat.' " *Editor & Publisher*, 20 Dec. 1986, pp. 15, 24.

Laing, Mack. "The Art of Science Reporting." *Content*, Jan./Feb. 1986, p. 18.

---- "Covering Science: More Useful Tips." *Content*, Nov./Dec. 1986, pp. 17-19.

LaRocque, Paula. "Despite Writing Woes, Journalists Are Not Destroying the English Language." *presstime*, Sept. 1986, p. 34.

---- "The Problems in Coaching Our Writers." *APME News*, Feb./March 1986, p. 24.

---- "To Editors: Suggestions for Coaching Reporters." *The Coaches' Corner*, Dec. 1986, pp. 1, 9.

Levins, Harry. "Copy Editors Can Have a Role in Coaching, Too." *The Coaches' Corner*, Sept. 1986, pp. 2, 6.

Levy, Mark R. "*WJR* Readers Name the Best in the Business." *Washington Journalism Review*, Feb. 1986, pp. 16-17.

Long, Kate. "How to Help Reporters Fill Their Dreams as Writers." *The Coaches' Corner*, March 1986, p. 7.

McGlashan, Zena Beth. "Women Witness the Russian Revolution: Analyzing Ways of Seeing." *Journalism History* 12 (Summer 1986): 54-61.

"Major Journalism Awards." *The Quill*, June 1986, pp. 34-37.

Mann, Raleigh C. "Expectations Must Be Clear to Coaches." *Journalism Educator*, Summer 1986, pp. 13, 15-18.

Martin, Nita. "Mining the Asbestos Lode: One Reporter's Guide to Tracking the Toxic Substance." *The IRE Journal*, Summer 1986, pp. 12-18.

Milne, Lorus J. and Margery Milne. "So You Want to Write About Science." *The Writer*, Nov. 1986, pp. 11-13, 42.

Murray, Donald M. "One Writer's Secrets." *College Composition and Communication* 37 (May 1986): 146-153.

---- "Tackling the Lead, Winning Out in the End." *The Coaches' Corner*, Sept. 1986, pp. 4, 5.

Neustein, Amy. "New Ways to Interview Effectively." *The IRE Journal*, Summer 1986, pp. 8-9.

"Newspaper Lesson Aids." *Communication: Journalism Education Today (C:JET)*, Winter 1986, pp. 2-22.

O'Neal, Donna. "Covering a Military Installation: A Resource Guide." *Ideas*, Spring 1986, pp. 1-22.

Perkins, Jay. "When the Truth Is Elusive II: The Case of the Serpent Man." *The IRE Journal*, Fall 1986, pp. 14-19.

Provost, Gary. "How to Make the Reader Like You." *Writer's Digest*, Sept. 1986, pp. 36-38.

Reed, Donald. "How Editors View Writing Coaches." *Editor & Publisher*, 10 May 1986, pp. 44, 30.

Reeder, Daniel L. "Newspapers and Language." *presstime*, Sept. 1986, pp. 24-30.

Reigstad, Tom. "How To: Improve a Reporter's Sentence Fluency." *The Coaches' Corner*, June 1986, pp. 2, 5.

Renfro, Paula C. and John P. Maittlen-Harris. "Study Suggests Computer Time Won't Help Writing." *Journalism Educator*, Autumn 1986, pp. 49-51.

"Rick Zahler: The Coach as Counselor." *The Coaches' Corner*, March 1986, p. 3.

Robertson, Michael. "The Reporter as Novelist: The Case of William Kennedy." *Columbia Journalism Review*, Jan./Feb. 1986, pp. 49-50, 52.

Robinson, Don W. "Editorials Should Analyze the Facts, Evaluate the Issues and Offer Ideas on What to Do." *ASNE Bulletin*, Sept./Oct. 1986, pp. 30-31.

Safire, William. "In 750 Words." *ASNE Bulletin*, April 1986, p. 36.

Salsini, Paul. "Keeping the Flow Going Through the Middle." *The Coaches' Corner*, Dec. 1986, p. 3.

---- "To Improve Newspaper Writing, All Editors Must Play a Role." *APME News*, Feb./March, 1986, p. 16.

---- "Traditional Methods, But Coaches Get Results." *The Coaches' Corner*, Sept. 1986, p. 1.

---- "Writing Coaches—Growing in Stature." *Editor & Publisher*, 1 March 1986, pp. 52, 41.

Sanborn, Jean. "Grammar: Good Wine Before Its Time." *English Journal*, March 1986, pp. 72-80.

Schlosberg, Jeremy. "The Writer's Organizational Toolbox." *Writer's Digest*, July 1986, pp. 25-27.

Seeger, Arthur. "Use a Checklist for Features." *Journalism Educator*, Autumn 1986, pp. 43-44.

Shannon, Paul. "When the Truth Is Elusive I: The Case of the Dying Child." *The IRE Journal*, Fall 1986, pp. 12-13.

Shear, Marie. "Solving the Great Pronoun Problem: 14 Ways to Avoid the Sexist Singular." *ASNE Bulletin*, July/Aug. 1986, pp. 16-18.

Seigenthaler, John. "Howard Cosell: Sportswriters 'Not Prepared' to Cover Current Sports Scene." *ASNE Bulletin*, Sept./Oct. 1986, pp. 13-15.

Sims, Norman. "*House*: A Text for Dramatic Narrative." *The Coaches' Corner*, March 1986, p. 8.

Singer, Eleanor. "Social Science Stories Often Report Limited Research as 'Universal Truths.' " *ASNE Bulletin*, Feb. 1986, pp. 26-27, 30.

Spikol, Art. "Column Right." *Writer's Digest*, Feb. 1986, pp. 20-23.

Stein, M.L. "Baseball Manager Learns a Lesson." *Editor & Publisher*, 23 Aug. 1986, pp. 16-17.

---- "Could the Media Have Prevented Shuttle Disaster?" *Editor & Publisher*, 12 July 1986, pp. 11, 35.

---- "Risking Their Lives for a Story." *Editor & Publisher*, 15 March 1986, pp. 12-13, 37.

Steiner, Linda and Susanne Gray. "Genevieve Forbes Herrick: A Front-Page Reporter 'Pleased to Write About Women.' " *Journalism History* 12 (Spring 1986): 8-16.

Stempel, Guido H. III. "Study Shows Reporters Now More Careful in Use of Confidential Sources." *presstime*, Feb. 1986, p. 43.

Streitmatter, Rodger. "AIDS Coverage: Rewriting the Rules." *feed/back*, Spring 1986, pp. 20-25.

"The Top 10 News Stories of 1985." *Editor & Publisher*, 4 Jan. 1986, pp. 18, 31.

Thomasson, Dan. "In Public Affairs Reporting, We Can Rightly Be Accused of Taking 'Cheap Shots.' " *ASNE Bulletin*, Feb. 1986, pp. 26, 28-29.

Trillin, Calvin. "Covering the Cops." *New Yorker*, 17 Feb. 1986, pp. 39-57. [on Edna Buchanan]

"What Do Writers Want from Writing Coaches?" *The Coaches' Corner*, Sept. 1986, pp. 10-11.

"What To Do When You've Been Shut Out." *The Coaches' Corner*, March 1986, pp. 5-6.

Wolf, Rita and Tommy Thomason. "Writing Coaches: Their Strategies for Improving Writing." *Newspaper Research Journal* 7 (Spring 1986): 43-49.

Wolfson, Lewis. "Some Advice on Covering the White House." *Editor & Publisher*, 22 March 1986, pp. 48, 37.

"Writing Aids from Penney-Missouri Workshop." *Press Woman*, April 1986, pp. 6-7.

Wushke, Ralph. "Going Back to Church." *Content*, July/Aug. 1986, pp. 2-3.

Yarish, Alice. "North Bay Narcs: A Reporter Recalls Her Coverage of a Drug Enforcement Agency." *feed/back*, Spring 1986, pp. 12-16.

Zucchino, David. "Digging Out the...Why." *The Quill*, Jan. 1986, pp. 10-17.

RESEARCH REPORTS
AND CONFERENCE PAPERS

Buddenbaum, Judith M. "The Religious Journalism of James Gordon Bennett." Paper presented at the annual meeting of the Association for Education in Journalism and Mass Communication (69th, Norman, OK, August 1986). 36p. ERIC Document 270803.

Covert, Douglas C. "Science Communication Lessons from Environmental Education." Paper presented at the annual meeting of the Association for Education in Journalism and Mass Communication (69th, Norman, OK, August 1986). 24p. ERIC Document 272862.

Olasky, Marvin N. "When World Views Collide: Journalists and the Great Monkey Trial." Paper presented at the annual meeting of the Association for Education in Journalism and Mass Communication (69th, Norman, OK, August 1986). 28p. ERIC Document 272925.

Post, James F., et al. "Reporting on Radon: The Role of Local Newspapers." Paper presented at the annual meeting of the Association for Education in Journalism and Mass Communication (69th, Norman, OK, August 1986). 38p. ERIC Document 270784.

"The Well-Edited Newspaper: Putting the Pieces Together." Report of the APME Writing and Editing Committee (Cincinnati, OH, October 1986). 19p.

Former ASNE Award Winners

1986

Deadline writing: Bradley Graham, *The Washington Post*
Non-deadline writing: John Camp, *St. Paul Pioneer Press-Dispatch,* and David Finkel, *St. Petersburg Times*
Commentary: Roger Simon, *The Sun,* Baltimore, Md.
Editorial Writing: Jonathan Freedman, *The Tribune,* San Diego, Calif.

1985

Deadline writing: Jonathan Bor, *The Post Standard,* Syracuse, N.Y.
Non-deadline writing: Greta Tilley, *Greensboro News & Record*
Commentary: Murray Kempton, *Newsday*
Editorial writing: Richard Aregood, *Philadelphia Daily News*

1984

Deadline writing: David Zucchino, *The Philadelphia Inquirer*
Non-deadline writing: James Kindall, *The Kansas City Star*
Commentary: Roger Simon, *The Chicago Sun-Times*
Business writing: Peter Rinearson, *The Seattle Times*

1983

Deadline writing: No awards made in this category.
Non-deadline writing: Greta Tilley, *Greensboro News & Record*
Commentary: Rheta Grimsley Johnson, *Memphis Commercial Appeal*
Business writing: Orland Dodson, *Shreveport Times*

1982

Deadline writing: Patrick Sloyan, *Newsday*
Non-deadline writing: William Blundell, *The Wall Street Journal*
Commentary: Theo Lippman Jr., *The Baltimore Sun*
Sports writing: Tom Archdeacon, *The Miami News*

1981

Deadline writing: Richard Zahler, *The Seattle Times*
Non-deadline writing: Saul Pett, Associated Press
Commentary: Paul Greenberg, *Pine Bluff Commercial*
Sports writing: Thomas Boswell, *The Washington Post*

1980

Deadline writing: Carol McCabe, *Providence Journal-Bulletin*
Non-deadline writing: Cynthia Gorney, *The Washington Post*
Commentary: Ellen Goodman, *The Boston Globe*

1979

Deadline writing: Richard Ben Cramer, *The Philadelphia Inquirer*
Non-deadline writing—News: Thomas Oliphant, *Boston Sunday Globe*
Non-deadline writing—Features: Mary Ellen Corbett, *Fort Wayne News Sentinel*
Grand Prize (Commentary): Everett S. Allen, *New Bedford Standard-Times*

LIQUID PAPER

Shaped like a robot, this little worker
buries my dead. Touch the brushtip
lightly and bingo! a clean slate.
There are those who boil their brains
by sniffing it, which shows
it erases more than ink
and with imagination anything
can be misapplied. In the Army,
our topsergeant drank aftershave, shaking
my Old Spice to the last slow drop.
It worked like liquid paper in his head
until he'd walk the streets of Nuremberg
looking for the house in Boise, Idaho,
where he was born. If I were God
I'd authorize Celestial Liquid Paper
every seven years to whiten our mistakes.
We should be sorry and live with what we've done
but seven years is long enough and everyone
deserves a visit now and then
to the home where he was born
before everything got written so far wrong.

—Peter Meinke